MOUS PowerPoint 2000 Exam Prep

David W. Beskeen

MOUS PowerPoint 2000 Exam Prep **is published by Certification Insider™ Press and Course Technology.**

Limits Of Liability And Disclaimer Of Warranty

The author and publisher of this book have used their best efforts in preparing the book and the programs contained in it. These efforts include the development, research, and testing of the theories and programs to determine their effectiveness. The author and publisher make no warranty of any kind, expressed or implied, with regard to these programs or the documentation contained in this book.

The author and publisher shall not be liable in the event of incidental or consequential damages in connection with, or arising out of, the furnishing, performance, or use of the programs, associated instructions, and/or claims of productivity gains.

Trademarks

Trademarked names appear throughout this book. Rather than list the names and entities that own the trademarks or insert a trademark symbol with each mention of the trademarked name, the publisher states that it is using the names for editorial purposes only and to the benefit of the trademark owner, with no intention of infringing upon that trademark.

The Coriolis Group, LLC
14455 N. Hayden Road, Suite 220
Scottsdale, Arizona 85260

480/483-0192
FAX 480/483-0193
http://www.coriolis.com

ISBN: 1-57610-579-2

Printed in the United States of America
10 9 8 7 6 5 4 3 2 1

President, CEO
Keith Weiskamp

Publisher
Steve Sayre

Acquisitions Editor
Jeff Kellum

Marketing Managers
Cynthia Caldwell
Karen Bartlett

Product Managers
Sharon Sanchez McCarson
Jennifer Duffy
Rebecca VanEsselstine

Production Editors
Kim Eoff
Ellina Beletsky

Editorial Assistants
Hilary Long
Stacie Parillo

Cover Design
Jesse Dunn

Layout Design
April Nielsen

CD-ROM Developer
Robert Clarfield

CORIOLIS

14455 North Hayden Road • Suite 220 • Scottsdale, Arizona 85260

Coriolis: The Smartest Way To Get Certified™

To help you reach your goals, we've listened to readers like you, and we've designed our entire product line around you and the way you like to study, learn, and master challenging subjects.

In addition to our highly popular *Exam Cram* and *Exam Prep* books, we offer several other products to help you pass certification exams. Our *Practice Tests* and *Flash Cards* are designed to make your studying fun and productive. Our *Audio Reviews* have received rave reviews from our customers— and they're the perfect way to make the most of your drive time!

The newest way to get certified is the *Exam Cram Personal Trainer* —a highly interactive, personalized self-study course based on the best-selling *Exam Cram* series. It's the first certification-specific product to completely link a customizable learning tool, exclusive *Exam Cram* content, and multiple testing techniques so you can study what, how, and when you want.

Exam Cram Insider —a biweekly newsletter containing the latest in certification news, study tips, and announcements from Certification Insider Press—gives you an ongoing look at the hottest certification programs. (To subscribe, send an email to **eci@coriolis.com** and type "subscribe insider" in the body of the email.) We also sponsor the Certified Crammer Society and the Coriolis Help Center—two other resources that will help you get certified even faster!

Help us continue to provide the very best certification study materials possible. Write us or email us at **cipq@coriolis.com** and let us know how our books have helped you study. Tell us about new features that you'd like us to add. Send us a story about how we've helped you; if we use it in one of our books, we'll send you an official Coriolis shirt!

Good luck with your certification exam and your career. Thank you for allowing us to help you achieve your goals.

Keith Weiskamp

Keith Weiskamp
President and CEO

Preface

Welcome to *MOUS PowerPoint 2000 Exam Prep.* This highly visual book offers users a hands-on introduction to basic through advanced aspects of Microsoft PowerPoint 2000 and also serves as an excellent reference for future use.

▶ Organization and Coverage

This text contains eight units that cover basic to advanced PowerPoint skills. In these units, you learn how to create, modify, customize, and enhance presentations and charts.

▶ About this Approach

What makes this approach so effective at teaching software skills? It's quite simple. Each skill is presented on two facing pages, with the step-by-step instructions on the left page, and large screen illustrations on the right. You can focus on a single skill without having to turn the page. This unique design makes information extremely accessible and easy to absorb, and provides a great reference for after the course is over.

Each lesson, or "information display," contains the following elements:

Each 2-page spread focuses on a single skill.

Clear step-by-step directions explain how to complete the specific task. When you follow the numbered steps, you quickly learn how each procedure is performed and what the results will be.

Concise text that introduces the basic principles discussed in the lesson. Procedures are easier to learn when concepts fit into a framework.

PowerPoint 2000

Changing Master Text Indents

The master text placeholder in every presentation has five levels of text, called **indent levels.** You can use the horizontal slide ruler to control the space between the bullets and the text or to change the position of the whole indent level. Each indent level is represented by two small triangles called **indent markers** on the ruler that identify the position of each indent level in the master text placeholder. You can also set tabs on the horizontal ruler by clicking the tab indicator to the left of the horizontal ruler. Table E-1 describes the indent and tab markers on the ruler. Scenario Maria decides to change the distance between the bullet symbols and the text in the first two indent levels of her presentation to emphasize the bullets.

Steps

1. Click **View** on the menu bar, point to **Master**, then click **Slide Master**
   The Slide Master appears.
2. Click anywhere in the master text placeholder to place the insertion point, click **View** on the menu bar, then click **Ruler**
   The rulers and indent markers for the Master text placeholder appear. The indent markers are set so that the first line of text in each level, in this case the bullet, begins to the left of subsequent lines of text. This is a **hanging indent.**
3. Position the pointer over the left indent marker of the first indent level, then drag to the right to the ½" mark
   Compare your screen to Figure E-6.
4. Position the pointer over the left indent marker of the second indent level, then drag to the right to the 1¼" mark
   See Figure E-7. The rulers take up valuable screen area.
5. Click the right mouse button in a blank area of the Presentation window, then click **Ruler** on the pop-up menu
   The rulers are no longer visible.
6. Click **Close** on the Master toolbar
   Slide Master view closes and slide 2 appears, showing the increased indents in the main text object.
7. Click the **Save button** on the Standard toolbar

Trouble? If your rulers are already

Trouble? If you accidentally drag an indent marker into another marker, Click the Undo button to restore the indent levels to their original position.

QuickTip You can add tabs to any level text by clicking on the ruler where you want the tab. Click the tab indicator to the left of the ruler to cycle through the different tab alignment options.

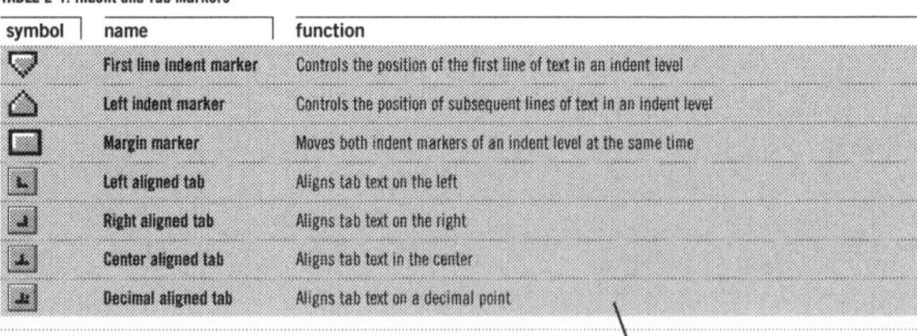

TABLE E-1: Indent and Tab Markers

symbol	name	function
	First line indent marker	Controls the position of the first line of text in an indent level
	Left indent marker	Controls the position of subsequent lines of text in an indent level
	Margin marker	Moves both indent markers of an indent level at the same time
	Left aligned tab	Aligns tab text on the left
	Right aligned tab	Aligns tab text on the right
	Center aligned tab	Aligns tab text in the center
	Decimal aligned tab	Aligns tab text on a decimal point

▶ POWERPOINT E-6 **CUSTOMIZING YOUR PRESENTATION**

Hints as well as trouble-shooting advice, right where you need it – next to the step itself.

Quickly accessible summaries of key terms, toolbar buttons, or keyboard alternatives connected with the lesson material. You can refer easily to this information when working on your own projects at a later time.

Features

The two-page lesson format featured in this book provides the new user with a powerful learning experience. Additionally, this book contains the following features:

- **MOUS Certification Coverage**
  Each unit opener has a MOUS next to it to indicate where Microsoft Office User Specialist (MOUS) skills are covered. This book thoroughly prepares you to learn the skills needed to pass the PowerPoint Core and Expert 2000 exams.

- **End of Unit Material**
  Each unit concludes with a Concepts Review that tests your understanding of what you learned in the unit. The Concepts Review is followed by a Skills Review, which provides you with additional hands-on practice of the skills. The Visual Workshops that follow the Skills Reviews helps you develop critical thinking skills. You are shown completed Web pages or screens and are asked to recreate them from scratch.

Every lesson features large-size, two-color representations of what your screen should look like after completing the numbered steps.

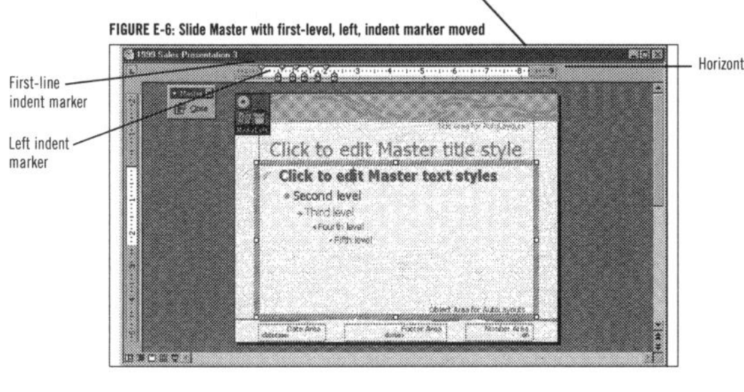

FIGURE E-6: Slide Master with first-level, left, indent marker moved

FIGURE E-7: Slide Master with second-level, left, indent marker moved

Second-level left indent marker moved

Second-level indent increased

PowerPoint 2000

CLUES TO USE

Exceptions to the Slide Master

If you change the format of text on a slide and then apply a different template to the presentation, the slide that you formatted retains the text formatting changes you made. These format changes that differ from the Slide Master are known as **exceptions**. Exceptions can only be changed on the individual slides where they occur. For example, you might change the font and size of a particular piece of text on a slide to make it stand out and then decide later to add a different template to your presentation. The text you formatted before you applied the template is an exception, and it is unaffected by the new template. Another way to override the slide master is to remove the master graphics on one or more slides. You might want to do this to get a clearer view of your slide text. Click Format on the menu bar, click Background, then click the Omit background graphics from master check box to select it.

CUSTOMIZING YOUR PRESENTATION POWERPOINT E-7

Clues to Use boxes provide concise information that either expands on one component of the major lesson skill or describes an independent task that is in some way related to the major lesson skill.

The page numbers are designed like a road map. PowerPoint indicates the PowerPoint section, E indicates the fifth unit, and 7 indicates the page within the unit.

Brief Contents

Contents

Contents

Enhancing a Presentation

Contents

Working with Embedded and Linked Objects and Hyperlinks POWERPOINT G-1

Contents

Getting Started with PowerPoint 2000

Objectives

- MOUS ► Define presentation software
- ► Start PowerPoint 2000
- MOUS ► Use the AutoContent Wizard
- MOUS ► View the PowerPoint window
- ► View a presentation
- MOUS ► Save a presentation
- MOUS ► Get Help
- MOUS ► Print and close the file, and exit PowerPoint

Microsoft PowerPoint 2000 is a presentation program that transforms your ideas into professional, compelling presentations. With PowerPoint, you can create slides to use as an electronic slide show, as 35-mm slides, and as transparency masters to display on an overhead projector. Scenario ► Maria Abbott is the general sales manager at MediaLoft, a nationwide chain of bookstore cafés that sells books, CDs, and videos at eight locations. Maria needs to familiarize herself with the basics of PowerPoint and learn how to use PowerPoint to create professional presentations.

PowerPoint 2000

Defining Presentation Software

Presentation software is a computer program you use to organize and present information. Whether you are giving a sales pitch or explaining your company's goals and accomplishments, presentation software can help make your presentation effective and professional. You can use PowerPoint to create 35-mm slides, overheads, speaker's notes, audience handouts, outline pages, or on-screen presentations. Table A-1 explains the items you can create using PowerPoint. Scenario Maria wants to create a presentation to review sales techniques at a monthly meeting of store managers. She is not familiar with PowerPoint, so she gets right to work exploring its capabilities. Figure A-1 shows an overhead she created using a word processor for a recent presentation. Figure A-2 shows how the same overhead might look in PowerPoint.

Maria can easily complete the following tasks using PowerPoint:

Create slides to display information

With PowerPoint, you can present information on full-color slides with interesting backgrounds, layouts, and clip art. Full-color slides have a more powerful impact than traditional black-and-white overheads.

Enter and edit data easily

Using PowerPoint, you can enter and edit data quickly and efficiently. When you need to change a part of your presentation, you can use the advanced word-processing and outlining capabilities of PowerPoint to edit your content rather than re-create your slides.

Change the appearance of information

By exploring the capabilities of PowerPoint, you will discover how easy it is to change the appearance of your presentation. PowerPoint has many features that can transform the way text, graphics, and slides look.

Organize and arrange information

Once you start using PowerPoint, you won't have to spend a lot of time making sure your information is correct and in the right order. With PowerPoint, you can quickly and easily rearrange and modify any piece of information in your presentation.

Incorporate information from other sources

Often, when you create presentations, you use information from other sources. With PowerPoint, you can import information from spreadsheet, database, and word-processing files prepared in programs such as Microsoft Excel, Microsoft Access, Microsoft Word, and Corel WordPerfect, as well as graphics from a variety of sources.

Show a presentation on any computer running Windows 98 or Windows 95

PowerPoint has a powerful feature called the PowerPoint Viewer that you can use to show your presentation on computers running Windows 98 or Windows 95 that do not have PowerPoint installed. The PowerPoint Viewer displays a presentation as an on-screen slide show.

FIGURE A-1: Traditional overhead

Forecast for 2000

- New stores in Austin, Madison, and Denver
- 75 new employees
- Sales up 32%
- Expanded CD and video offerings
- Test market online sales
- Another record year!

FIGURE A-2: PowerPoint overhead

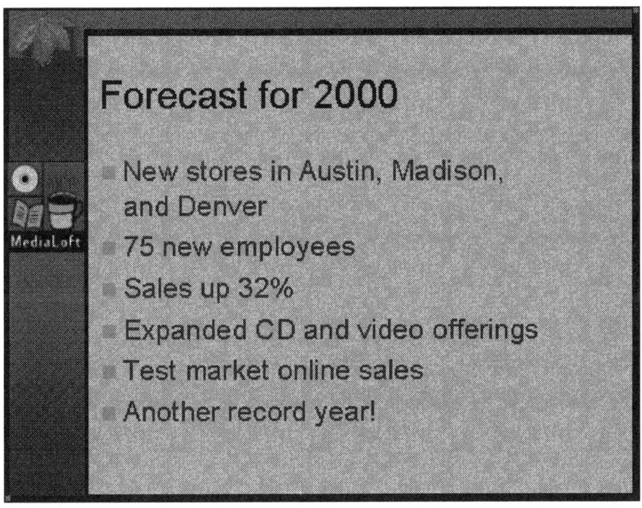

TABLE A-1: Items you can create using PowerPoint

item	use
On-screen presentations	Run a slide show directly from your computer
Web presentations	Broadcast a presentation on the Web or on an intranet that others can view, complete with video and audio
Online meetings	View or work on a presentation with your colleagues in real time
35-mm slides	Use a film-processing bureau to convert PowerPoint slides to 35-mm slides
Black-and-white overheads	Print PowerPoint slides directly to transparencies on your black-and-white printer
Color overheads	Print PowerPoint slides directly to transparencies on your color printer
Speaker notes	Print notes that help you remember points about each slide when you speak to a group
Audience handouts	Print handouts with two, three, or six slides on a page
Outline pages	Print the outline of your presentation to show the main points

PowerPoint 2000

Starting PowerPoint 2000

To start PowerPoint, you must first start Windows, and then click the Start button on the taskbar and point to the Programs folder, which usually contains the PowerPoint program icon. If the PowerPoint icon is not in the Programs folder, it might be in a different location on your computer. If you are using a computer on a network, you might need to use a different starting procedure. Scenario Maria starts PowerPoint to familiarize herself with the program.

Steps

1. **Make sure your computer is on and the Windows desktop is visible**
   If any program windows are open, close or minimize them.
2. **Click the Start button on the taskbar, then point to Programs**
   The Programs menu opens, showing a list of icons and names for all your programs, as shown in Figure A-3. Your screen might look different, depending on which programs are installed on your computer.
3. **Click Microsoft PowerPoint on the Programs menu**
   PowerPoint starts, and the PowerPoint startup dialog box opens, as shown in Figure A-4. This allows you to choose how you want to create your presentation or to open an existing presentation.
4. **If a dialog balloon connected to the Office Assistant appears, click OK to close it**

Trouble?

If you have trouble finding Microsoft PowerPoint on the Programs menu, check with your instructor or technical support person.

Clues to Use: Creating a PowerPoint shortcut icon on the desktop

You can make it easier to start PowerPoint by placing a shortcut on the desktop. To create the shortcut, click the Start button, then point to Programs. On the Programs menu, point to Microsoft PowerPoint, then right-click Microsoft PowerPoint. In the pop-up menu that appears, click Create Shortcut. Windows places a shortcut icon named PowerPoint (2) on the Programs menu. Drag this icon to your desktop where it will look like [icon]. In the future, you can start PowerPoint by simply double-clicking this icon, instead of using the Start menu. You can edit or change the name of the shortcut by right-clicking the shortcut icon, clicking Rename on the pop-up menu, and then editing as you would any item name in Windows.

FIGURE A-3: Programs menu

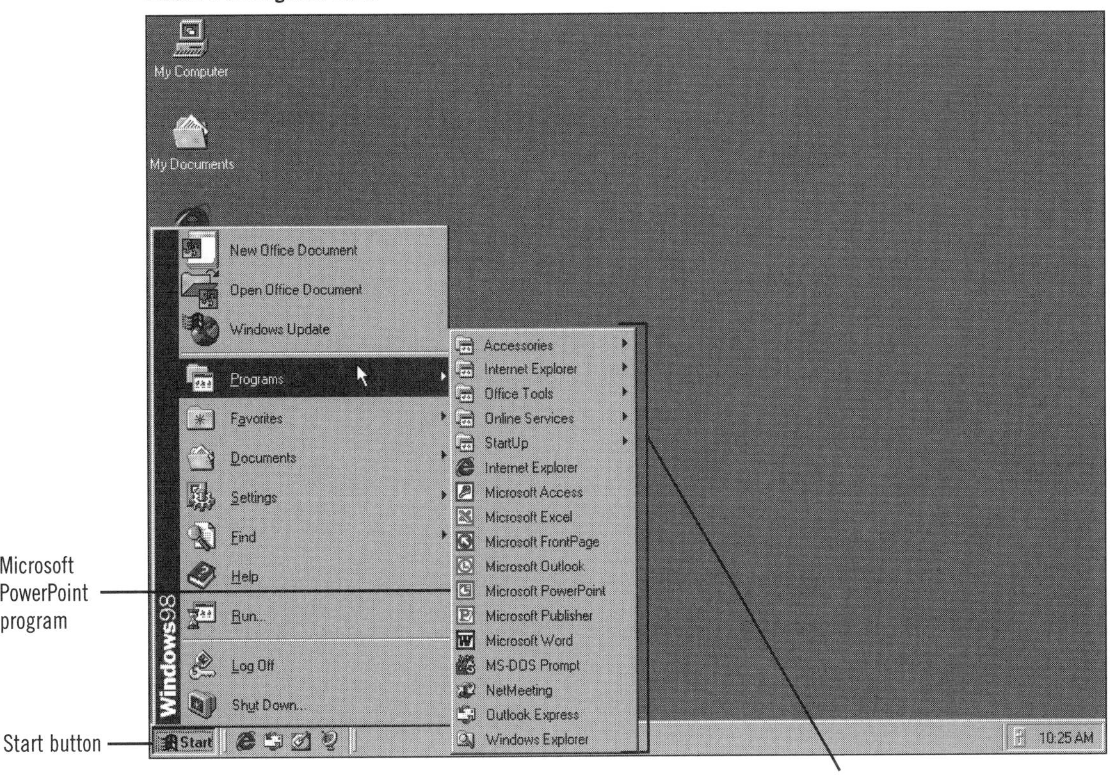

FIGURE A-4: PowerPoint startup dialog box

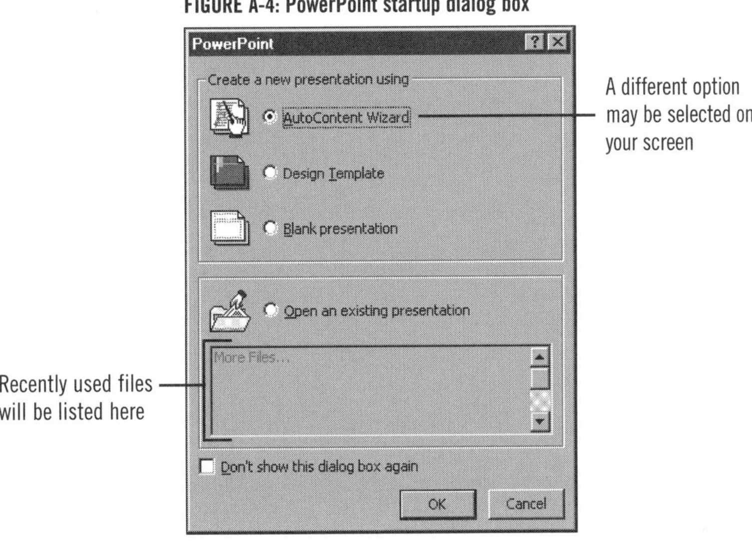

PowerPoint 2000

PowerPoint 2000

Using the AutoContent Wizard

When PowerPoint first starts, the startup dialog box opens. The startup dialog box gives you four options for starting your presentation. See Table A-2 for an explanation of all the options in the PowerPoint startup dialog box. The first option, the AutoContent Wizard, is the quickest way to create a presentation. A **wizard** is a series of steps that guides you through a task (in this case, creating a presentation). Using the AutoContent Wizard, you choose a presentation type from the wizard's list of sample presentations. Then you indicate what type of output you want. Next, you type the information for the title slide and the footer. The AutoContent Wizard then creates a presentation with sample text you can use as a guide to help formulate the major points of your presentation. Scenario Maria decides to start her presentation by opening the AutoContent Wizard.

1. In the startup dialog box, click the **AutoContent Wizard option button** to select it, then click **OK**
   The AutoContent Wizard dialog box opens, as shown in Figure A-5. The left section outlines the contents of the AutoContent Wizard and places a green box next to the current screen name. The text on the right side explains the purpose of the wizard.
2. Click **Next**
   The Presentation type screen appears. This screen contains category buttons and types of presentations. Each presentation type contains suggested text for a particular use. By default, the presentation types in the General category are listed.
3. Click the category **Sales/Marketing**, click **Selling a Product or Service** in the list on the right, then click **Next**
   The Presentation style screen appears, asking you to choose an output type.
4. If necessary, click the **On-screen presentation option button** to select it, then click **Next**
   The Presentation options screen requests information that will appear on the title slide of the presentation and in the footer at the bottom of each slide.
5. Click in the **Presentation title text box**, then type **Selling MediaLoft Products**
6. Press **[Tab]**, then type your name in the Footer text box
7. Make sure the **Date last updated** and **Slide number check boxes** are selected
8. Click **Next**, then click **Finish**
   The AutoContent Wizard opens the presentation based on the Selling a Product or Service presentation type you chose. Sample text for each slide is listed on the left, and the title slide appears on the right side of the screen. Compare your screen to Figure A-6.

Trouble?

If the Office Assistant is in your way, drag it out of the way.

QuickTip

To start the AutoContent Wizard when PowerPoint is already running, click File on the menu bar, click New, click the General tab, then double-click the AutoContent Wizard icon.

CLUES TO USE

About Wizards and the PowerPoint installation

As you use PowerPoint, you may find that not all AutoContent Wizards are available to you. The wizards available depend on your PowerPoint installation. A basic installation gives you a minimal set of wizards, templates, and other features. Some may be installed so that the program requests the CD "on first use" the first time you request that feature. If you find that a feature you want is not installed, insert the Office CD as directed. If you are working on a networked computer or in a lab, see your technical support person for assistance.

FIGURE A-5: AutoContent Wizard opening screen

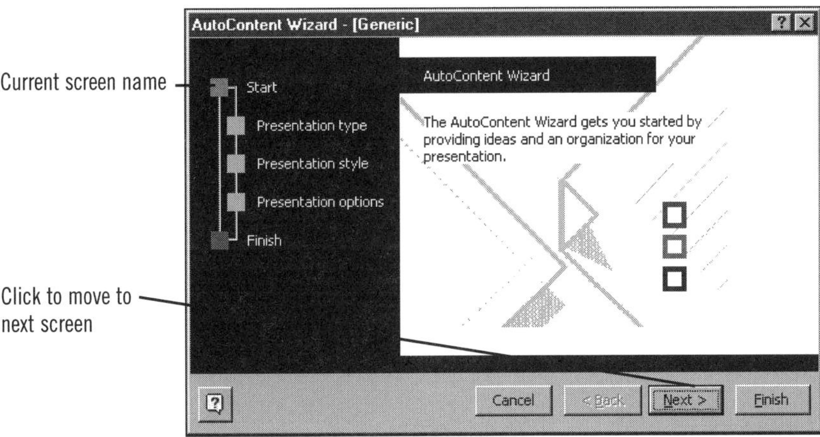

FIGURE A-6: Presentation created with the AutoContent Wizard

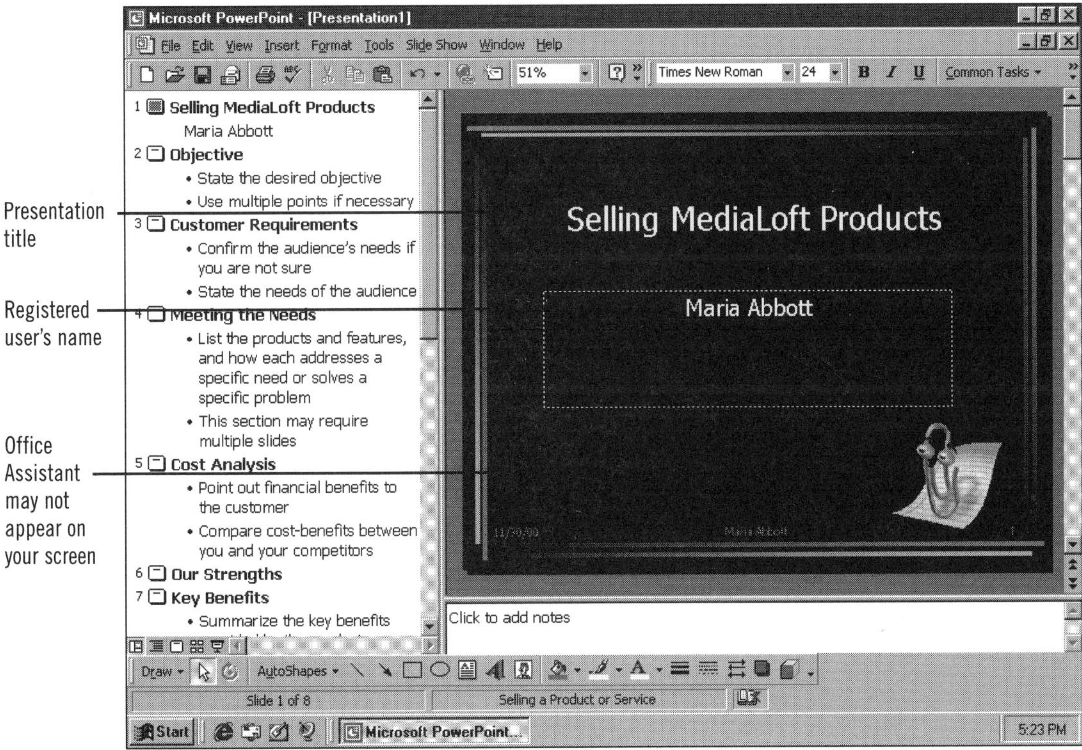

TABLE A-2: PowerPoint startup dialog box options

option	description
AutoContent Wizard	Helps you determine the content and organization of your presentation by creating a title slide and an outline using ready-made text for the category you choose
Design Template	Opens the New Presentation dialog box, containing PowerPoint design templates; you can click a template to see a preview of it
Blank presentation	Opens the New Slide dialog box, allowing you to choose a predesigned slide layout for the first slide, then opens a presentation with no predefined content or design
Open an existing presentation	Opens the Open dialog box, allowing you to open a previously created presentation; you can preview a selected presentation before opening it

PowerPoint 2000

Viewing the PowerPoint Window

After you make your selection in the PowerPoint startup dialog box, the Presentation window opens within the PowerPoint window, and the presentation you just created or opened appears. PowerPoint has different **views** that allow you to see your presentation in different forms. By default, the PowerPoint window opens in **Normal view**, which is divided into three **panes** or sections: the Outline pane, the Notes pane, and the Slide pane. Each pane is described below. You move around in each pane by using its scroll bars. Scenario Maria examines the elements of the PowerPoint window. Find and compare the elements described below, using Figure A-7 as a guide.

The **title bar** contains the program name, the title of the presentation, a program Control Menu button, resizing buttons, and the program Close button.

The **menu bar** contains the names of the menus you use to choose PowerPoint commands, as well as the resizing and Close buttons for the maximized presentation window. When you click a menu name, a list of commands from which you can choose opens.

The **toolbar** contains buttons for commonly used commands. There are actually two toolbars in this row: **Standard**, which contains buttons for the most frequently used commands, such as copying and pasting; and **Formatting**, which contains buttons for the most frequently used formatting commands, such as changing font type and size, as well as the Common Tasks drop-down menu. The **Common Tasks menu** contains three tasks typically performed in PowerPoint: New Slide, Slide Layout, and Assign Design Template. The Common Tasks menu button may be the only button visible on the Formatting toolbar. By default, the two toolbars appear on one row on your screen when PowerPoint first opens. The contents of the toolbars change depending on which options you have recently selected, but you can reset the toolbars back to their default options if you wish. Be sure to read the Clues to Use in this lesson to learn more about working with PowerPoint's toolbars.

The **Presentation window** contains the Outline, Slide, and Notes panes. It is the "canvas" where you type text, organize your content, work with lines and shapes, and view your presentation.

The **Outline pane** displays your presentation text in the form of an outline, without graphics. In this pane, it is easy to move text on or among slides by dragging to reorder the information.

The **Slide pane** contains the current slide in your presentation, including all text and graphics. You can use this pane's vertical scroll bar to view other slides in the presentation.

The **Notes pane** lets you type in speaker notes for any slide. Speaker notes are for your reference as you make a presentation, such as reminders of other points you want to make during the presentation. They are not visible to the audience when you make a slide presentation. You can print a copy of your presentation with your notes showing under each slide and refer to this copy as you speak.

The **Office Assistant** is an animated character that provides help. The character on your screen might be different. You can hide the Office Assistant, but it will reappear if you use the Help system. If another user turned off the Office Assistant, it may not appear on your screen. When the Office Assistant has a style tip, a light bulb appears in the presentation window.

The **Drawing toolbar**, located below the Presentation window, contains buttons and menus that let you create lines, shapes, and special effects.

The **view buttons**, at the bottom of the Outline pane, allow you to quickly switch between PowerPoint views.

The **status bar**, located at the bottom of the PowerPoint window, shows messages about what you are doing and seeing in PowerPoint, including which slide you are viewing.

FIGURE A-7: Presentation window in Normal view

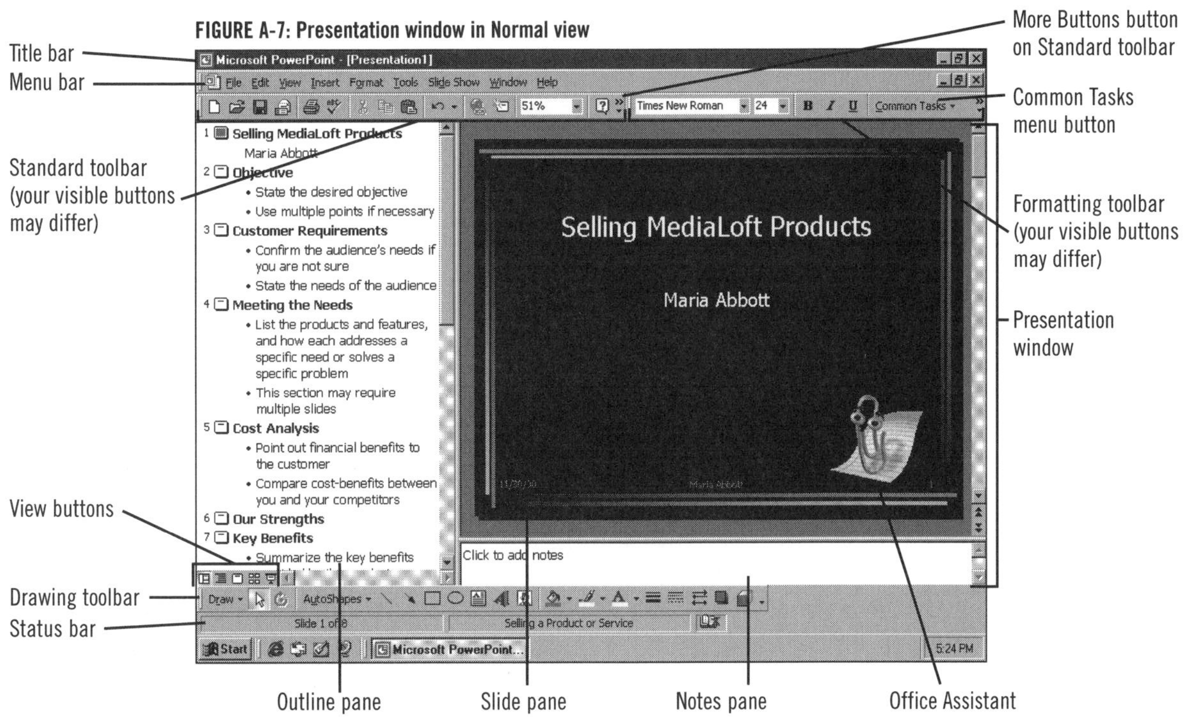

Personalized toolbars and menus in PowerPoint 2000

PowerPoint toolbars and menus modify themselves to your working style. The Standard and Formatting toolbars you see when you first start PowerPoint include the most frequently used buttons. To locate a button not visible on a toolbar, click the **More Buttons button** at the right end of each toolbar to see the list of additional toolbar buttons. (Because the Standard and Formatting toolbars are on the same line, there are two More Buttons buttons in the row below the menu bar, one for the Standard toolbar and one for the Formatting toolbar.) Throughout the lessons in this book, you will need to remember to click the More Buttons button if a button you are instructed to click is not visible on your screen. As you work, PowerPoint adds the buttons you use to the visible toolbars, and moves the buttons you haven't used in a while to the More Buttons list. Similarly, PowerPoint menus adjust to your work habits. Short menus appear when you first click a menu command. To view additional menu commands, point to the double-arrow at the bottom of the menu, leave the pointer on the menu name after you've clicked the menu, or double-click the menu name. You can return toolbars and menus to their default settings. Click Tools on the menu bar, click Customize, then click the Options tab in the Customize dialog box. On the Options tab, click Reset my usage data. An alert box or the Office Assistant appears asking if you are sure you want to do this. Click Yes to close the alert box or the dialog balloon, then click Close in the Customize dialog box. Resetting your usage data erases changes made automatically to your menus and toolbars. It does not affect the options you customize.

PowerPoint 2000

Viewing a Presentation

This lesson introduces you to the six PowerPoint views: Normal view, Slide view, Outline view, Slide Sorter view, Notes Page view, and Slide Show view. Each PowerPoint view shows your presentation in a different way and allows you to manipulate your presentation differently. To move easily among the PowerPoint views, use the view buttons located to the left of the horizontal scroll bar, as shown in Figure A-8. Table A-3 provides a brief description of the PowerPoint view buttons and views. Scenario Maria examines each PowerPoint view, starting with Normal view.

Steps

1. **In the Outline pane, click the small slide icon next to slide 3 to view the Customer Requirements slide in the Slide pane**
   Notice that in Normal view you can easily view the Outline, Slide, and Notes panes.
2. **Click the Previous Slide button at the bottom of the vertical scroll bar twice so that slide 1 (the title slide) appears**
   The scroll box in the vertical scroll bar moves back up the scroll bar. The gray slide icon in the Outline pane indicates which slide is displayed in the Slide pane. Both the status bar and the Outline pane indicate the number of the slide you are viewing. As you scroll through the presentation, notice the sample text on each slide created by the AutoContent Wizard.
3. **Click the Outline View button to the left of the horizontal scroll bar**
   PowerPoint switches to Outline view, which is simply the Outline pane enlarged. See Figure A-8. The Slide pane contains a miniature view of the selected slide.
4. **Click the Slide View button**
   The Slide pane enlarges, the Notes pane disappears, and the Outline pane is reduced to a list of slide numbers and icons that you can click to view other slides. Compare your screen to Figure A-9.
5. **Click the Slide Sorter View button**
   A miniature image of each slide in the presentation appears in this view. You can examine the flow of your slides and easily move them to change their order.
6. **Click the Slide Show button**
   The first slide fills the entire screen. In this view, you can practice running through your slides as they would appear in an electronic slide show.
7. **Click the left mouse button, press [Enter], or press [Spacebar] to advance through the slides one at a time until you see a black slide, then click once more to return to Slide Sorter view**
   After you view the last slide in Slide Show view, a black slide indicating that the slide show is finished appears. When you click the black slide (or press [Spacebar] or [Enter]), you automatically return to Slide Sorter view, the view you were in before you ran the slide show.
8. **Click View on the menu bar, then click Notes Page**
   Notes Page view appears, showing a reduced image of the title slide above a large box. You can enter text in this box and then print the notes page for your own use to help you remember important points about your presentation.

QuickTip

Double-click any slide in Slide Sorter view to return to that slide in the previous view.

QuickTip

To switch to Notes Page view, you must choose Notes Page from the View menu. To switch to Slide and Outline views, you must use the view buttons.

FIGURE A-8: Outline View

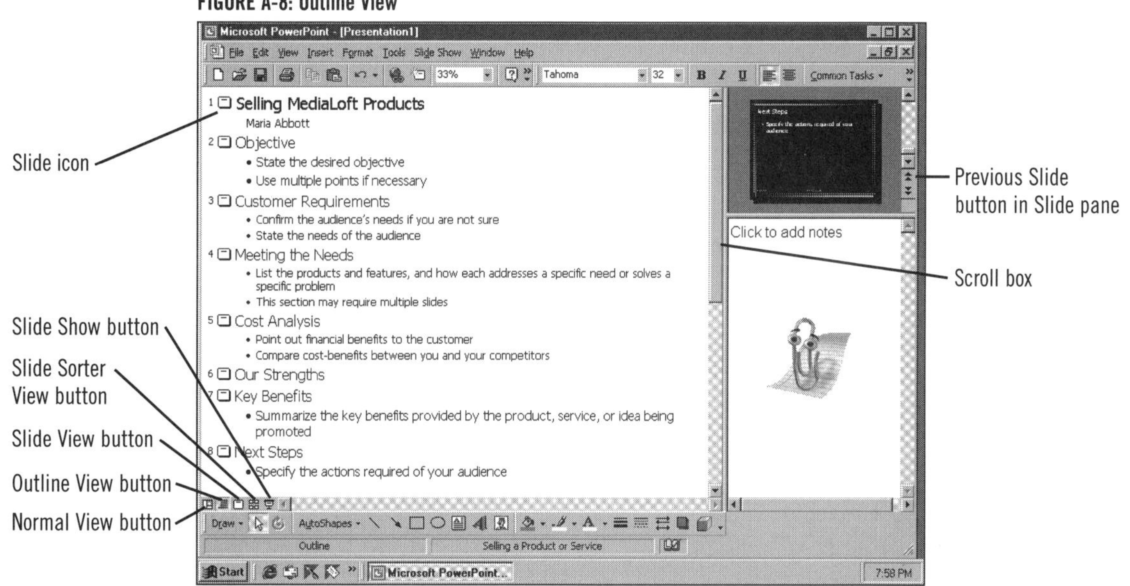

FIGURE A-9: Slide view

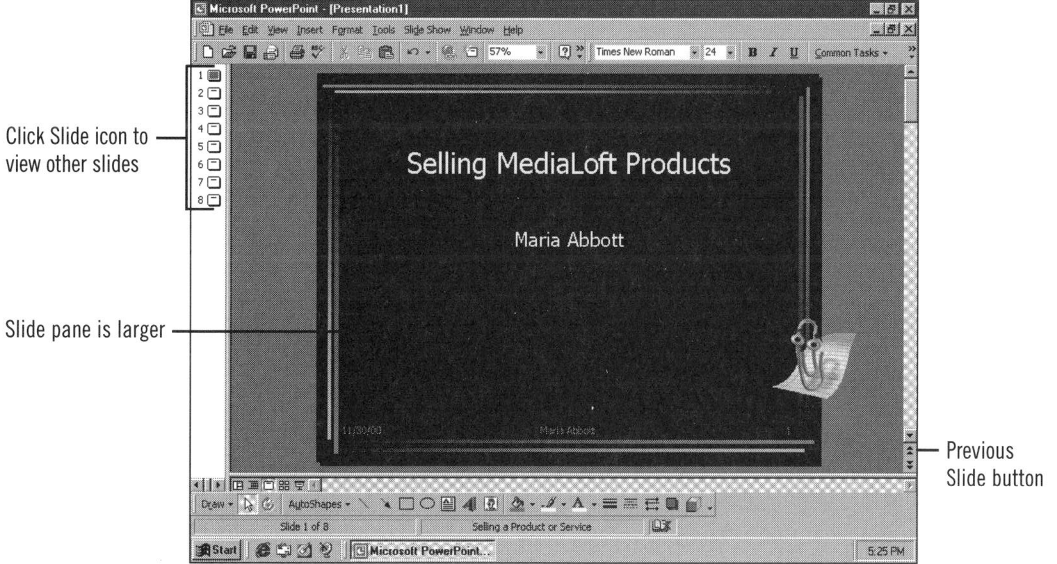

TABLE A-3: View buttons

button	button name	description
	Normal View	Displays the Outline, Slide, and Notes panes at the same time; use this view to work on your presentation's content, layout, and notes concurrently
	Outline View	Widens the outline pane to view the title and main topics in the form of an outline; use this view to enter and edit the text of your presentation
	Slide View	Widens the slide pane so it occupies most of the presentation window; displays one slide at a time; use this view to modify slide content and enhance a slide's appearance
	Slide Sorter View	Displays a miniature picture of all slides in the order in which they appear in your presentation; use this view to rearrange and add special effects to your slides
	Slide Show	Displays your presentation as an electronic slide show

PowerPoint 2000

Saving a Presentation

To store your presentation permanently, you must save it as a file on a disk. As a general rule, you should save your work about every 10 or 15 minutes and before printing. You use the Save As command on the File menu to save your presentation for the first time or to save an existing presentation under a different name. Use the Save command to save your changes to a file without changing its name. In this lesson, you save your presentation to your Project Disk. Scenario ▶ Maria saves her presentation as "Sales Presentation."

Steps 1 2 3 4

1. **Click File on the menu bar, then click Save As**
   The Save As dialog box opens. See Figure A-10.
2. **Make sure your Project Disk is in the appropriate drive, click the Save in list arrow, then click the drive that contains your Project Disk**
   A default file name placeholder, which PowerPoint takes from the presentation title you entered, appears in the File name text box. If your disk contains any PowerPoint files, their file names appear in the white area in the center of the dialog box.
3. **In the File name text box, drag to select the default presentation name if necessary, type Sales Presentation, then click Save**
   Windows 98 allows you to have file names up to 255 characters long and permits you to use lower- or uppercase letters, symbols, numbers, and spaces. The Save As dialog box closes, and the new file name appears in the title bar at the top of the Presentation window. You decide you want to save the presentation in Outline view instead of in Notes Page view.
4. **Click the Outline View button**
   The presentation view changes from Notes Page view to Outline view.
5. **Click the Save button on the Standard toolbar**
   The Save command saves any changes you made to the file to the same location you specified when you used the Save As command. Save your file frequently while working with it to protect the presentation.

Trouble?

Don't worry if you see the extension .ppt after the file name in the title bar or in the list of file names, even though you didn't type it. Windows can be set up to show or not show the file extensions.

QuickTip

To save a file quickly, you can press the shortcut key combination [Ctrl][S].

Saving fonts with your presentation

When you create a presentation, it uses the fonts that are installed on your computer. If you need to open the presentation on another computer, the fonts might look different if that computer has a different set of fonts. To preserve the look of your presentation on any computer, you can save, or **embed**, the fonts in your presentation. Click File on the menu bar, then click Save As. The Save As dialog box opens. Click Tools, then click Embed TrueType fonts from the drop-down list. Finally, click Save. Now the presentation will look the same on any computer that opens it. This option, however, significantly increases the size of your presentation on disk, so only use this option when necessary. You can freely embed any TrueType font that comes with Windows. You can embed other TrueType fonts only if they have no license restrictions.

FIGURE A-10: Save As dialog box

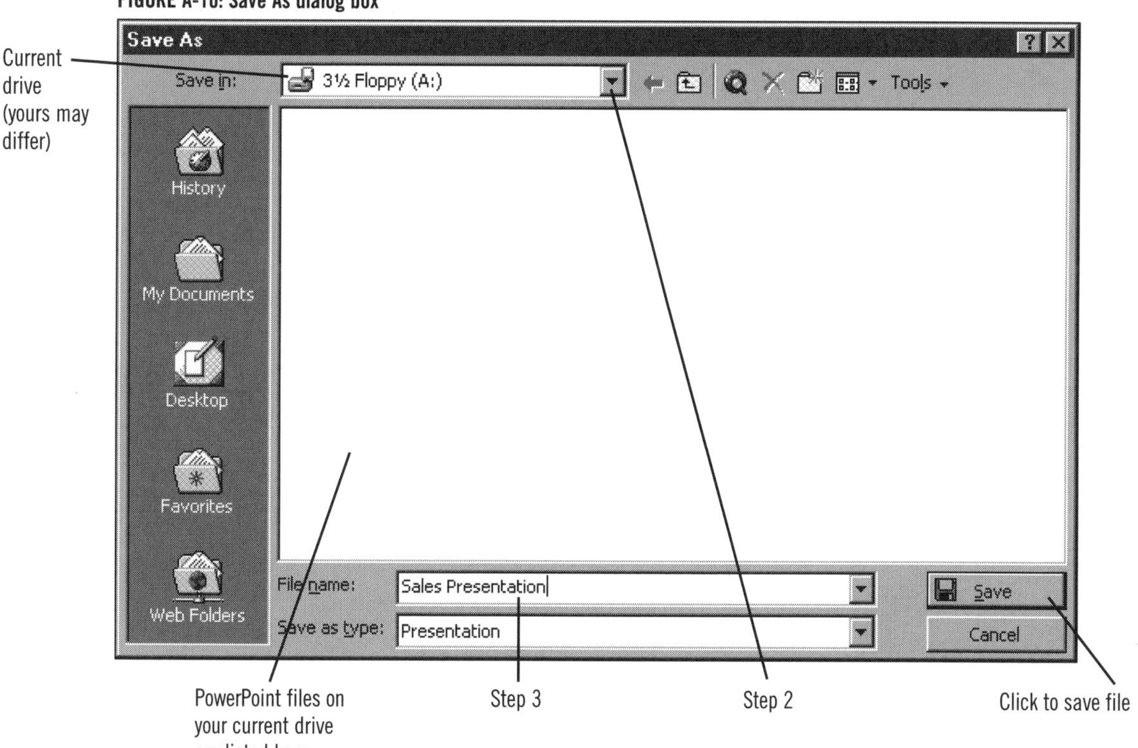

PowerPoint 2000

PowerPoint 2000

Getting Help

PowerPoint has an extensive Help system that gives you immediate access to definitions, reference information, and feature explanations. Help information appears in a separate window that you can move and resize. Scenario Maria likes the way the AutoContent Wizard helped her create a presentation quickly, and she decides to find out more about it.

Steps

Trouble?

If the Microsoft PowerPoint Help dialog box opens instead of the Office Assistant, someone turned the Office Assistant off. Click the Close button in the Help window, click Help on the menu bar, click Show the Office Assistant, then repeat step 1. If there is no space in the dialog balloon to type the question, click OK, then repeat Step 1.

QuickTip

To quickly open the Office Assistant dialog balloon, click the animated character, click the Microsoft PowerPoint Help button on the Standard toolbar, or press [F1].

QuickTip

To turn off the Office Assistant completely, right-click the Assistant, click Options, deselect the Use the Office Assistant checkbox, then click OK.

1. Click **Help** on the menu bar, then click **Microsoft PowerPoint Help**
   If the Office Assistant wasn't already open, it opens. A balloon-shaped dialog box opens near the Office Assistant. The dialog balloon may contain a tip related to the current slide. The question "What would you like to do?" appears at the top of the dialog balloon. It also contains topics related to what is currently on-screen and the last few commands you executed. Below this list is a space for you to type your question. Finally, at the bottom of the dialog balloon are two buttons. Clicking the Options button opens a dialog box that allows you to change Office Assistant options. Clicking the Search button searches PowerPoint Help topics for topics related to the question you type.
2. Type **AutoContent Wizard**, then click **Search**
   The dialog balloon closes and reopens with five topics related to the AutoContent Wizard listed under "What would you like to do?" See Figure A-11. If you click the See more option, two more topics appear. The mouse pointer changes to when it is positioned over the topics.
3. Click **Create a new presentation**
   The Microsoft PowerPoint Help window opens, containing information about creating a new presentation. See Figure A-12. Read the information in the window.
4. Click **Create a presentation based on suggested content and design** in the Microsoft PowerPoint Help window
   You may need to scroll down to see this. Another Help window opens listing the steps to follow for using the AutoContent Wizard. Read through the steps.
5. Click the **Show button** at the top of the window
   The Help window expands to include three tabs: Contents, Answer Wizard, and Index. The Contents tab contains Help topics organized in outline form. To open a Help window about a topic, double-click it. On the Answer Wizard tab, you can search for a key word in all the Help topics. The Index tab contains an alphabetical list of Help topics. Type the word you want help on in text box 1, and the list in box 2 scrolls to that word. Click Search to view related subjects in text box 3, then click the topic you want to read about.
6. Click the **Close button** on the Microsoft PowerPoint Help Window to close it
   The Help Topics dialog box closes, and you return to your presentation. The rest of the figures in this text will not show the Office Assistant.
7. Click **Help** on the menu bar, then click **Hide the Office Assistant**
   If you have hidden the Office Assistant several times, it may open a dialog balloon asking if you want to turn it off permanently.
8. If a dialog balloon opens asking if you want to turn off the Office Assistant permanently, click the option you prefer in the Office Assistant dialog balloon, then click **OK**
   Selecting Hide the Office Assistant only hides it temporarily; it will reappear later to give you tips.

FIGURE A-11: Office Assistant dialog balloon

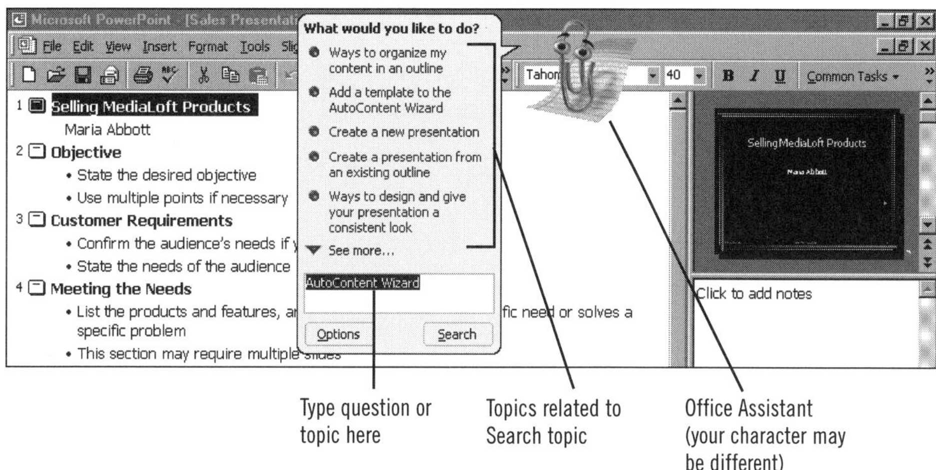

FIGURE A-12: Help window

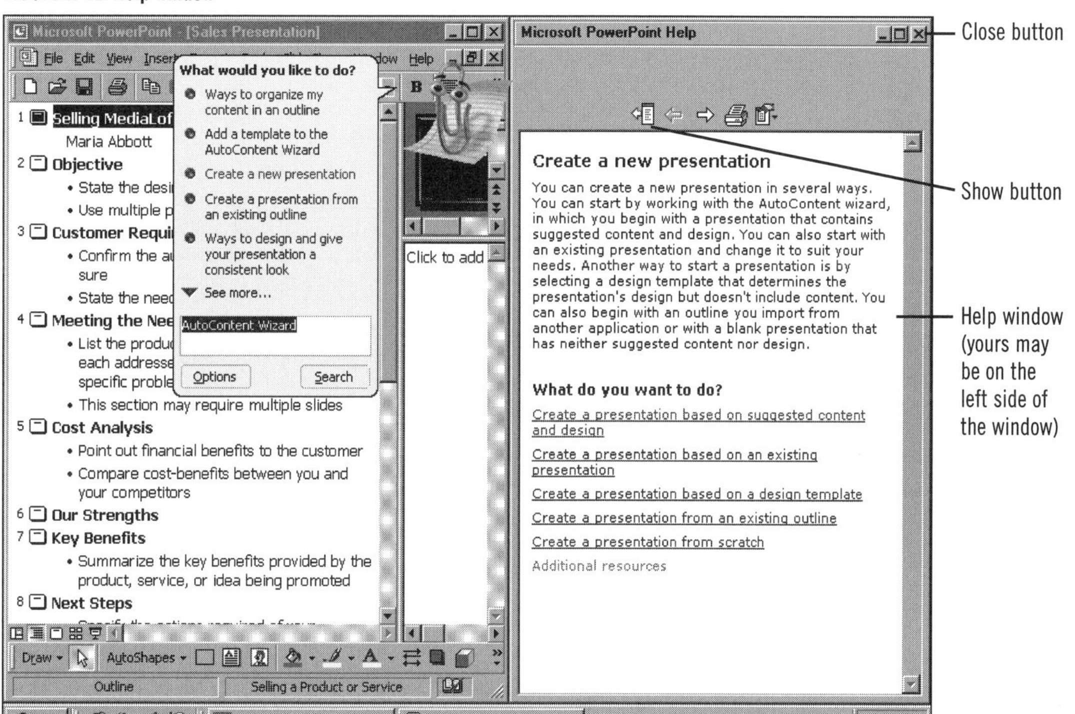

PowerPoint 2000

What do I do if I see a lightbulb on a slide?

If you have the Office Assistant on, you may see a yellow lightbulb in your presentation window. The lightbulb is part of the PowerPoint Help system and it can mean several things. First, the Office Assistant might have a suggestion for appropriate clip art for that slide. Second, the Office Assistant might have a helpful tip based on the task you are performing. This is known as a context-sensitive tip. Third, the Office Assistant might have detected a style, such as a word in the slide title that should be capitalized, which is inconsistent with preset style guidelines. When you see a lightbulb, you can click it, read the dialog balloon, then click the option you prefer, or you can ignore it. If the Office Assistant is hidden or turned off, the lightbulbs do not appear.

PowerPoint 2000

Printing and Closing the File, and Exiting PowerPoint

You print your presentation when you have completed it or when you want to review your work. Reviewing hard copies of your presentation at different stages of production gives you an overall perspective of its content and look. When you are finished working on your presentation, close the file containing your presentation and exit PowerPoint. Scenario Maria needs to go to a meeting, so after saving her presentation, she prints the slides and notes pages of the presentation so she can review them later; then she closes the file and exits PowerPoint.

Steps

1. Click **File** on the menu bar, then click **Print**
   The Print dialog box opens, similar to Figure A-13. In this dialog box, you can specify which slide format you want to print (slides, audience handouts, notes pages, etc.) as well as the number of pages to print and other print options. The default option, Slides, and the Grayscale check box are already selected in the Print what area at the bottom of the dialog box.

2. In the Print range section in the middle of the dialog box, click the **Slides option button** to select it, type **3** to print only the third slide, then click **OK**
   The third slide prints. Because the Grayscale check box is selected by default, the black background does not print. If you have a black-and-white printer, the slide prints in shades of gray. To save paper, it's often a good idea to print in handout format, which lets you print up to nine slides per page.

QuickTip

If the Office Assistant appears offering you help with printing, click No in the dialog balloon.

3. Click **File** on the menu bar, then click **Print**
   The Print dialog box opens again.

4. Click the **All option button** in the Print range section, click the **Print what list arrow**, click **Handouts**, click the **Slides per page list arrow** in the Handouts section, then click **6**
   The PowerPoint black-and-white option can help you save toner.

QuickTip

The options you choose in the Print dialog box remain there until you close the presentation. To quickly print the presentation with the current Print options, click the Print button on the Standard toolbar.

5. Click the **Pure black and white check box** to select it, then click **OK**
   The presentation prints as audience handouts on two pages. If you have a black-and-white printer, the presentation prints without any gray tones.

6. Click **File** on the menu bar, then click **Print**
   The Print dialog box opens again.

7. Click the **Print what list arrow**, click **Outline View**, then click **OK**
   The presentation outline prints. Notice that you can print any view from the Print dialog box, regardless of the current view.

QuickTip

To print slides in a size appropriate for overhead transparencies, click File, click Page Setup, and click the Slides sized for list arrow. Select Overhead. Then print or copy your slides onto transparency film.

8. Click **File** on the menu bar, then click **Close**
   If you have made changes to your presentation, a Microsoft PowerPoint alert box opens asking you if you want to save changes you have made to the Sales Presentation file, as shown in Figure A-14.

9. If necessary, click **Yes** to close the alert box

10. Click **File** on the menu bar, then click **Exit**
    The Presentation window and the PowerPoint program close, and you return to the Windows desktop.

FIGURE A-13: Print dialog box

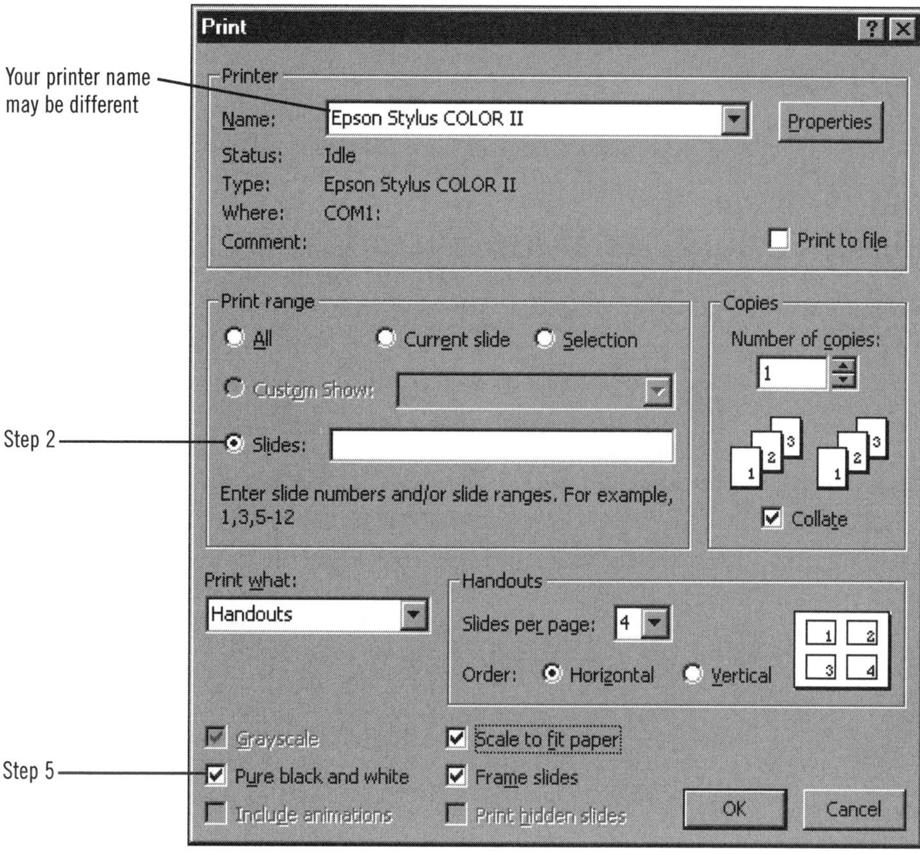

FIGURE A-14: Save changes alert box

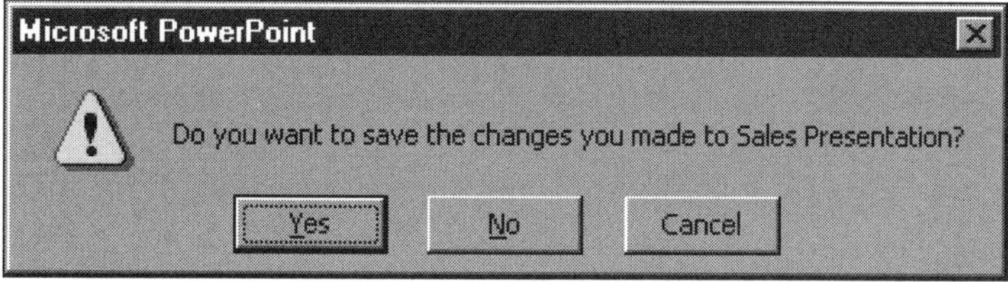

Viewing your presentation in gray scale or black and white

Viewing your presentation in pure black and white or in grayscale (using shades of gray) is very useful when you will be printing a presentation on a black-and-white printer and you want to make sure your text will be readable. To see how your color presentation looks in grayscale when you are in any view (except Slide Show View), click the Grayscale Preview button on the Standard toolbar. To see how your slide looks in pure black and white, hold down [Shift] and press , which is now called the Pure Black and White button. If you don't like the way an object looks in black and white or grayscale view, you can change its shading. Right-click a slide object, point to Black and White, and choose from the options on the pop-up menu.

PowerPoint 2000

Practice

► Concepts Review

Label the elements of the PowerPoint window shown in Figure A-15.

FIGURE A-15

Match each term with the statement that describes it.

11. AutoContent Wizard
12. Presentation window
13. Slide Sorter view
14. Normal view
15. Outline pane

a. Displays the Outline, Slide, and Notes panes
b. Shows slide numbers and small slide icons
c. Series of dialog boxes that guides you through creating a presentation and produces a presentation with suggestions for content
d. The area where you work on your presentation
e. Shows all your slides in the same window

Practice

Select the best answer from the list of choices.

16. PowerPoint can help you create all of the following, *except*
- **a.** Outline pages.
- **b.** A movie.
- **c.** An on-screen presentation.
- **d.** 35-mm slides.

17. The buttons you use to switch between the PowerPoint views are called
- **a.** Toolbar buttons.
- **b.** View buttons.
- **c.** Screen buttons.
- **d.** PowerPoint buttons.

18. All of the following are PowerPoint views, *except*
- **a.** Current Page view.
- **b.** Notes Page view.
- **c.** Outline view.
- **d.** Slide view.

19. The animated character that appears on the screen when you click the Microsoft PowerPoint Help button is the
- **a.** PowerPoint Assistant.
- **b.** Office Assistant.
- **c.** Assistant Paper Clip.
- **d.** Office Helper.

20. The view that allows you to view your electronic slide show with each slide filling the entire screen is called
- **a.** Slide Show view.
- **b.** Slide Sorter view.
- **c.** Presentation view.
- **d.** Electronic view.

21. Which wizard helps you create and outline your presentation?
- **a.** OrgContent Wizard
- **b.** Presentation Wizard
- **c.** AutoContent Wizard
- **d.** Pick a Look Wizard

22. How do you switch to Notes Page view?
- **a.** Press [Shift] and click in the Notes pane
- **b.** Click View on the menu bar, then click Notes Page
- **c.** Click the Notes Page View button to the left of the horizontal scroll bar
- **d.** All of the above

23. **How do you save changes to your presentation after you have saved it for the first time?**
    a. Click Save As on the File menu, specify a new location and file name, then click Save
    b. Click the Save button on the Standard toolbar
    c. Click Save As on the File menu, then click Save
    d. Click Save As on the File menu, select a file name from the list, then assign it a new name

Skills Review

1. **Start PowerPoint and use the AutoContent Wizard.**
    a. Start the PowerPoint program, selecting the AutoContent Wizard option.
    b. In the AutoContent Wizard, select a presentation category and type. (*Hint:* If you see a message saying you need to install the feature, insert your Office 2000 CD in the appropriate drive and click OK. See your technical support person for assistance.)
    c. Select the output options of your choice.
    d. Enter appropriate information for the opening slide, enter your name as the footer text, and complete the wizard to show the first slide of the presentation.

2. **View the PowerPoint window.**
    a. Identify as many elements of the PowerPoint window as you can without referring to the unit material.
    b. For any elements you cannot identify, refer to the unit.

3. **View a presentation.**
    a. View each slide in the presentation to become familiar with its content.
    b. When you are finished, return to slide 1.
    c. Change to Outline view and review the presentation contents.
    d. Change to Notes Page view and see if the notes pages in the presentation contain text, then return to slide 1.
    e. Examine the presentation contents in Slide Sorter view.
    f. View all the slides of the presentation in Slide Show view, and end the slide show to return to Slide Sorter view.

4. **Save a presentation.**
    a. Change to the view in which you would like to save your presentation.
    b. Open the Save As dialog box.
    c. Make sure your Project Disk is in the correct drive.
    d. Save your presentation as "Practice."
    e. Embed the fonts in your presentation.
    f. Save your changes to the file.
    g. Go to a different view than the one you saved your presentation in.
    h. Save the changed presentation.

5. Get Help.

- **a.** If the Office Assistant is open, click it. If it is not on your screen, open it.
- **b.** In the text box, type "Tell me about Help" and click Search.
- **c.** Select the topic, "Display tips and messages through the Office Assistant."
- **d.** Click the Show button to open the Help window containing the Contents, Answer Wizard, and Index tabs.
- **e.** On the Contents tab, double-click any book icon to view the Help subjects (identified by page icons), then click the page icons to review the Help information. Explore a number of topics that interest you.
- **f.** When you have finished exploring the Contents tab, switch to the Index tab.
- **g.** In the Type keywords text box, type a word you want help with.
- **h.** Click a word in the list in box 2 if it did not jump to the correct word, then click Search.
- **i.** Click a topic in the list in box 3 and read about it.
- **j.** Explore a number of topics that interest you.
- **k.** When you have finished exploring the Index tab, close the Help window and hide the Office Assistant.

6. Print and close the file, and exit PowerPoint.

- **a.** Print slides 2 and 3 as slides in grayscale. (*Hint:* In the Slides text box, type 2-3.)
- **b.** Print all the slides as handouts, 6 slides per page, in pure black and white.
- **c.** Print all the slides in Outline view.
- **d.** Resize the slides for overhead transparencies then print slides 1 and 2 in grayscale.
- **e.** Close the file, saving your changes.
- **f.** Exit PowerPoint.

 Visual Workshop

Create the presentation shown in Figure A-16 using the Business Plan AutoContent Wizard in the Corporate category. Save the presentation as "Web Plan" on your Project Disk. Print the slides as handouts, six slides per page, in black and white.

FIGURE A-16

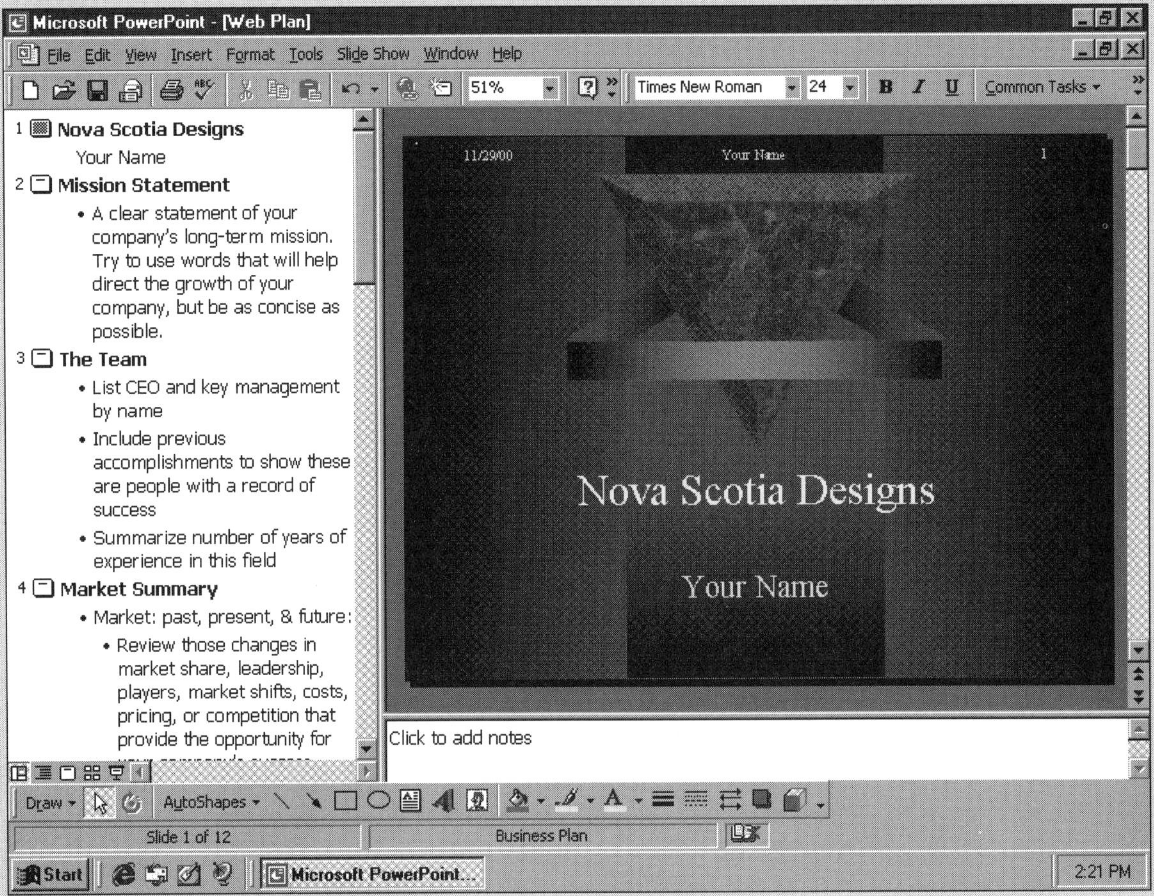

PowerPoint 2000

Creating a Presentation

Objectives

- ▶ Plan an effective presentation
- MOUS ▶ Choose a look for a presentation
- MOUS ▶ Enter slide text
- MOUS ▶ Create a new slide
- MOUS ▶ Work in Outline view
- MOUS ▶ Enter notes
- MOUS ▶ Check spelling in the presentation
- MOUS ▶ Evaluate a presentation

Now that you are familiar with PowerPoint basics, you are ready to plan and create your own presentation. To do this, you enter and edit text and choose a slide design. PowerPoint helps you accomplish these tasks with the AutoContent Wizard and with a collection of professionally prepared slide designs, called **design templates**, which can enhance the look of your presentation. In this unit, you create a presentation using a design template. Scenario ▶ Maria Abbott needs to prepare a presentation on MediaLoft's sales for the upcoming annual meeting for store managers. She begins by planning her presentation.

PowerPoint 2000

Planning an Effective Presentation

Before you create a presentation using PowerPoint, you need to plan and outline the message you want to communicate and consider how you want the presentation to look. When preparing the outline, you need to consider where you are giving the presentation and who your audience will be. It is also important to know what resources you might need, such as a computer or projection equipment. Scenario Using Figure B-1 and the planning guidelines below, follow Maria as she outlines the presentation message.

In planning a presentation it is important to:

Determine the purpose of the presentation, the location, and the audience
Maria needs to present the highlights of MediaLoft's 1999 sales at the yearly company meeting for store managers in a large room at a business center.

Determine the type of output—black-and-white or color overhead transparencies, on-screen slide show, or 35-mm slides—that best conveys your message, given time constraints and computer hardware availability
Because Maria is speaking in a large room and has access to a computer and projection equipment, an on-screen slide show is the best choice.

Determine a look for your presentation that will help communicate your message
You can choose one of the professionally designed templates that come with PowerPoint, modify one of these templates, or create one of your own. Maria wants to establish an upbeat, friendly relationship with the store managers, so she will choose an artistic template.

Determine the message you want to communicate, then give the presentation a meaningful title and outline your message
Maria wants to highlight the previous year's accomplishments. See Figure B-1.

Determine what additional materials will be useful in the presentation
You need to prepare not only the slides themselves but supplementary materials, including speaker notes and handouts for the audience. Speaker notes will allow Maria to stay on track and deliver a concise message.

FIGURE B-1: Outline of the text in the presentation

1. Media Loft
   - -1999 Sales Report to Managers
   - -Maria Abbott
   - -General Sales Manager
   - -January 26, 2000
2. 1999: A Banner Year
   - -Overall sales set new record
   - -3 new locations
   - -Book sales post biggest increase
   - -CDs and videos close behind
   - -Café sales steady
3. 1999 Sales by Division
   - -Overall product sales up 22%
   - -MediaLoft East sales up 25%
   - -MediaLoft West sales up 21%
4. The Star: MediaLoft East
   - -Book sales up 29%
   - -CD sales up 25%
   - -Video sales up 20%

PowerPoint 2000

Choosing a Look for a Presentation

To help you design your presentation, PowerPoint provides 44 design templates so you don't have to spend time creating the right presentation look. A **design template** has borders, colors, text attributes, and other elements arranged in a specific format that you can apply to all the slides in your presentation. You can use a design template as is, or you can modify any element to suit your needs. Unless you know something about graphic design, it is often easier and faster to use or modify one of the templates supplied with PowerPoint. No matter how you create your presentation, you can save it as a template for future use. Scenario Maria doesn't have a lot of time but wants to create a good-looking presentation, so she uses an existing PowerPoint template.

QuickTip

If PowerPoint is already running, click File on the menu bar, then click New.

1. Start PowerPoint, click the **Design Template option button** in the PowerPoint startup dialog box, then click **OK**

   The New Presentation dialog box opens, containing three tabs. See Table B-1 for an overview of the tabs.
2. Click the **Design Templates tab**

   This lists the 44 PowerPoint design templates.
3. Click the **right scroll arrow** if necessary, then click the **Sumi Painting icon** once

   A miniature version of the selected template appears in the Preview box on the right side of the dialog box, as shown in Figure B-2.
4. Click **OK**

   The New Slide dialog box opens, showing 24 AutoLayouts. An **AutoLayout** is a slide containing placeholders for text and graphics. The first AutoLayout is selected, and its name, Title Slide, appears on the right side of the dialog box. Because the first slide of the presentation is the title slide, this layout is appropriate.
5. Click **OK**

   A blank title slide, containing placeholders for title and subtitle text, appears in the Slide pane. The background of the slide and the graphics are part of the Sumi Painting design template you chose. Notice that the name of the template is in the status bar. Notice also that there is a slide icon for slide 1 in the Outline pane.
6. Click **Window** on the menu bar, then click **Arrange All**

   This step adjusts your presentation window so it matches the figures in this book. Compare your screen to Figure B-3.
7. Click **Tools** on the menu bar, click **Customize**, click the **Options tab** in the Customize dialog box, click **Reset my usage data** to restore your toolbars to the default settings, click **Yes**, then click **Close**
8. Click the **Save button** on the Standard toolbar, then save your presentation as **1999 Sales Report** to your Project Disk

TABLE B-1: New Presentation dialog box tabs

tab	contains	use
General	A blank presentation and the AutoContent Wizard	To create a presentation from scratch, or to use one of 24 preformatted presentations with suggested content
Design Templates	44 design templates with backgrounds and text formats	To create a presentation with a predesigned template that contains text and graphic designs that coordinate well with each other
Presentations	24 design templates that contain suggested content for specific uses	To create a presentation based on suggested content

FIGURE B-2: Design Templates tab in the New Presentation dialog box

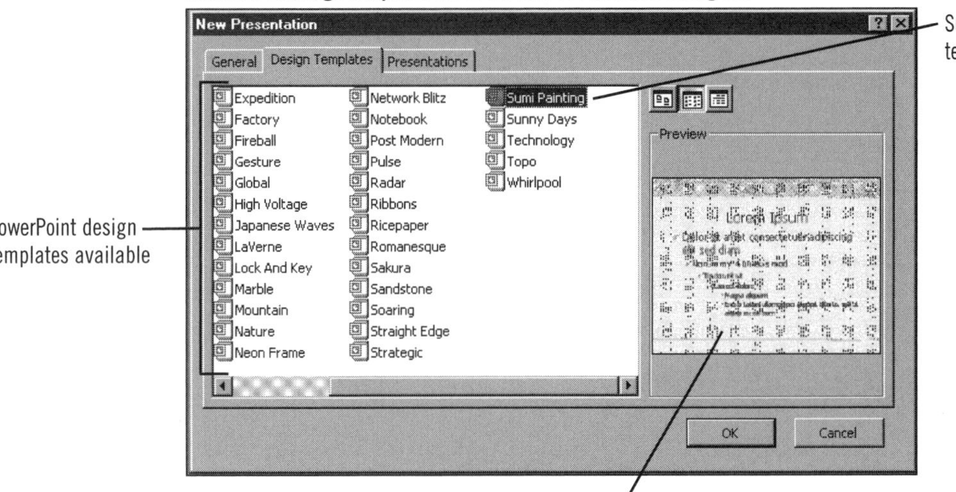

FIGURE B-3: Title slide with template design

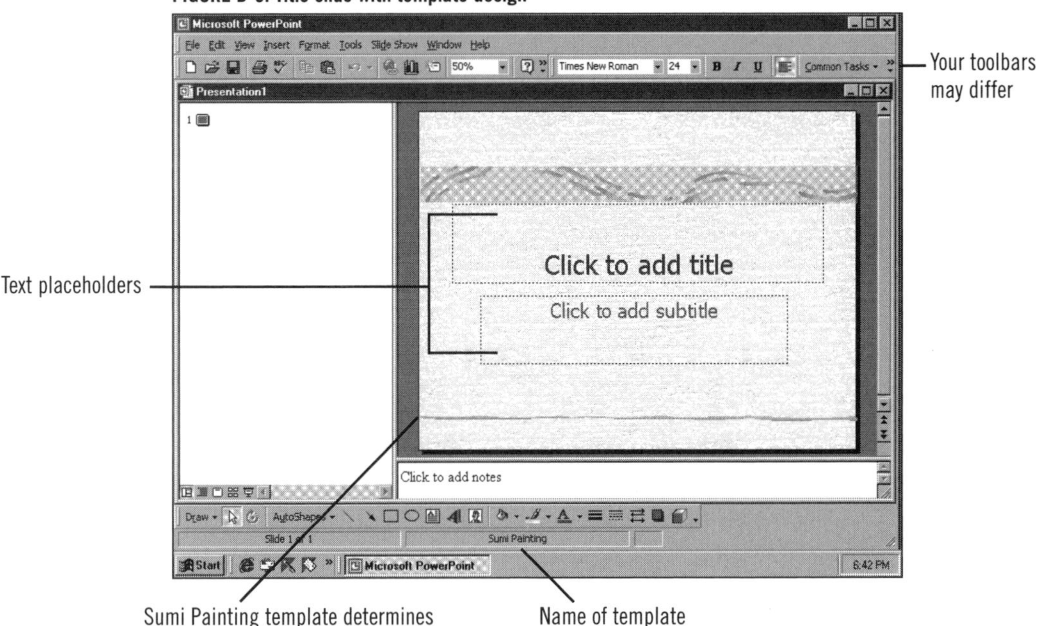

PowerPoint 2000

CLUES TO USE

Applying a design template to an existing presentation

You can apply a design template to a presentation at any time. Open the presentation to which you want to apply the template. Click the Common Tasks menu button on the Formatting toolbar, then click Apply Design Template on the drop-down menu. You can also select Apply Design Template on the Format menu. The Apply Design Template dialog box opens with the Presentations Designs folder open. This list of templates is similar to the list that appears on the Design Templates tab in the New Presentation dialog box. Select the template you want to apply. A preview appears in the preview box on the right. Then click Apply. The Apply Design Template dialog box closes and the slide text and background now reflect the template you chose.

PowerPoint 2000

Entering Slide Text

Now that you have applied a template to your new presentation, you are ready to enter text into the title slide. The title slide has two **text placeholders**, boxes with dashed line borders where you enter text. The first text placeholder on the title slide is the **title placeholder** labeled "Click to add title." The second text placeholder on the title slide is the **main text placeholder** labeled "Click to add subtitle." To enter text in a placeholder, simply click the placeholder and then type your text. After you enter text in a placeholder, the placeholder becomes a text object. An **object** is any item on a slide that can be manipulated. Objects are the building blocks that make up a presentation slide. Scenario Maria begins working on her presentation by entering the title of the presentation in the title placeholder.

Steps 1 2 3 4

1. Move the pointer over the title placeholder labeled "Click to add title" in the Slide pane
   The pointer changes to I when you move the pointer over the placeholder. In PowerPoint, the pointer often changes shape, depending on the task you are trying to accomplish. Table B-2 describes the functions of the most common PowerPoint mouse pointer shapes.
2. Click the **title placeholder**
   The **insertion point**, a blinking vertical line, indicates where your text will appear in the title placeholder. A **selection box**, the slanted line border, appears around the title placeholder, indicating that it is selected and ready to accept text. See Figure B-4.
3. Type **MediaLoft**
   In the Slide pane, PowerPoint center-aligns the title text within the title placeholder, which is now a text object. Notice that the text appeared in the Ouline pane as you typed.
4. Click the **main text placeholder** in the Slide pane
   A wavy, red line may appear under the word "MediaLoft" in the title object indicating that the automatic spellchecking feature in PowerPoint is active. Don't worry if it doesn't appear on your screen.
5. Type **1999 Sales Report to Managers**, then press **[Enter]**
   In the Outline pane, this text appears indented under the slide title.
6. Type **Maria Abbott**, press **[Enter]**, type **General Sales Manager**, press **[Enter]**, then type **January 26, 2000**
   Compare your title slide to Figure B-5.
7. Click outside the main text object in a blank area of the slide
   Clicking a blank area of the slide deselects all selected objects on the slide.
8. Click the **Save button** on the Standard toolbar to save your changes

Trouble?

If you press a wrong key, press [Backspace] to erase the character, then continue to type.

FIGURE B-4: Selected title placeholder

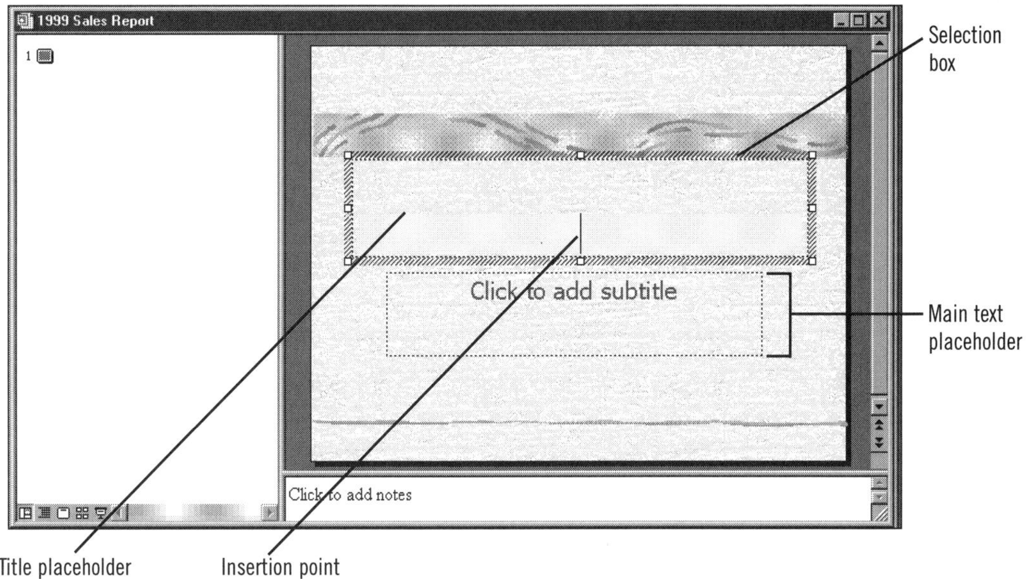

FIGURE B-5: Title slide with text

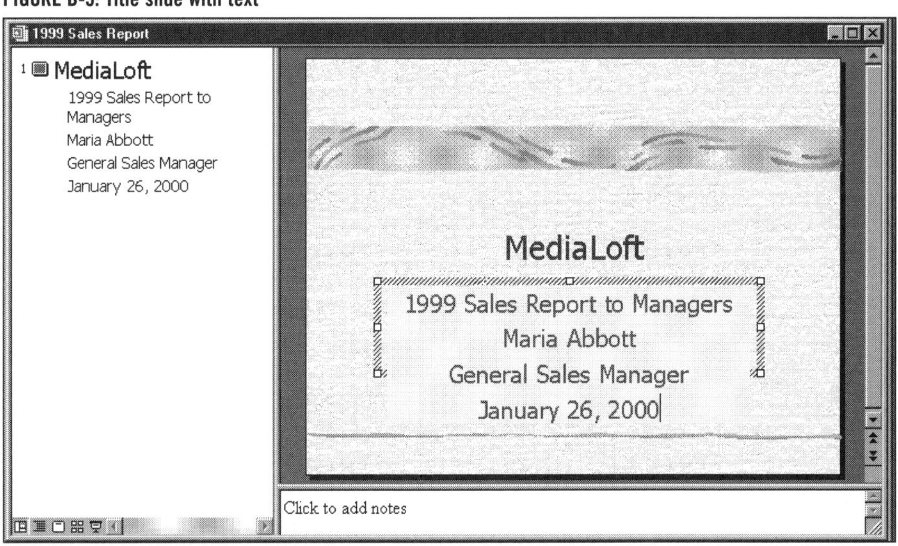

PowerPoint 2000

TABLE B-2: PowerPoint mouse pointer shapes

shape	description
(arrow)	Appears when you select the Selection tool; use this pointer to select one or more PowerPoint objects
(I-beam)	Appears when you move the pointer over a text object; use this pointer, called the I-beam, to place the insertion point where you want to begin typing or selecting text
(four-headed arrow)	Appears when you move the pointer over a bullet, slide icon, or object; use this pointer to select title or paragraph text
(cross-hair)	Appears when you select a drawing tool; use this pointer, called the cross-hair cursor, to draw shapes

PowerPoint 2000

Creating a New Slide

To help you create a new slide easily, PowerPoint offers 24 predesigned AutoLayouts, which include a variety of placeholder arrangements for objects including titles, main text, clip art, graphs, charts, and media clips. You have already used the title slide AutoLayout. Table B-3 describes the different placeholders you'll find in the AutoLayouts. Scenario To continue developing the presentation, Maria needs to create a slide that states the main theme of her presentation.

Trouble?

If you don't see the New Slide button on your toolbar, click the More Buttons button on the Standard toolbar.

QuickTip

To delete a slide, select it in the Outline pane, display it in the Slide pane or select it in Slide Sorter view, click Edit on the menu bar, and then click Delete Slide.

1. Click the **New Slide button** on the Standard toolbar
   The New Slide dialog box opens, showing the different AutoLayouts. (Click the down scroll arrow to view more.) This is the same dialog box from which you chose the title slide layout. The title for the selected AutoLayout appears in a Preview box to the right of the layouts, as shown in Figure B-6. You can choose a layout by clicking it. The Bulleted List AutoLayout is already selected.
2. Click **OK**
   A new slide appears after the current slide in your presentation. In the Slide pane, it contains a title placeholder and a main text placeholder for the bulleted list. Notice that the status bar indicates Slide 2 of 2. A new slide icon for slide 2 appears in the Outline pane.
3. Click next to the **slide icon** for slide 2 in the Outline pane, then type **1999: A Banner Year**
   As you type, the text appears in the Slide pane also.
4. Click the **main text placeholder** in the Slide pane
   You can type text in either pane. The insertion point appears next to a bullet in the main text placeholder.
5. Type **Overall sales set new record**, then press **[Enter]**
   A new bullet automatically appears when you press [Enter].
6. Press **[Tab]**
   The new first-level bullet indents and becomes a second-level bullet.
7. Type **3 new locations**, then press **[Enter]**
   This bullet should actually be a first-level bullet.
8. Click to the left of the **3** that you just typed, then press **[Shift][Tab]**
   The item changes back to a first-level bullet.
9. Click after the word **locations**, press **[Enter]**, then enter the next three bulleted items as shown in Figure B-7
10. Click the **Save button** on the Standard toolbar
    Your changes are saved to your Project Disk.

FIGURE B-6: New Slide dialog box

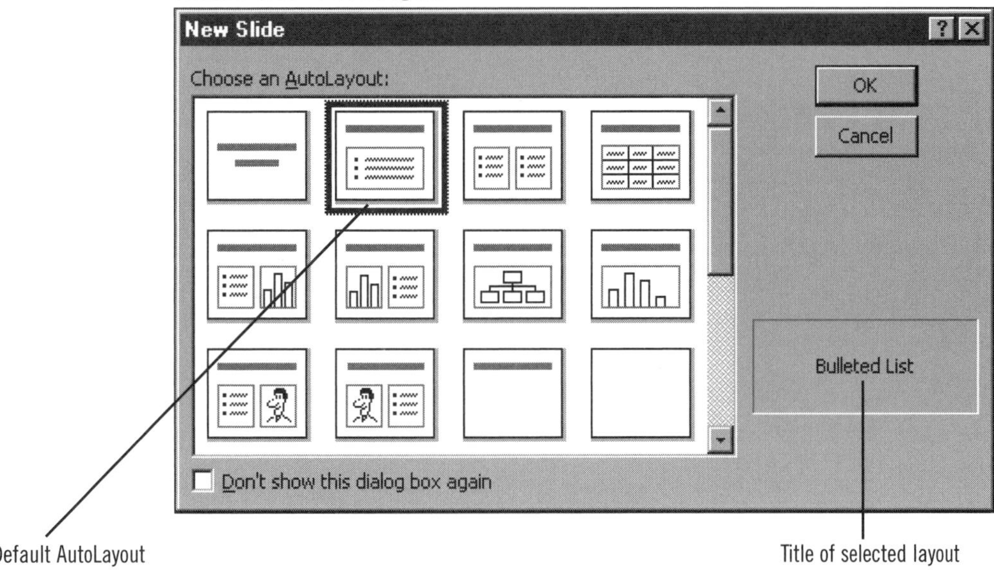

FIGURE B-7: New slide with bulleted list

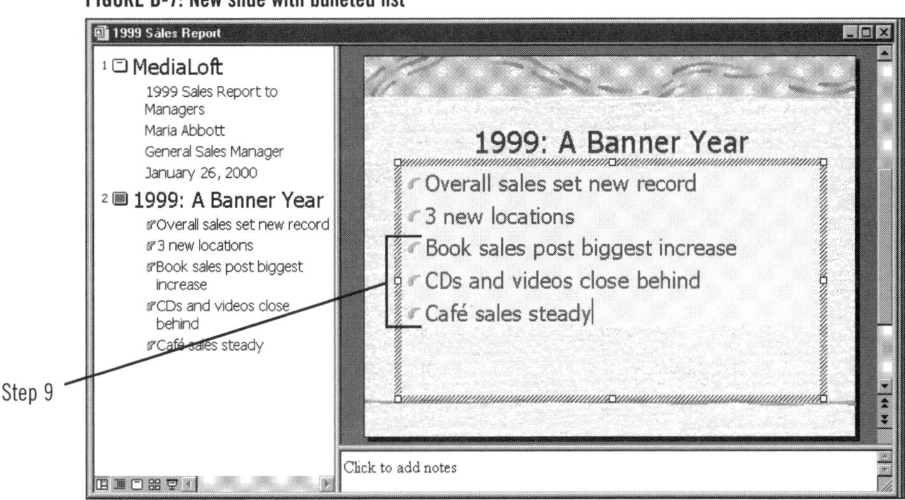

TABLE B-3: AutoLayout placeholder types

placeholder	symbol	description
Bulleted List		Inserts a short list of related points
Clip Art		Inserts a picture from the Clip Gallery
Chart		Inserts a chart created with Microsoft Graph
Organization Chart		Inserts an organizational chart
Table		Inserts a table
Media Clip		Inserts a music, sound, or video clip
Object		Inserts an external object such as WordArt, an equation, a spreadsheet, or a picture

PowerPoint 2000

Working in Outline View

As you have learned, you can enter your presentation text in the Slide or Outline pane in Normal view. You can also enter text in Slide or Outline view. If you want to focus on the presentation text without worrying about how it looks, Outline view can be a good choice. As in a regular outline, the headings, or **titles**, appear first; then under them, the subpoints, or **main text**, appear. The main text appears as one or more lines of bulleted text indented under a title. Scenario ▶ Maria switches to Outline view to enter text for two more slides.

Steps 1 2 3 4

QuickTip

You can work in the Outline pane in Normal view if you prefer.

Trouble?

If the Outlining toolbar is not visible, click View on the menu bar, point to Toolbars, then click Outlining.

QuickTip

You can also drag slide icons or bullets to a new location.

1. Click the **Outline View button** to the left of the horizontal scroll bar
   Switching to Outline view enlarges the Outline pane; the Slide and Notes panes become smaller and move to the right side of the screen. The blinking insertion point is in the title of slide 2 (the slide you just created). The Outlining toolbar appears on the left side of the screen.
2. Click anywhere in the last text bullet, press **[Shift]**, then click the **New Slide button** on the Standard toolbar
   Pressing [Shift] while clicking inserts a new slide with the same AutoLayout as the current slide. A slide icon appears next to the slide number when you add a new slide to the outline. See Figure B-8. Text you enter next to a slide icon becomes the title for that slide. The Outlining toolbar is helpful when working in Outline view.
3. Right-click any toolbar, then click **Outlining**
   Table B-4 describes the buttons available on the Outlining toolbar. Because the third slide is a bulleted list like the second slide, you can insert a new slide with the same layout as Slide 2.
4. Type **1999 Sales by Division**, press **[Enter]**, then click the **Demote button** on the Outlining toolbar
   A new slide was inserted when you pressed [Enter], but because you want to enter the main text for the slide you just created, you indented this line to make it part of slide 3. You can also press [Tab] to indent text one level.
5. Type **Overall product sales up 22%**, then press **[Enter]**; type **MediaLoft East sales up 25%**, then press **[Enter]**; type **MediaLoft West sales up 21%**, then press **[Enter]**
6. Press **[Shift][Tab]**
   The bullet changes to a new slide icon.
7. Type **The Star: MediaLoft East**, press **[Ctrl][Enter]**, type **Book sales up 29%**, press **[Enter]**, type **CD sales up 25%**, press **[Enter]**, then type **Video sales up 20%**
   Pressing [Ctrl][Enter] while the cursor is in title text creates a bullet. Pressing [Ctrl][Enter] while the cursor is in the main text creates a new slide with the same layout as the previous slide. Two of the bulleted points you just typed for slide 4 are out of order.
8. Position the pointer to the left of the last bullet in slide 4, then click
   The pointer changes from I to ✥. PowerPoint selects the entire line of text.
9. Click the **Move Up button** on the Outlining toolbar
   The third bullet point moves up one line and trades places with the second bullet point, as shown in Figure B-9.
10. Right-click any toolbar, click **Outlining** to close the Outlining toolbar, click the **Normal View button**, click the **Previous Slide button** below the vertical scroll bar in the Slide pane three times to view each slide, then save your work
    When you are finished viewing all the slides, Slide 1 of 4 should appear in the status bar.

FIGURE B-8: Outline view

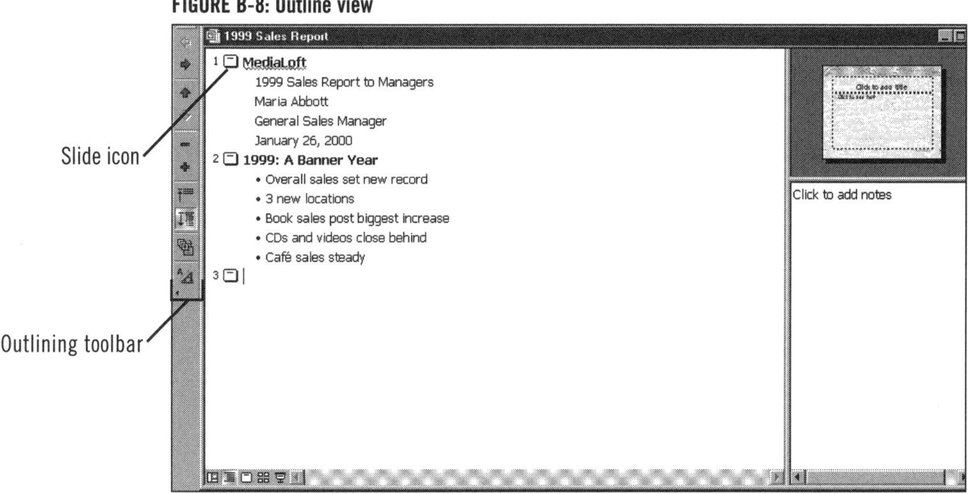

FIGURE B-9: Bulleted item moved up in Outline view

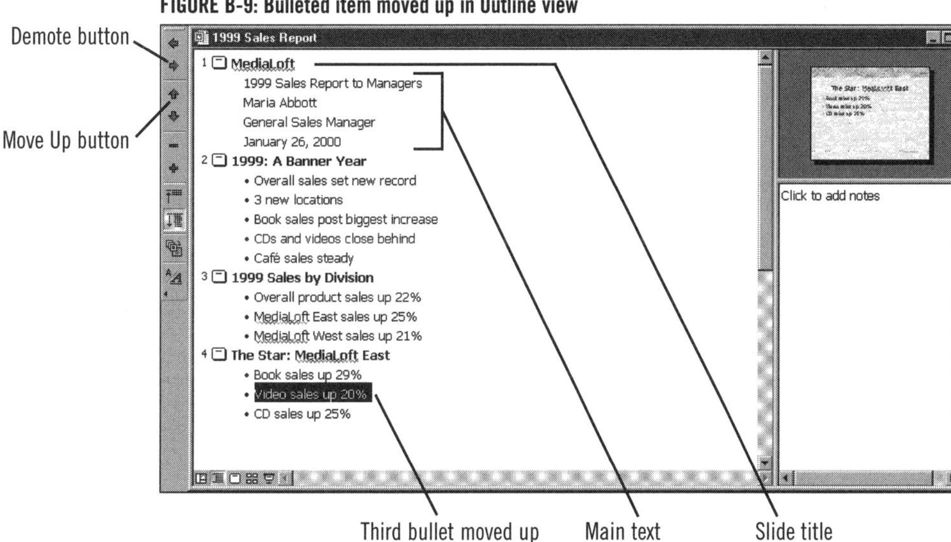

TABLE B-4: Outlining toolbar commands

button	button name	description
	Promote	Indents selected text one tab to the left
	Demote	Indents selected text one tab to the right
	Move Up	Moves the selection above the previous line
	Move Down	Moves the selection below the next line
	Collapse	Shows only the titles of the selected slide
	Expand	Shows all levels of the selected slide
	Collapse All	Shows only the titles of all slides
	Expand All	Shows all levels of all slides
	Summary Slide	Creates a new bulleted slide containing only the titles of selected slides; good for creating an agenda slide
	Show Formatting	Shows or hides all character formatting

PowerPoint 2000

Entering Notes

So you don't have to rely on your memory when you give your presentation in front of a group, you can create notes that accompany your slides. You can enter notes in either the Notes pane or in Notes Page view. The notes you enter do not appear on the slides themselves; they are private notes. You can print these pages and refer to them during your presentation. If you want to provide pages on which your audience can take notes, print the notes pages, but leave the text placeholder blank. You can also insert graphics on the notes pages if you use Notes Page view. Scenario To make sure she doesn't forget how she will present the slide information, Maria enters notes to her slides.

Steps 1 2 3 4

1. Click in the **Notes pane**
   The placeholder text in the Notes pane disappears and the blinking insertion point appears, as shown in Figure B-10.
2. Type **Welcom to MediaLoft's Year 2000 company meeting.**
   Make sure you typed "Welcome" without the "e" as shown. The red, wavy line under the words "MediaLoft" and "Welcom" means that these words are not in the Microsoft Office dictionary.
3. Click the **Next Slide button**, click in the **Notes pane**, then type **I'm happy to share with you a brief overview of the success MediaLoft has achieved in the last year.**
   As you type, text automatically wraps to the next line.
4. Click to go to the third slide, click the **Notes pane**, then type **Due to our record year in 1998, MediaLoft's 1999 goals were very aggressive. Our overall product sales were up an amazing 22%, with the eastern division edging out the western division. Of course, they did get 2 of the 3 new stores, so they had an advantage there.**
5. Click **View** on the menu bar, click **Notes Page**, click the **Zoom list arrow** on the Standard toolbar, then click **100%**
   Because the note on slide 3 is so long, it is easier to read in Notes Page view. See Figure B-11.
6. Click , click in the **notes placeholder**, then type **As you can see, the book sales for MediaLoft East were remarkable. We had been concerned about the growth of online booksellers, but there appears to be no substitute for actually holding a book and sipping a cup of cappuccino.**
7. Press **[Enter]**, then type **Thank you all for your hard work and support, and I look forward to working with you all in the new millennium!**
8. Click the **Normal View button**, then drag the scroll box in the Slide pane vertical scroll bar all the way to the top to return to slide 1

Trouble?

If you don't see a red, wavy line under the words "MediaLoft" and "Welcom," don't worry. Someone else may have turned this feature off on your machine.

Trouble?

If you don't see Notes Page on the View menu, point to the double arrow at the bottom of the menu. If you don't see the Zoom list arrow, click the More Buttons button on the Standard toolbar

QuickTip

You can also increase the size of the Notes pane in Normal view by dragging the separator line between the Notes pane and the Slide pane.

FIGURE B-10: Insertion point in the Notes pane

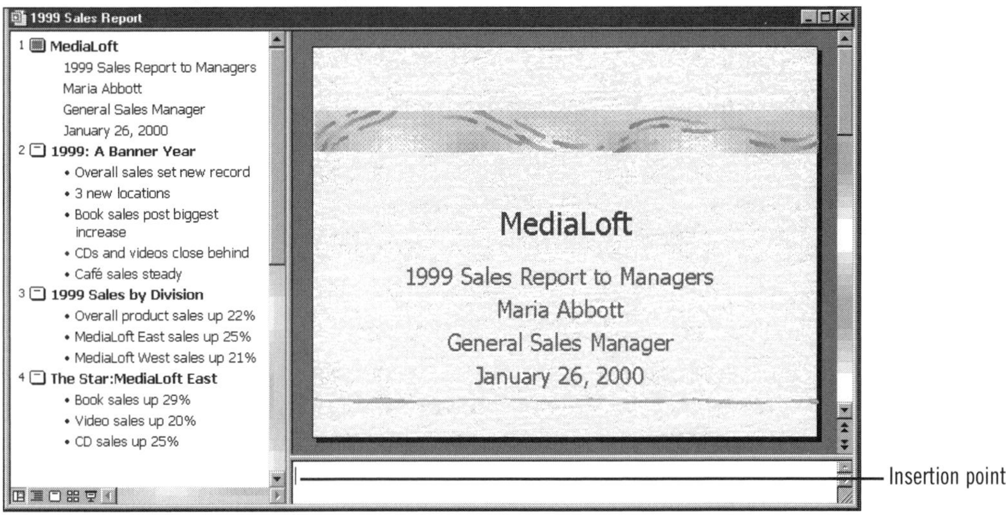

FIGURE B-11: Slide 3 in Notes Page view

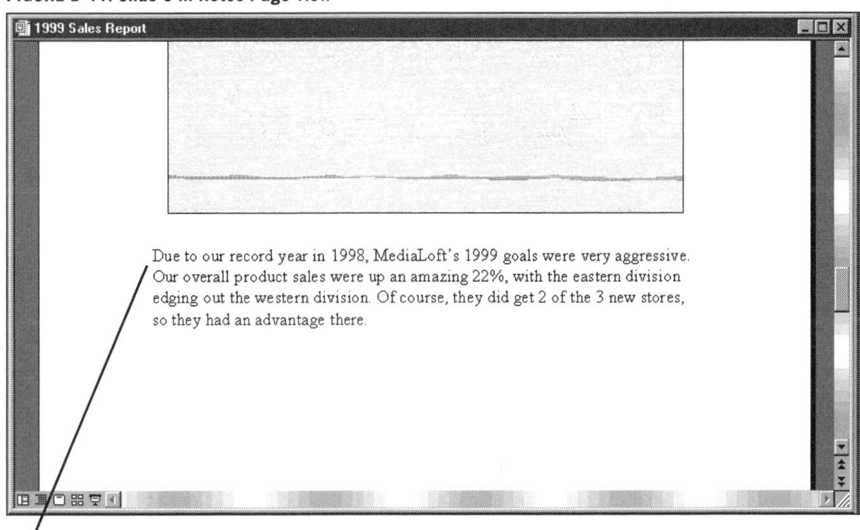

PowerPoint 2000

Adding slide footers and headers

To customize your slides, notes pages, or handouts with information, such as your company or product name, the slide number, or the date, you can add headers and footers. To add a header or footer, click View on the menu bar, then click Header and Footer. Each checked element in the Header and Footer dialog box is included as part of the header or footer. Each check box corresponds to a different footer area. The date and time appear in the left footer area. The slide number appears in the right footer area, and any footer text you add appears in the middle. Click the check boxes and watch to see in which of the three footer areas the footer element appears. On the Slide tab, you can add only footers. To have the footer appear on only the current slide, click Apply; to have footers appear on all the slides, click Apply to All. On the Notes and Handouts tab, you can choose to add headers and footers, so they appear on all the pages.

PowerPoint 2000

Checking Spelling in the Presentation

As your work nears completion, you need to review and proofread your presentation thoroughly for errors. You can use the spellchecking feature in PowerPoint to check for and correct spelling errors. The spellchecking feature compares the spelling of all the words in your presentation against the words contained in its electronic dictionary. You still must proofread your presentation for punctuation, grammar, and word-usage errors, however. The spellchecker recognizes only misspelled words, not misused words. For example, the spellchecker would not identify "The Test" as an error even if you had intended to type "The Best." Scenario Maria has finished adding and changing text in the presentation, so she checks her work.

Steps

1. **Click the Spelling button on the Standard toolbar**
   PowerPoint begins to check the spelling in your entire presentation. When PowerPoint finds a misspelled word or a word it doesn't recognize, the Spelling dialog box opens, as shown in Figure B-12. For an explanation of the commands available in the Spelling dialog box, see Table B-5. In this case, PowerPoint does not recognize "MediaLoft" on slide 1. It suggests that you replace it with two separate words "Media" and "Loft," which it does recognize. You want the word to remain as you typed it.

2. Click **Ignore all**
   Clicking Ignore All tells the spellchecker to ignore all instances of this word in this presentation. The next word the spellchecker identifies as an error is the word "Welcom" on the notes for slide 1. In the Suggestions list box, the spellchecker suggests "Welcome."

3. Click **Welcome** in the Suggestions list box, then click **Change**
   If PowerPoint finds any other words it does not recognize, either change them or ignore them. When the spellchecker finishes checking your presentation, the Spelling dialog box closes, and a PowerPoint alert box opens with a message saying the spelling check is complete.

4. Click **OK**
   The alert box closes.

5. Click **View** on the menu bar, then click **Header and Footer**
   Before you print your final presentation, placing your name in the footer helps you identify your printout if you are sharing a printer.

6. On the Slide tab, make sure the **Footer check box** is selected, click in the **Footer text box**, then type your name

7. Click the **Notes and Handouts tab**, type your name in the Footer text box, then click **Apply to All**
   Now your name will print on slides, notes pages, and handouts.

8. Click **File** on the menu bar, then click **Print**

9. Click the **Print what list arrow**, click **Notes Pages**, click the **Pure black and white check box** to select it, click the **Frame Slides check box** to select it, then click **OK**
   The notes pages print with a frame around each page.

10. Save your presentation, then return to **slide 1** in Normal view

QuickTip

If your spellchecker doesn't find the word "MediaLoft," then a previous user may have accidentally added it to the custom dictionary. Skip steps 1 and 2 and continue with the lesson.

QuickTip

The spellchecker does not check the text in pictures or embedded objects. You'll need to spell check text in imported objects, such as charts or Word documents, using their original application.

FIGURE B-12: Spelling dialog box

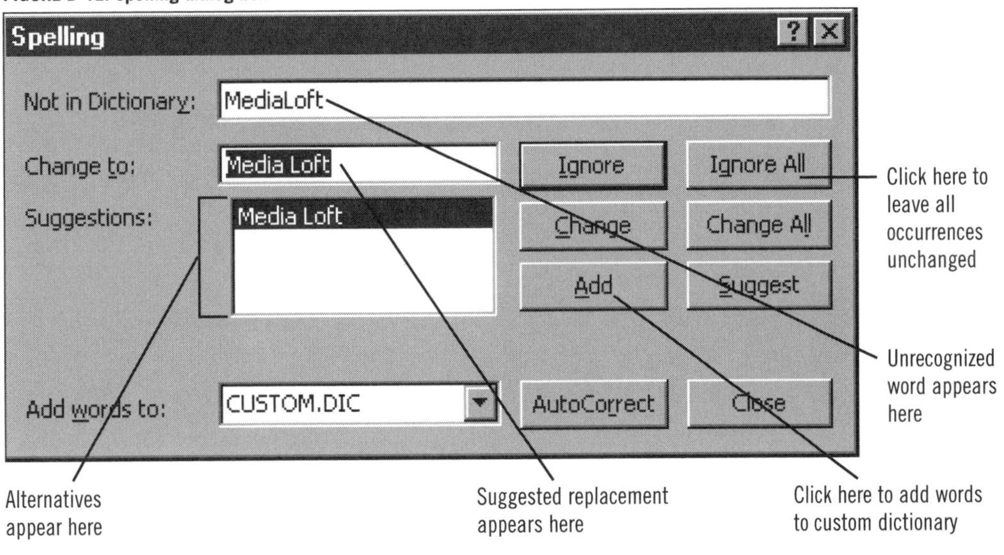

TABLE B-5: Spelling dialog box commands

command	description
Ignore/Ignore all	Continues spellchecking, without making any changes to the identified word (or all occurrences of the identified word)
Change/Change All	Changes the identified word (or all its occurrences) to the suggested word
Add	Adds the identified word to your custom dictionary; spellchecker will not flag it again
Suggest	Suggests an alternative spelling for the identified word
AutoCorrect	Adds suggested word as an AutoCorrect entry for the highlighted word
Add words to	Lets you choose a custom dictionary where you store words you often use but that are not part of the PowerPoint dictionary

Checking spelling as you type

PowerPoint checks your spelling as you type. If you type a word that is not in the electronic dictionary, a wavy, red line appears under it. To correct the error, right-click the misspelled word. A pop-up menu appears with one or more suggestions. You can select a suggestion, add the word you typed to your custom dictionary, or ignore it. To turn off automatic spellchecking, click Tools on the menu bar, then click Options to open the Options dialog box. Click the Spelling and Style tab, and in the Spelling section click the Check spelling as you type check box to deselect it. To temporarily hide the wavy, red lines, select the Hide spelling errors in this document check box.

Evaluating a Presentation

As you create a presentation, keep in mind that good design involves preparation. An effective presentation is both focused and visually appealing. A planned presentation is easy for the speaker to present and easy for the audience to comprehend. The visual elements (colors, graphics, and text) can strongly influence audience attention and interest and can determine the success of your presentation. Scenario Maria evaluates her presentation's effectiveness. Her final presentation is shown in Slide Sorter view in Figure B-13. For contrast, Figure B-14 shows a poorly designed slide.

1. Click the **Slide Show button**, then press **[Enter]** to move through the slide show
2. When you are finished viewing the slide show, click the **Slide Sorter View button**
   Maria decides that slide 4 should come before slide 3.
3. Drag **slide 4** to the left until you see a thin black line between slides 2 and 3, then release the mouse button
   The thin, black line indicates the slide's position.
4. When you are finished evaluating your presentation according to the following guidelines, exit PowerPoint, saving changes when prompted

In evaluating a presentation it is important to:

Keep your message focused

Don't put everything you are going to say on your presentation slides. Keep the audience anticipating further explanations to the key points shown on your slides. For example, Maria's presentation focuses the audience's attention on last year's sales numbers and sales by division because she included only the sales percentage increases and the breakdown of the sales by division. She supplemented the slides with notes that explain the reasons for the increases.

Keep the design simple, easy to read, and appropriate for the content

Use appropriate fonts, font sizes, and background colors. A design template makes the presentation consistent. If you design your own layout, do not add so many elements that the slides look cluttered. Use the same design elements consistently throughout the presentation; otherwise, your audience will get confused. The design template Maria used for the sales presentation is simple; the horizontal bar on each slide gives the presentation an interesting, somewhat artistic look, appropriate for a friendly presentation to company employees.

Choose attractive colors that make the slide easy to read

Use contrasting colors for slide background and text, so that the slides are easy to read. If you are giving your presentation on a computer, you can use almost any combination of colors.

Keep your text concise

Limit each slide to six words per line and six lines per slide. Use lists and symbols to help prioritize your points visually. Your presentation text provides only the highlights; use notes to give more detailed information.

Choose fonts and styles that are easy to read and emphasize important text

As a general rule, use no more than two fonts in a presentation and vary font size. Use bold and italic selectively. Do not use text smaller than 18 points. In the design template Maria used, the titles are 44-point Tahoma and the main text is 32-point Tahoma.

Use visuals to help communicate the message of your presentation

Commonly used visuals include clip art, photographs, charts, worksheets, tables, and movies. Whenever possible, replace text with a visual, but be careful not to overcrowd your slides.

FIGURE B-13: The final presentation

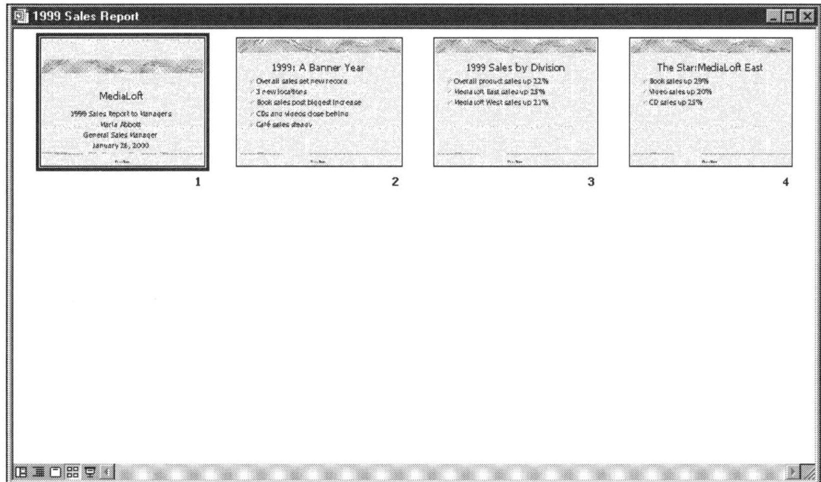

FIGURE B-14: A poorly designed slide in Slide view

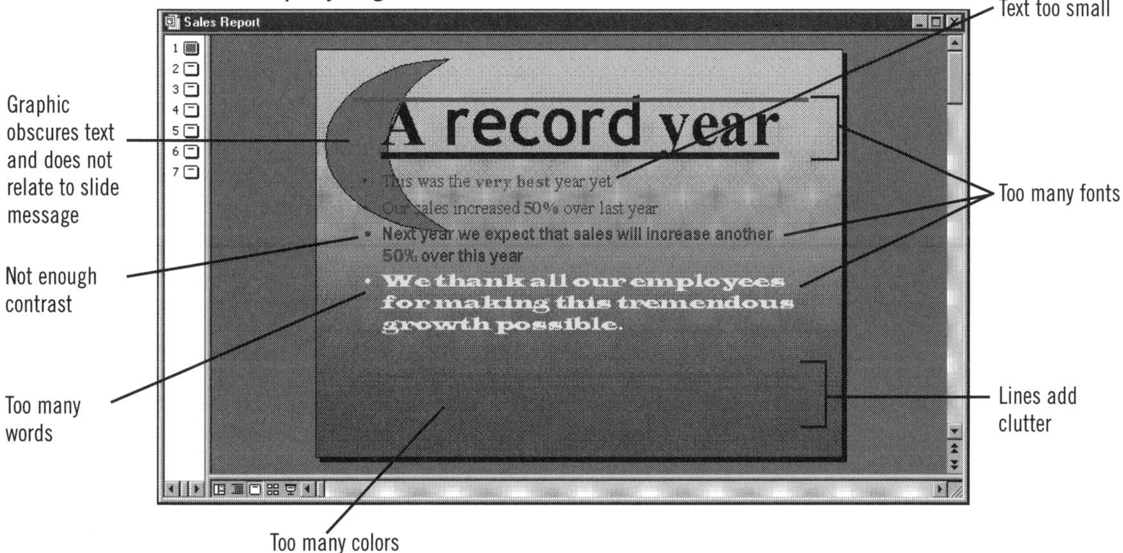

Using design templates

You are not limited to the templates in PowerPoint; you can either modify a PowerPoint template or create your own presentation template. For example, you might want to use your company's color as a slide background or incorporate your company's logo on every slide. If you modify an existing template, you can keep, change, or delete any color, graphic, or font. To create a new template, click File on the menu bar, then click New. On the General tab, double-click Blank Presentation, then select the Blank AutoLayout. Add the design elements you want, then use the Save As command on the File menu to name and save your customized design. Click the Save as type list arrow, and choose Design template, then name your template. PowerPoint will automatically add a .pot file extension to the file name. You can then use your customized template as a basis for future presentations. To apply a template from another presentation, open the presentation you want to change, then choose Apply Design Template from the Format menu. In the Apply Design Template dialog box, choose Presentations and Shows in the Files of type list box. Then navigate to and double-click the presentation whose design you want to apply. That presentation's template will be applied to your current presentation.

Practice

► Concepts Review

Label each element of the PowerPoint window shown in Figure B-15.

FIGURE B-15

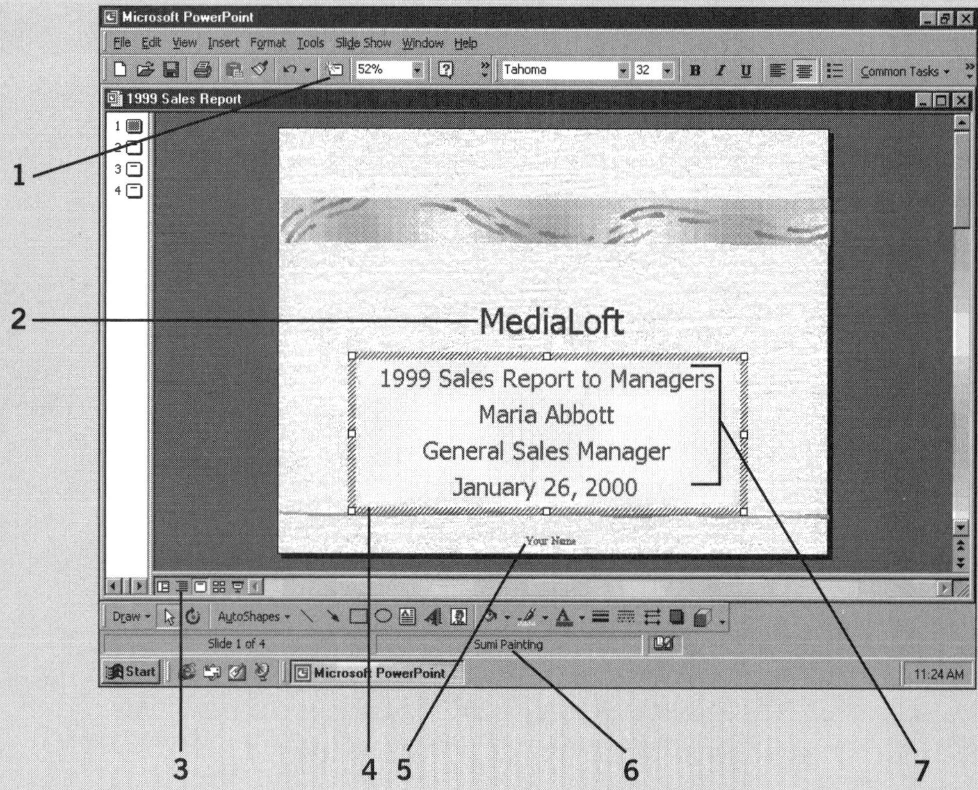

Match each term with the statement that describes it.

8. **Selection box**
9. **Insertion point**
10. **Slide icon**
11. **Design template**

a. In Outline view, the symbol that represents a slide
b. A blinking vertical line that indicates where your text will appear in a text object
c. A box of slanted lines containing prompt text in which you can enter text
d. A specific design, format, and color scheme that is applied to all the slides in a presentation

Select the best answer from the list of choices.

12. The I pointer shape appears for which one of the following tasks?

a. Inserting a new slide
b Switching views
c. Choosing a new layout
d. Entering text

13. To move a slide up to a new position in Outline view

a. Click
c. Press [Tab]
b. Click
d. Click

14. When the spellchecker identifies a word as misspelled, which of the following is not a choice?

a. To ignore all occurrences of the error in the presentation
b. To change the misspelled word to the correct spelling
c. To have the spellchecker automatically correct all the errors it finds
d. To ignore this occurrence of the error

15. When you evaluate your presentation, you should make sure it follows which of the following criteria?

a. The message should be clearly outlined without a lot of extra words
b. The slides should use as many colors as possible to hold the audience's attention
c. Lots of different typefaces will make the slides more interesting
d. The slides should include every piece of information to be presented so the audience can read it

16. According to the unit, which of the following is *not* a guideline for planning a presentation?

a. Determine who else can give the final presentation
b. Determine what you want to produce when the presentation is finished
c. Determine which type of output you will need to best convey your message
d. Determine the purpose of the presentation

17. Which of the following statements is *not* true?

a. PowerPoint has many colorful templates from which to choose
b. The spellchecker will identify "there" as misspelled if the correct word for the context is "their"
c. Speaker notes do not appear during the slide show
d. You can customize any PowerPoint template

18. Which of the following is *not* a method for changing text levels in the Outline pane or Outline view

a. Drag selected text
c.
b.
d.

Skills Review

1. Choose a look for a presentation.

a. Start PowerPoint if necessary and open a new presentation by clicking the Design Template option button or by clicking New on the File menu.
b. Display the Design Templates tab.
c. Review the PowerPoint design templates and examine the preview of each one when the template is available.
d. When you have finished reviewing the templates, open a new presentation using the Mountain template. (*Hint:* If you see a message saying you need to install additional templates, insert the Office 2000 CD in the appropriate drive and click OK. See your technical support person for assistance.)
e. In the New Slide dialog box, select the Title Slide AutoLayout.
f. Save the presentation as "Weekly Goals" to your Project Disk.

g. Go to Slide view and apply the Bold Stripes template from the Design Templates folder.
h. Apply the template from the 1999 Sales Report presentation you created in the unit, and print slides 1 and 2 as Handouts in Grayscale, 6 slides per page.
i. Save the presentation.

2. Enter slide text.

a. In the Slide pane in Normal view or in Slide view, enter the text "Product Marketing" in the title placeholder.
b. In the main text placeholder, enter "Les Bolinger."
c. On the next line of the placeholder, enter "Manager."
d. On the next line of the placeholder, enter "Aug. 2, 2000."
e. Display and examine the different pointer shapes in PowerPoint. Refer back to Table B-2 to help you display the pointer shapes.
f. Deselect the text objects.

3. Create new slides.

a. Open the New Slide dialog box, and click each of the AutoLayouts. Identify each AutoLayout by its name in the Preview box.
b. Select the Bulleted List AutoLayout.
c. Type "Weekly Meeting for Marketing Groups" in the title placeholder.
d. Create a new bulleted list slide.
e. Enter the text from Table B-5 into the new slide.

f. Move slide 5 up to the slide 4 position.

TABLE B-5

(Slide title)	Goals for the Week
(Main text object, first indent level)	Les
(Main text object, second indent level)	Interview for new marketing rep Discuss new procedures with Pacific Rim marketing reps
Prepare for weekly division	meeting next Mon.

4. Work in Outline view.

a. Switch to Outline view
b. Create a new bulleted list slide after the last one.
c. Enter the text from Table B-6 into the new slide.
d. Create a new bulleted list slide after the last one.
e. Enter the text from Table B-7 into the new slide.

TABLE B-6

(Slide title)	Goals for the Week
(Main text object, first indent level)	John
(Main text object, second indent level)	Revise product marketing report Set up plan for the annual
sales meeting	Thurs.—fly to Phoenix for sales meeting planning session

5. Enter notes.

a. Go to slide 3 and place the insertion point in the Notes pane.
b. Enter the following notes:
I am interviewing new candidates for the product marketing position.
The following week, each of you will interview the candidates who meet initial qualifications.
I need all reports for the weekly meeting by Fri.
Reminder of the company profit sharing party next Fri. Work half day.
Open agenda for new division items.

TABLE B-7

(Slide title)	Goals for the Week
(Main text object, first indent level)	April
(Main text object, second indent level)	Complete division advertising plan for next year Establish preliminary advertising budget for division VP Investigate new advertising agencies for company

c. View slide 5.
d. Enter the following notes:
I need the marketing report by Wed.
John: Come by my office later this afternoon to review the sales meeting plan.
Open agenda for new division items.
e. View slide 4.
f. Enter the following speaker's notes:
I need to review the advertising company list by Fri.
April: See me about weekly division report after this meeting.
Status on the advertising budget and next year's advertising plan.
Open agenda for new division items.
g. Switch to Slide view.

6. Check spelling in the presentation.

a. Perform a spelling check on the document and change any misspelled words. Ignore any words that are correctly spelled but that the spellchecker doesn't recognize.
b. Add your name to the footer on all sides and on all notes and handouts.
c. Add "Product Marketing Presentation" to the left side of the header for Notes and Handouts.
d. Save the presentation.

7. Evaluate your presentation.

a. View slide 1 in Slide Show view, then move through the slide show.
b. Go to Slide Sorter view, then delete slide 2.
c. Drag slide 4 so that it comes before slide 3.
d. Evaluate the presentation using the points described in the lesson as criteria.
e. Print the Notes pages in Pure black and white, with a frame around the page.
f. Customize the template text by adding the date and time to the left side of the slide footer, then save your new design as a template called Weekly Goals Template.
g. Print the Notes pages in Grayscale with a frame around the page.

Visual Workshop

Create the marketing presentation shown in Figures B-16 and B-17. Save the presentation as "Sales Project" to your Project Disk. Review your slides in Slide Show view, add your name as a footer, then print the first slide of your presentation in Slide view and print the outline.

FIGURE B-16

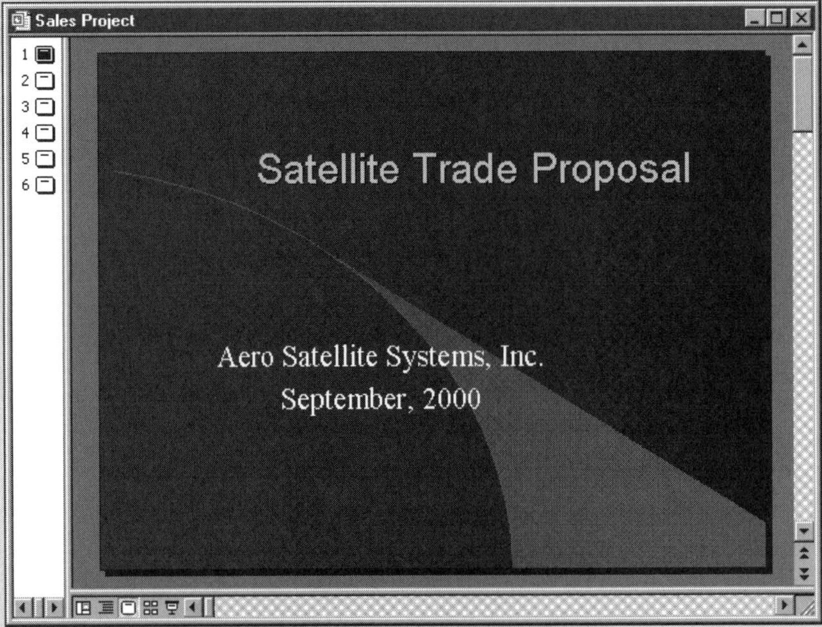

FIGURE B-17

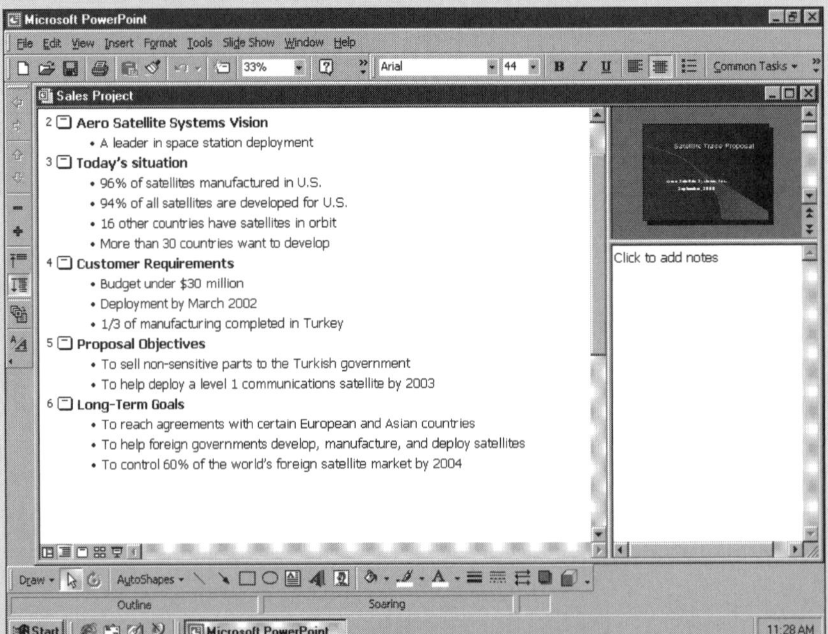

PowerPoint 2000

Modifying a Presentation

Objectives

- MOUS ► Open an existing presentation
- MOUS ► Draw and modify an object
- MOUS ► Edit drawing objects
- ► Understand aligning, grouping, and stacking objects
- MOUS ► Align and group objects
- MOUS ► Add and arrange text
- MOUS ► Format text
- MOUS ► Customize the color scheme and background
- ► Correct text automatically

After you create the basic outline of your presentation and enter text, you need to add visuals to your slides to communicate your message in the most effective way possible. In this unit, you open an existing presentation; draw and modify objects; add, arrange, and format text; change a presentation color scheme; and automatically correct text. Scenario After Maria Abbott reviews her presentation, she continues to work on the Sales Report presentation. Maria uses the PowerPoint drawing and text-editing features to bring the presentation closer to a finished look.

PowerPoint 2000

Opening an Existing Presentation

Sometimes the easiest way to create a new presentation is by changing an existing one. Revising a presentation saves you from typing duplicate information. You simply open the file you want to change, then use the Save As command to save a copy of the file with a new name. Whenever you open an existing presentation in this book, you will save a copy of it with a new name to your Project Disk—this keeps the original file intact. Saving a copy does not affect the original file. Scenario Maria wants to add visuals to her presentation, so she opens the presentation she has been working on.

1. Start PowerPoint and insert your Project Disk into the appropriate disk drive
2. Click the **Open an existing presentation option button** in the PowerPoint startup dialog box, click **More Files** in the scrollable window, then click **OK**
   The Open dialog box opens. See Figure C-1.
3. Click the **Look in list arrow**, then locate the drive that contains your Project Disk
4. Click the drive that contains your Project Disk
   A list of the files on your Project Disk appears in the Open dialog box.
5. Click **PPT C-1**
   The first slide of the selected presentation appears in the preview box on the right side of the dialog box.
6. Click **Open**
   The file named PPT C-1 opens in Slide view.
7. Click **File** on the menu bar, then click **Save As**
   The Save As dialog box opens. See Figure C-2. The Save As dialog box works just like the Open dialog box.
8. Make sure the Save in list box shows the drive containing your Project Disk and that the current file name in the File name text box is selected, then type **1999 Sales Report 1**
   Compare your screen to the Save As dialog box in Figure C-2.
9. Click **Save** to close the Save As dialog box and save the file
   PowerPoint creates a copy of PPT C-1 with the name 1999 Sales Report 1 on your Project Disk and closes PPT C-1.
10. Click **Window** on the menu bar, then click **Arrange All**
    Your screen now matches those shown in this book. If you have another PowerPoint presentation open and it appears next to this presentation, close it, then repeat step 10.

QuickTip

If PowerPoint is already running, click the Open button on the Standard toolbar.

Trouble?

If the Open dialog box on your screen does not show a preview box, click the Views list arrow in the toolbar at the top of the dialog box, then select Preview.

QuickTip

When you save copies of files, you may want to use a naming system to help you stay organized and differentiate different versions of a document. Many people use the name of the original file followed by consecutive numbers (1, 2, 3. . .) or letters (a, b, c. . .) to designate revisions of the same document or presentation.

FIGURE C-1: Open dialog box

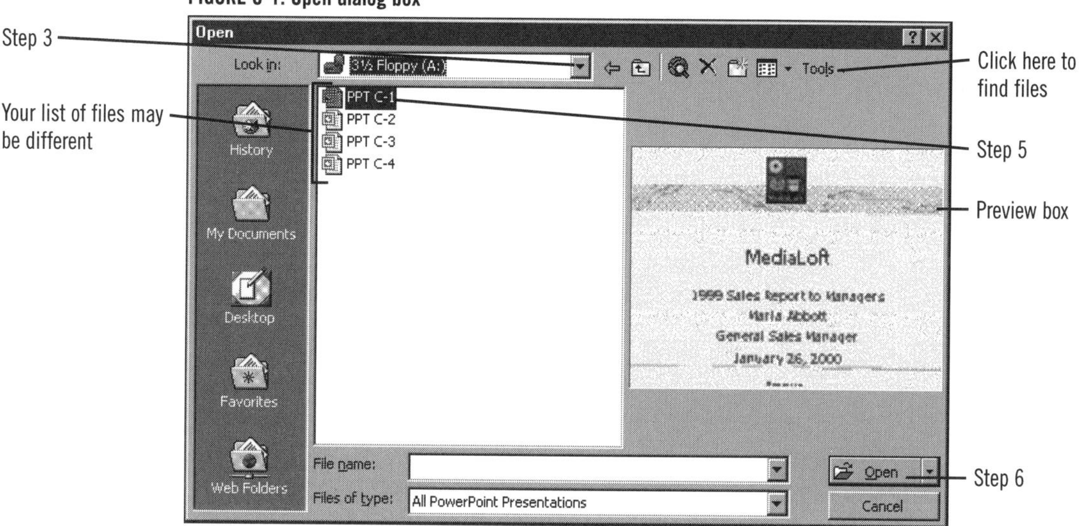

FIGURE C-2: Save As dialog box

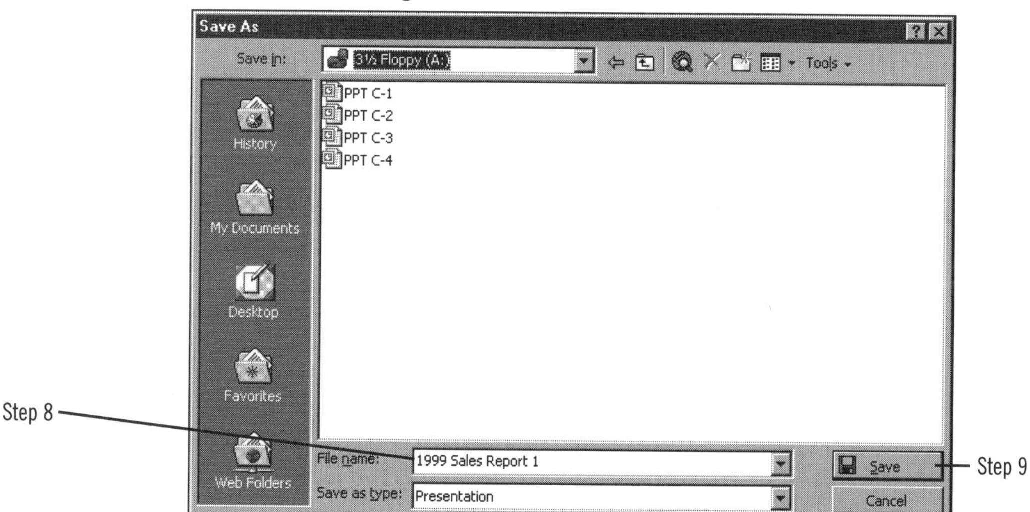

CLUES TO USE

Searching for a file by properties

If you can't find a file, you can search for it using the PowerPoint Find dialog box, which you open from the Tools menu in the Open dialog box. (See Figure C-1.) To search for a file, open the Open dialog box, click the Tools menu button on the toolbar at the top of the dialog box, then click Find on the drop-down list. The Find dialog box opens. You can specify criteria PowerPoint should use to search by clicking the list arrows in the Property, Condition, and Value boxes at the bottom of the dialog box. A property is any aspect of a presentation, such as its file name, title, contents, size, or format. For example, you can specify that you want to find a presentation whose file name (property) includes (condition) the words "sales presentation" (value). Once you've specified criteria, click Add to List. To specify where PowerPoint should search for the file, click the Look in list arrow and select the drive or folder you want to search. To include subfolders in the search, click the Search subfolders check box to select it. Click Find Now to start the search. PowerPoint closes the Find dialog box and lists the folders and files that meet your criteria in the Look in list box in the Open dialog box.

PowerPoint 2000

Drawing and Modifying an Object

The drawing capabilities of PowerPoint allow you to draw and modify lines, shapes, and pictures to enhance your presentation. Lines and shapes that you create with the PowerPoint drawing tools are objects that you can modify and move at any time. These drawn objects have graphic attributes that you can change, such as fill color, line color, line style, shadow, and 3-D effects. To add drawing objects to your slides, use the buttons on the Drawing toolbar at the bottom of the screen above the status bar. Scenario Maria decides to draw an object on slide 4 of her sales report presentation to add impact to her message.

Steps

1. Click **Tools** on the menu bar, click **Customize**, click the **Options tab** in the Customize dialog box, click **Reset my usage data** to restore the default settings, click **Yes** in the alert box or dialog balloon that opens, then click **Close**
   This restores the default settings to your toolbars.
2. In the Outline pane, click the **slide icon** for slide 4
   The 1999 Sales by Division slide appears.
3. Press and hold **[Shift]**, then click the **main text object**
   A dotted selection box with small boxes called **sizing handles** appears around the text object. If you click a text object without pressing [Shift], a selection box composed of slanted lines appears indicating the object is active, but not selected. When an entire object is selected, you can change its size, shape, or attributes.
4. Position the pointer over the right, middle sizing handle, then drag the sizing handle to the left until the text object is about half its original size
   When you position the pointer over a sizing handle, it changes to ↔. It points in different directions depending on which sizing handle it is positioned over. When you drag a text object's sizing handle, the pointer changes to +, and a dotted outline representing the size of the text object appears. See Figure C-3.
5. Click the **AutoShapes menu button** on the Drawing toolbar, point to **Stars and Banners**, then click the **Up Ribbon button** (third row, first item)
   After you select a shape from the AutoShapes menu and move the pointer over the slide, the pointer changes to +.
6. Position + in the blank area of the slide to the right of the text object, press **[Shift]**, drag down and to the right to create a ribbon object, as shown in Figure C-4, then release the mouse button and release **[Shift]**
   When you release the mouse button, a ribbon object appears on the slide, filled with the default color and outlined with the default line style, as shown in Figure C-4. Pressing [Shift] while you create the object keeps the object's proportions as you change its size.
7. If your ribbon object is not approximately the same size as the one shown in Figure C-4, press **[Shift]** and drag one of the sizing handles to resize the object
8. Click the **Line Color list arrow** on the Drawing toolbar, then click the **light purple square** (the third square from the right, called Follow Accent Scheme Color)
   PowerPoint applies the purple color to the selected object's outline.
9. Click the **Fill Color list arrow** on the Drawing toolbar, then click the **dark purple square** (the fourth square from the left, called Follow Title Text Scheme Color)
   PowerPoint fills the ribbon with the dark purple color.

Trouble?
If you are not satisfied with the size of the text object, resize it again.

QuickTip
Position the pointer on top of a button to see its name.

QuickTip
To create a circle or square, click the Oval or Rectangle button on the Drawing toolbar, then press [Shift] while dragging the pointer.

FIGURE C-3: Resizing a text object

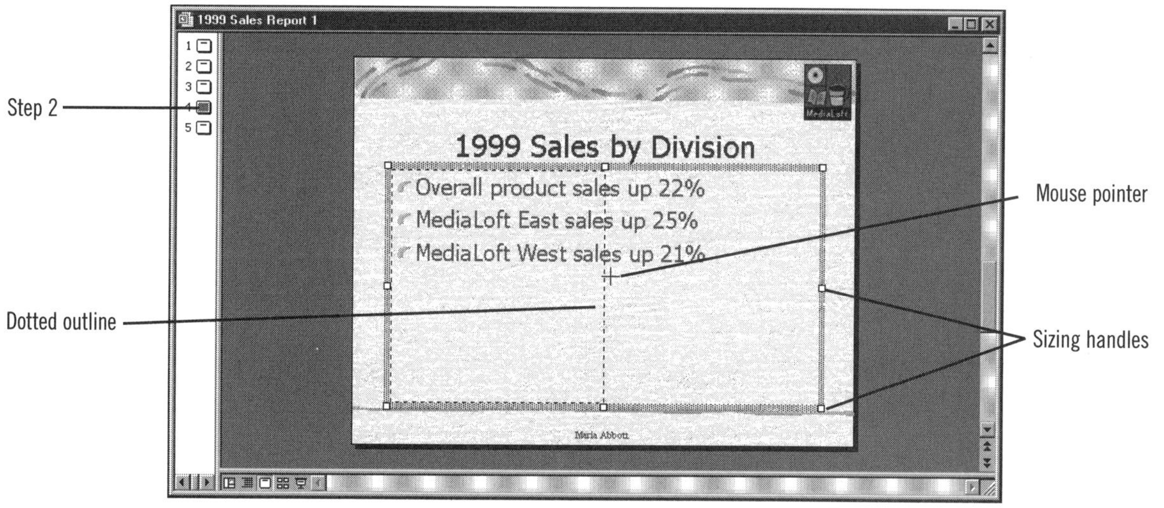

FIGURE C-4: Slide showing ribbon object

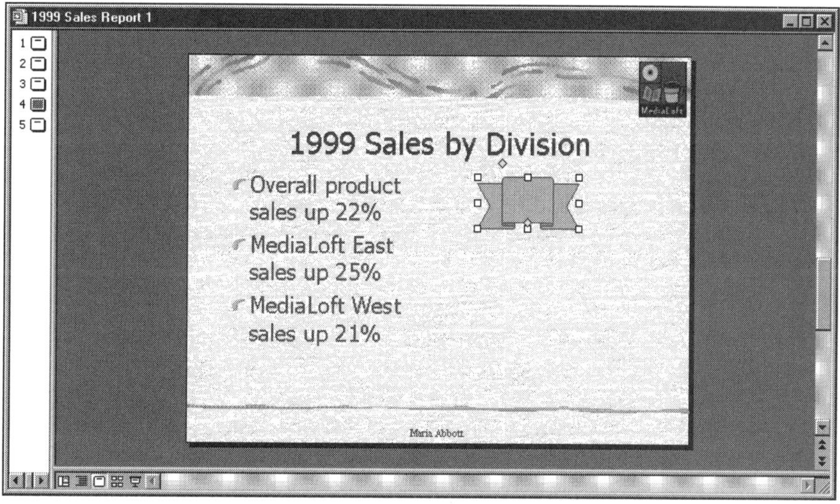

Using the Drawing toolbar

The Drawing toolbar contains many useful buttons for drawing and modifying objects on PowerPoint slides (See Figure C-5). You use the buttons on the left, including the Draw menu button, to manipulate objects. When you click the Draw menu button, a menu of commands useful for manipulating objects opens. The buttons in the middle section are used to create objects on your slides. You use the buttons in the far right section to modify objects once they have been created. To find out about a particular button, point to it to see its name in a ScreenTip, or click Help on the menu bar, click What's This, then click the button to see a brief description.

FIGURE C-5: The Drawing toolbar

PowerPoint 2000

Editing Drawing Objects

Often, a drawn object does not match the slide or presentation "look" you are trying to achieve. PowerPoint allows you to manipulate the size and shape of objects on your slide. You can alter the appearance of any object by changing its shape, as you did when you resized the text object in the previous lesson, or by adjusting the object's dimensions. You also can cut, copy, and paste objects and add text to most PowerPoint shapes. Scenario Maria changes the shape of the ribbon object, then makes two copies of it to help emphasize each point on the slide.

Steps

1. **Click the ribbon object to select it, if necessary**
   In addition to sizing handles, small yellow diamonds called **adjustment handles** appear. You change these handles to change the appearance of an object, usually its most prominent feature, like the size of an arrow head, or the proportion of a ribbon's center to its "tails."
2. **Drag the bottom, right sizing handle to the right about 1"**
3. **Position the pointer over the middle of the selected ribbon object so that it changes to ✥, then drag the ribbon so that the top of the ribbon aligns with the top of the first bullet**
   A dotted outline appears as you move the ribbon object to help you position it. Compare your screen to Figure C-6 and make any necessary adjustments.
4. **Position ✥ over the ribbon object, then press and hold [Ctrl]**
   The pointer changes to ⊞, indicating that PowerPoint will make a copy of the ribbon object when you drag the mouse.
5. **While holding down [Ctrl], drag the ribbon object down the slide until dotted lines indicate that the copy aligns with the second bullet, then release the mouse button**
   An exact copy of the first ribbon object appears. See Figure C-7.
6. **Position the pointer over the second ribbon object, press and hold [Ctrl], then drag a copy of the ribbon object down the slide until it aligns with the third bullet**
   Compare your screen to Figure C-7.
7. Click the **top ribbon object**, then type **22%**
   The text appears in the center of the object. The text is now part of the object, so if you move the object, the text will move with it.
8. Click the **middle ribbon object**, type **25%**, then click the **bottom ribbon object** and type **21%**
   The graphics you have added reinforce the slide text. The ribbon shape suggests achievement, and the numbers, which are the focus of this slide, are prominent. The dark text is hard to read on the dark background.
9. Press and hold **[Shift]**, click the **other two ribbon objects**, click the **Font Color list arrow** A on the Drawing toolbar, then click the **white square**
   Make sure the bottom ribbon object is still selected when you select the other two objects. The text changes to white.
10. **Click a blank area of the slide to deselect the objects, then save your presentation**

Trouble?

If you have trouble aligning the objects with the text, press and hold down [Alt] while dragging the object to turn off the automatic grid.

QuickTip

You can use PowerPoint rulers to help you align objects. To display the rulers, position the pointer in a blank area of the slide, right-click, then click Ruler in the pop-up menu. Or, click View on the menu bar, and then click Ruler.

QuickTip

Text entered in an AutoShape appears on one line unless you change it. With the AutoShape selected, click Format on the menu bar, click AutoShape, select the Word wrap text in the AutoShape check box, then click OK.

FIGURE C-6: Slide showing resized ribbon object

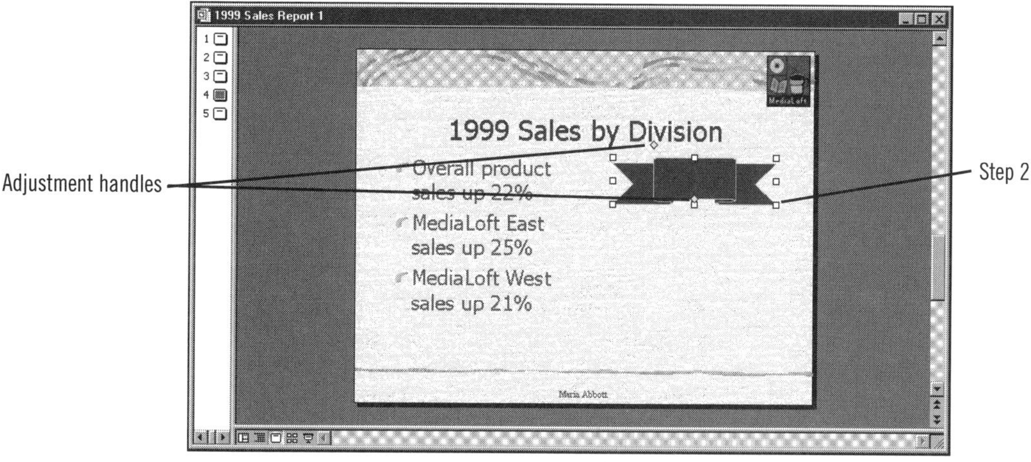

FIGURE C-7: Slide showing duplicated ribbon object

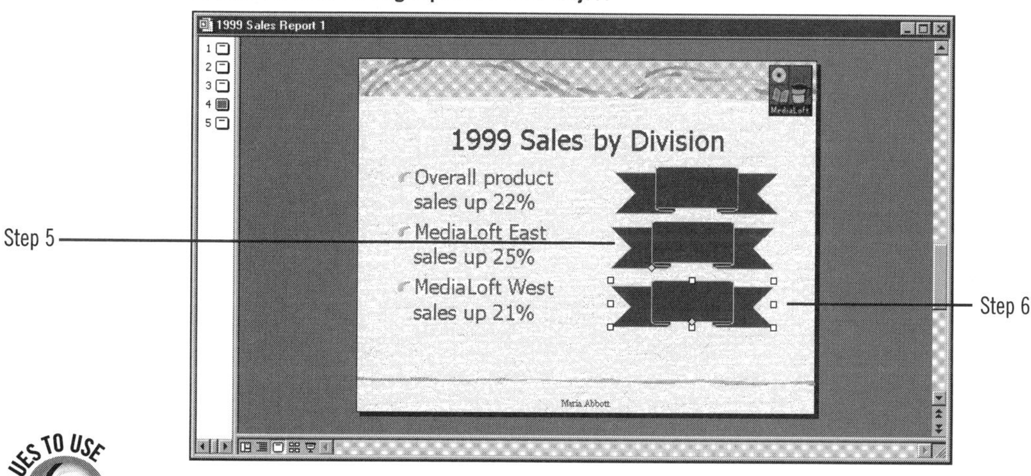

CLUES TO USE

Using the Office Clipboard

In this lesson, you copied objects using the Ctrl-Drag technique. You can also copy objects using the Office Clipboard, which lets you copy and paste multiple items. You can store up to 12 text or graphic items on the Office Clipboard. See Figure C-8. When you copy a second item within any Office program, the program automatically places the second item on the Office Clipboard. If you put 12 items on the Office Clipboard and then copy a thirteenth item, the program asks you if you want to remove the first item. You can check the contents of a particular item on the Office Clipboard by holding the pointer over it to display a ScreenTip. You can then paste one or more of the items from the Office Clipboard to a slide in your PowerPoint presentation. Just click the item you want to paste on the Clipboard toolbar and PowerPoint inserts it in the presentation. To paste all the items on the Clipboard, click Paste All on the Clipboard toolbar. The items you collect on the Office Clipboard remain there until you quit all Office programs. To clear the Office Clipboard, click Clear Clipboard on the Clipboard toolbar. You can copy and paste items among any of the Office programs.

FIGURE C-8: Clipboard toolbar

PowerPoint 2000

Understanding Aligning, Grouping, and Stacking Objects

As you work in PowerPoint, you often work with multiple objects on the same slide. These may be text objects or graphics objects, such as clip art, drawings, photos, tables, or charts. When you have more than one object on a slide, you want to make sure they look organized and neat and that they help communicate your message effectively. You can accomplish this by aligning, grouping, and stacking the objects using the commands on the Draw menu on the Drawing toolbar.

Aligning objects

When you **align** objects, you place their edges (or their centers) on the same plane. For example, you might align squares vertically so that their left edges are in a straight vertical line. Or you might align a series of circles horizontally so that their centers are in a straight horizontal line. You align objects in PowerPoint by first selecting the objects you want to align. Next, click the Draw menu button on the Drawing toolbar, point to Align or Distribute, then select one of the three horizontal alignment commands (Align Left, Align Center, or Align Right), or one of the three vertical alignment commands (Align Top, Align Middle, or Align Bottom). Aligning saves you time, because you don't have to drag each object individually. The PowerPoint Align commands make your slides look neater and more professional because they can do a better job than most people can do by manually dragging objects with the mouse and aligning them "by eye." See Figure C-9.

Grouping objects

When you **group** objects, you combine two or more objects into one object. For example, instead of having to move four squares, you could group them and then only have to move one object that contains the four squares. It's often helpful to group objects that you have aligned, so that when you move the group, the alignment among the objects remains the same. To group objects on a PowerPoint slide, you first select the objects, click the Draw menu button on the Drawing toolbar, and then click Group. You can easily ungroup objects by clicking a grouped object and then selecting the Ungroup command on the Draw menu. See Figure C-10.

Stacking objects

When you **stack** objects, you determine their order in a stack—that is, which ones are in the front and which are in back. You can easily move objects on top of each other to create effects. For example, you'll often want to place a word on top of a circle or square, or place graphics on top of other graphics. To control the stacking order of objects on a PowerPoint slide, you select the object whose order you want to adjust, click the Draw menu button on the Drawing toolbar, point to Order, and then click one of the four Order commands: Bring to Front, Send to Back, Bring Forward, or Send Backward. See Figure C-11.

FIGURE C-9: Aligning

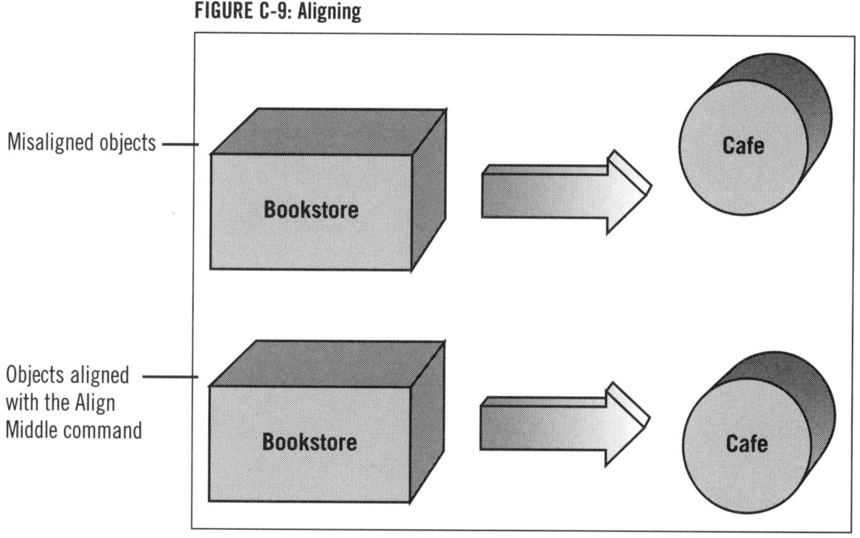

FIGURE C-10: Grouping

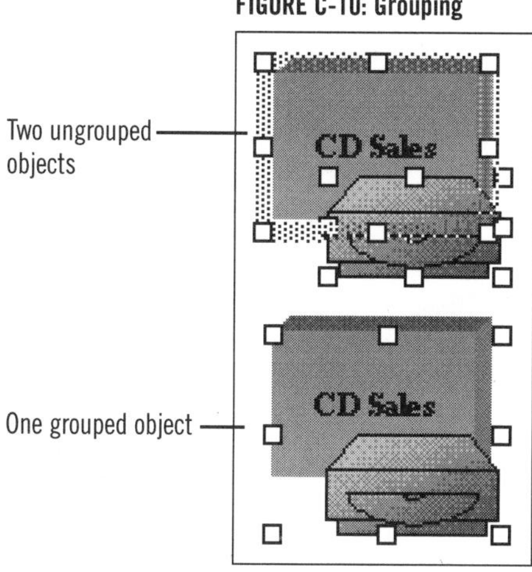

FIGURE C-11: Stacking

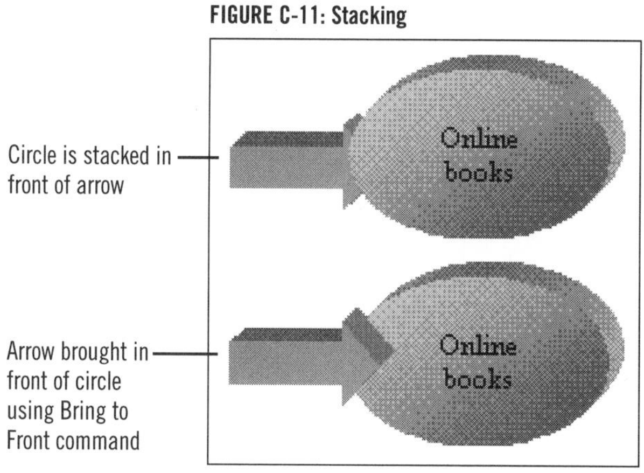

PowerPoint 2000

Aligning and Grouping Objects

After you create objects, modify their appearance, edit their size and shape, and position them on the slide, you can align and group them. The Align command aligns objects relative to each other by snapping the selected objects to an invisible grid of evenly spaced vertical and horizontal lines. The Group command groups objects into one object to make editing and moving them much easier. Scenario Maria aligns, groups, and positions the ribbon objects. Then she copies the grouped ribbon object and pastes it on the next slide.

Steps

1. Press and hold **[Shift]**, then click **each ribbon object** to select all three objects
2. Click the **Draw menu button** on the Drawing toolbar, then point to **Align or Distribute**
   A menu of alignment and distribution options appears. The top three options align objects horizontally; the next three options align objects vertically.
3. Click **Align Center**
   The ribbon objects align on their centers, as shown in Figure C-12.
4. Click the **Draw menu button**, then click **Group**
   The ribbon objects group to form one object without losing their individual attributes. Notice the sizing handles now appear around the outer edge of the grouped object, not around each individual object.
5. Right-click a blank area of the slide, then click **Guides** on the pop-up menu
   The PowerPoint guides appear as gray dotted lines on the slide. (The dotted lines might be very faint on your screen.) The guides intersect at the center of the slide. They will help you position the ribbon object on the slide.
6. Position over the **vertical guide** in a blank area of the slide, press and hold the mouse button until the pointer changes to a guide measurement box, then drag the guide to the right until the guide measurement box reads approximately **1.75**
7. Press **[Shift]**, drag the grouped ribbon object over the vertical guide until the center sizing handles are approximately centered over the vertical guide
   Pressing [Shift] while you drag an object constrains its movement to vertical or horizontal.
8. Right-click the ribbon object, click **Copy** on the pop-up menu, click the **Next Slide button**, then click the **Paste button** on the Standard toolbar
   Slide 5 appears and the grouped ribbon object from slide 4 is pasted onto slide 5. Notice that the position of the pasted ribbon object on slide 5 is the same as it was on slide 4.
9. Triple-click the **top ribbon object**, type **29%**, triple-click the **middle ribbon object**, type **20%**, triple-click the **bottom ribbon object**, type **25%**, then click in a blank area of the slide
   You do not have to ungroup the objects in order to change the text on them.
10. Click **View** on the menu bar, then click **Guides** to hide the guides
    Compare your screen to Figure C-13.

Trouble?

Click the More Buttons button to locate buttons that are not visible on a toolbar.

FIGURE C-12: Aligned ribbon objects

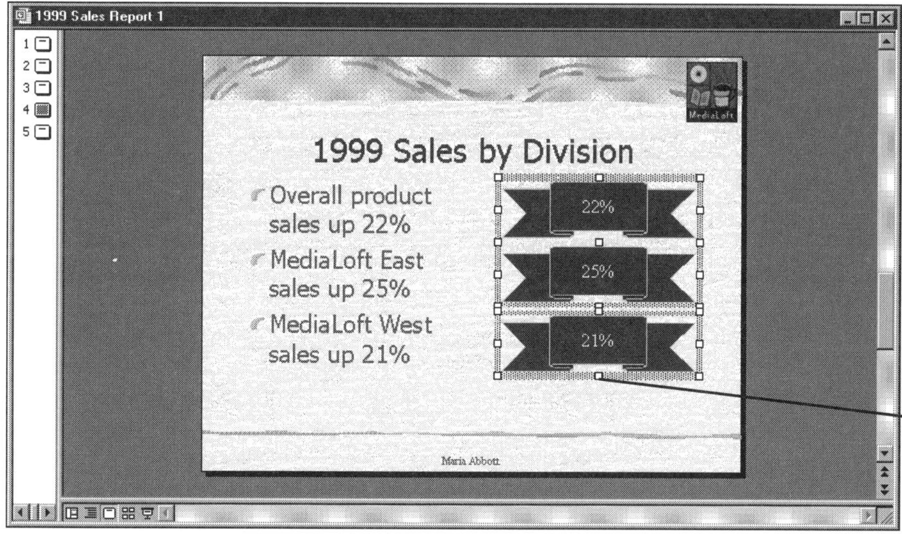

FIGURE C-13: Slide 5 showing pasted ribbon objects

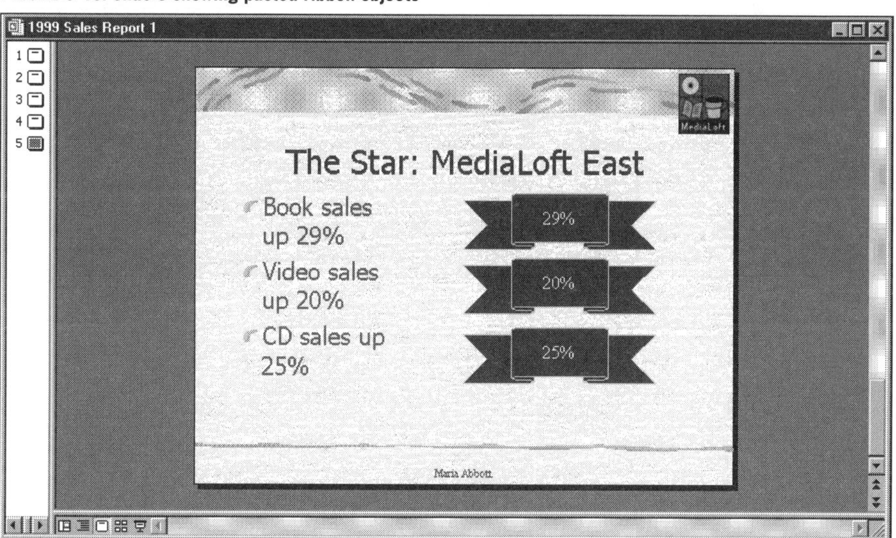

CLUES TO USE

More ways to change objects

You can change the appearance of an object by rotating or flipping it, or by making it three-dimensional. To rotate or flip an object, select it, click the Draw menu button on the Drawing toolbar, point to Rotate or Flip, then click one of the available menu commands, as shown in Figure C-14. Clicking a Flip command creates a mirror image. Clicking a Rotate command turns an object 90°. To make an object three-dimensional, select it, click the 3-D button, and click one of the options shown on the 3-D menu in Figure C-15. To add a shadow to an object, click the Shadow button on the Drawing toolbar, then click one of the buttons on the pop-up menu.

FIGURE C-14: Rotate or Flip submenu

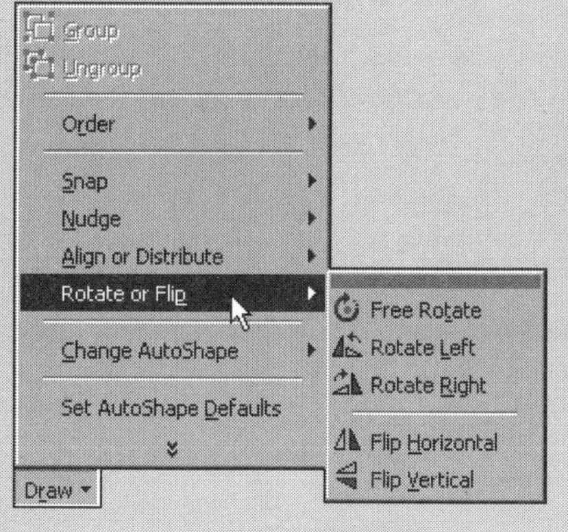

FIGURE C-15: 3-D menu

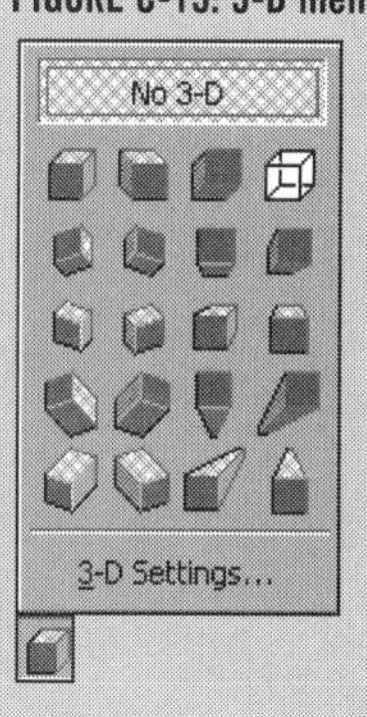

PowerPoint 2000

PowerPoint 2000

Adding and Arranging Text

Using the advanced text editing capabilities of PowerPoint, you can easily add, insert, or rearrange text. On a PowerPoint slide, you can enter text in prearranged text placeholders. If these text placeholders don't provide the flexibility you need, you can use the Text Box button on the Drawing toolbar to create your own text objects. With the Text Box button, you can create two types of text objects: a text label, used for a small phrase inside a box where text doesn't automatically wrap to the next line, and a word-processing box, used for a sentence or paragraph where the text wraps inside the boundaries of a box. Scenario Maria already added a slide to contain a quote from a recent review. Now, she uses the Text Box button to create a word-processing box on slide 3 in which to enter the quote.

1. Click the **slide icon** for slide 3 in the Outline pane
2. Click the **Text Box button** on the Drawing toolbar
3. Position the pointer about ½" from the left side of the slide and about even with the top of the picture already on the slide, then drag a word-processing box toward the picture so that your screen looks like Figure C-16
   After you click , the pointer changes to ↓. When you begin dragging, an outline of the box appears, indicating how wide a text object you are drawing. After you release the mouse button, an insertion point appears inside the text object, ready to accept text.
4. Type **Modeled on the café bookstore, MediaLoft takes the concept to new heights!**, press **[Enter]**, then type **Business Day, August 1999**
   Notice that the word-processing box increases in size as your text wraps inside the object. There is a mistake in the quote. It should read "bookstore café" not "café bookstore."
5. Double-click I on the word **bookstore** to select it
   When you select a word, the pointer changes from I to .
6. Position the pointer on top of the selected word and press and hold the mouse button
   The pointer changes to . A dotted insertion line indicates where PowerPoint will place the word when you release the mouse button.
7. Drag the word **bookstore** to the left of the word **café** in the quote, then release the mouse button
8. If necessary, drag the text box to reposition it so that it looks similiar to Figure C-17
9. Click a blank area of the slide outside the text object, then save your changes
   The text object is deselected. Your screen should look similar to Figure C-17.

QuickTip

Notice that after you type the word café and press [Spacebar], the PowerPoint AutoCorrect feature automatically inserts an accent over the e in café.

QuickTip

You also can use the Cut and Paste buttons on the Standard toolbar and the Cut and Paste commands on the Edit menu to move a word.

QuickTip

To create a text label in which text doesn't wrap, click , position ↓ where you want to place the text, then click once and enter the text.

Inserting slides from other presentations

To copy slides, open both presentations in Slide Sorter view, select the desired slides, then paste them into the current presentation. To insert slides, click Insert on the menu bar, then click Slides from Files. Click the Browse button in the Slide Finder dialog box, then locate the presentation from which you want to copy slides. In the Select slides section, select the slide(s) you want to insert, click Insert, then click Close. The new slides automatically take on the design of the current presentation.

FIGURE C-16: Slide showing word-processing box ready to accept text

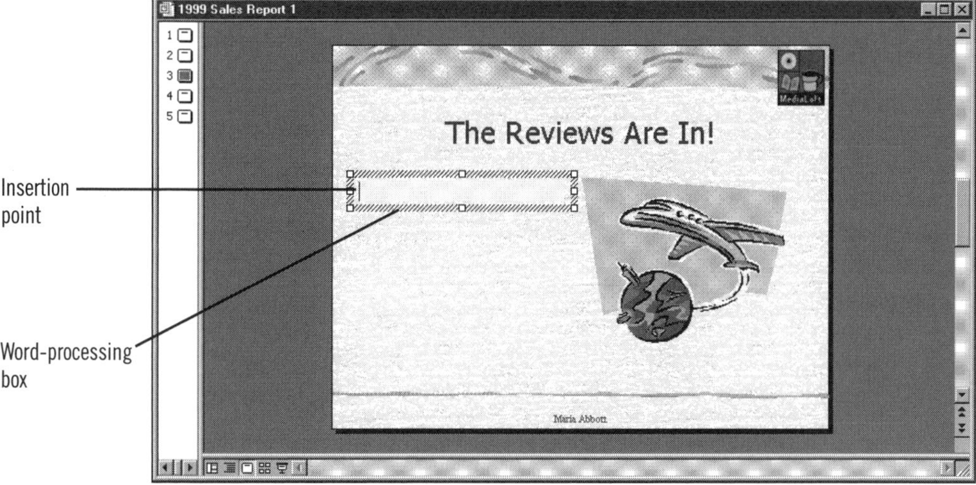

FIGURE C-17: Slide after adding text to the word-processing box

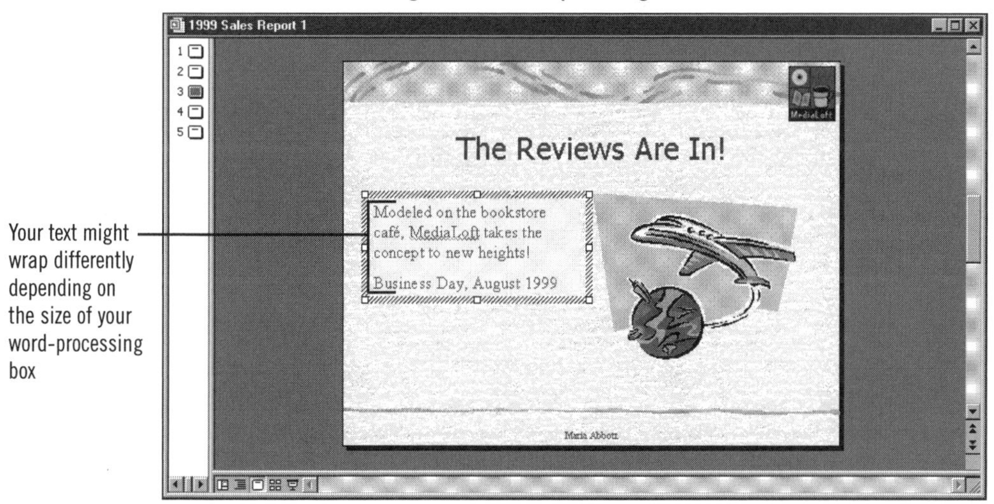

Importing text from Microsoft Word

You may want to create a presentation on a subject you wrote about earlier using Microsoft Word 2000. You can easily save time creating a presentation by importing the Word outline. You can import an outline to create a new presentation, or you can import an outline into an existing presentation. To create a new presentation from a Word outline, click the Open button on the Standard toolbar. Then in the Files of type list box, click All outlines, and double-click the name of the file you want to import. (You may receive a message asking you to insert the Office CD so the program can install a converter.) To insert an outline into an existing presentation, click the slide after which you want to insert the new information in the Outline pane or Outline view. Click Insert on the menu bar, then click Slides from Outline. Make sure the Files of type text box displays All Files, click the name of the file you want to import, then click Insert. When you import a Word outline, PowerPoint automatically creates slides containing the items from your outline, using the Outline level 1 heads as slide titles, and the lower level items as body text on the slides.

PowerPoint 2000

Formatting Text

Once you have entered and arranged the text in your presentation, you can change and modify the way the text looks to emphasize your message. Important text needs to be highlighted in some way to distinguish it from other text or objects on the slide. Less important information needs to be deemphasized. For example, if you have two text objects on the same slide, you could draw attention to one text object by changing its color or size. To change the way text looks, you need to select it, and then choose a Formatting command. Scenario Maria uses some of the commands on the Formatting and Drawing toolbars to change the way the review quote looks.

Steps 1 2 3 4

1. On slide 3, press **[Shift]**, then click the **text box**
   If a text box is already active because you have been entering text in it, you can select the entire text box by clicking on its edge with ✥. The entire text box is selected. Any changes you make will affect all the text in the selected text box. Changing the text's size and appearance will help emphasize it.

Trouble?

Click the More Buttons button » to locate buttons that are not visible on your toolbar.

2. Click the **Increase Font Size button** on the Formatting toolbar twice
   Note that after you click it once, it moves to the Formatting toolbar. The text increases in size to 32 points.
3. Click the **Italic button** on the Formatting toolbar
   The text changes from normal to italic text. The Italic button, like the Bold button, is a toggle button, which you click to turn the attribute on or off.
4. Click the **Font Color list arrow** on the Drawing toolbar
   The Font Color menu appears, showing the eight colors used in the current presentation and More Font Colors, which lets you choose additional colors.
5. Click **More Font Colors**, then in the Colors dialog box, click the **Standard tab**
6. In the color hexagon, click the **blue color cell** in the third row from the top, fourth from right, then click **OK**
   The Current color and the New color appear in the box in the lower-right corner of the dialog box. The text in the word-processing box changes to the blue color.
7. Click the **Font list arrow** on the Formatting toolbar
   A list of available fonts opens, as shown in Figure C-18. A double line at the top of the font list may separate the fonts most recently used from the complete list of available fonts.
8. Click the scroll arrows if necessary, then click **Arial**
   The Arial font replaces the original font in the text object.

QuickTip

To automatically wrap text in an AutoShape, drag a text box in the desired width, type your text, then group the two objects.

9. Drag the pointer over the text **Business Day, August 1999**, click the **Font Size list arrow** on the Formatting toolbar, click **18**, then click the **Align right button** on the Formatting toolbar
   The pointer changes to I when you drag it over text. The source text is now smaller and right-aligned. Only the selected text is affected by the formatting command, not the entire text object.
10. Drag the text box to center it vertically, click a blank area of the slide outside the text object to deselect it, then click the **Save button** on the Standard toolbar
    Compare your screen to Figure C-19.

FIGURE C-18: Font list open

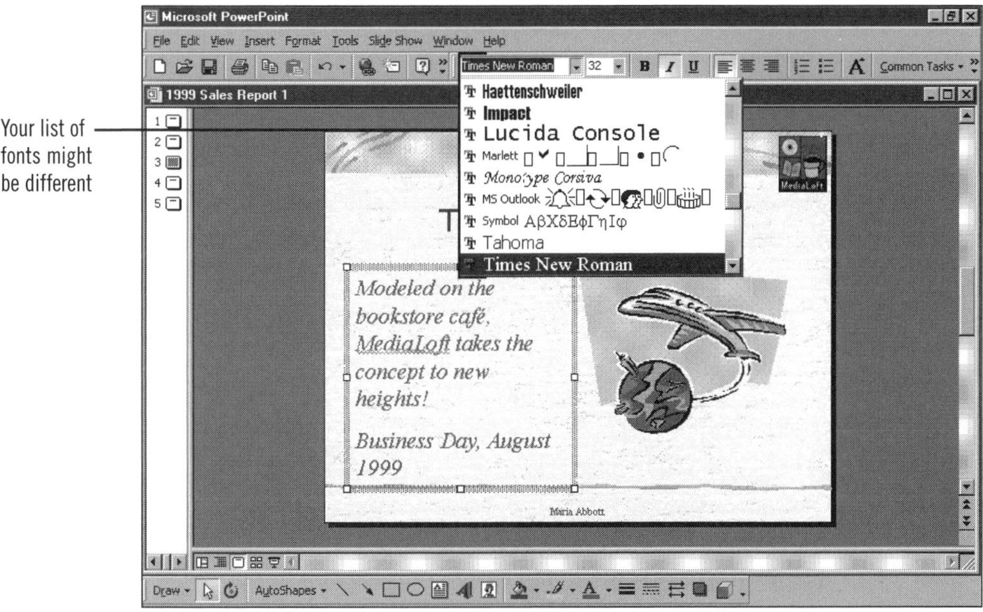

FIGURE C-19: Slide showing formatted text box

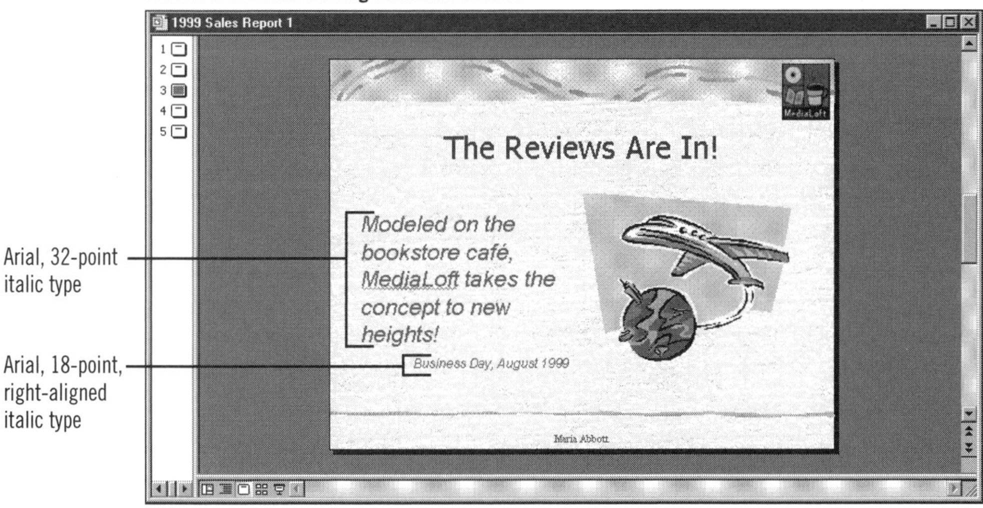

Replacing text and attributes

As you review your presentation, you may decide to replace certain words or fonts throughout the entire presentation. You can automatically modify words, sentences, fonts, text case, and periods. To replace specific words or sentences, use the Replace command on the Edit menu. To change a font, use the Replace Fonts command on the Format menu. To automatically add or remove periods from title or body text and to automatically change the case of title or body text, click Options on the Tools menu, click the Spelling and Style tab, then click Style Options to open the Style Options dialog box. Click the Case and End Punctuation tab. The options on the Visual Clarity tab in the Style Options dialog box control the legibility of bulleted text items on the slides.

PowerPoint 2000

Customizing the Color Scheme and Background

Every PowerPoint presentation has a set of eight coordinated colors, called a **color scheme**, that determines the main colors for the slide elements in your presentation: slide background, text and lines, title text, shadows, fills, and accents. See Table C-1 for a description of the slide color scheme elements. The **background** is the area behind the text and graphics. Every design template has a default color scheme that you can use, or you can create your own. You can also change the background color and appearance independent of changing the color scheme. Scenario Maria decides she doesn't like the color scheme or the white background, so she decides to change it.

1. Click **Format** on the menu bar, then click **Slide Color Scheme**
   The Color Scheme dialog box opens with the Standard tab active. See Figure C-20. The number of preset color schemes available depends on the elements in the current presentation. The current color scheme is selected with a black border.
2. Click the second color scheme in the top row, then click **Apply to All**
   The dialog box closes, and the new color scheme is applied to all the slides in the presentation. In this case, the new color scheme changes the color of the slide graphics, but the text and background remain the same.
3. Click **Format** on the menu bar, then click **Background**
   The Background dialog box opens.
4. In the Background fill section, click the **list arrow** below the preview of the slide, click **Fill Effects**, then click the **Gradient tab**, as shown in Figure C-21
5. In the Colors section, click the **Two colors option button**, click the **Color 2 list arrow**, click **More Colors** on the drop-down menu, click the **Standard tab**, click the **orange color cell** in the fifth row from the bottom, the sixth color from the right, then click **OK**
   The horizontal shading style is selected, as is the first of the four variants, showing that the background is shaded from color 1 (white) on the top to color 2 (orange) on the bottom.
6. In the Shading Styles section, click the **Diagonal up option button**, click the **upper-left variant**, click **OK**, then click **Apply to All**
   The background is now shaded from white (upper-left) to orange (lower-right).The ribbons on slides 4 and 5 would look better in plum.
7. Click the **slide icon** for slide 4, click **Format** on the menu bar, click **Slide Color Scheme**, then click the **Custom tab**
   The eight colors for the selected color scheme appear.
8. In the Scheme colors section, click the **Accent and hyperlink color box**, then click **Change Color**
   The Accent and Hyperlink Color dialog box opens.
9. Click the **Standard tab**, click the **plum color cell** in the fifth row from the bottom on the far right, as shown in Figure C-22
   The Current color and the New color appear in the box in the lower-right of the dialog box.
10. Click **OK**, click **Add As Standard Scheme**, then click **Apply to All**
    PowerPoint updates the color scheme on all your slides, and the ribbons change to plum. The next time you open the Color Scheme dialog box in this presentation, your new scheme will appear, along with the existing schemes.

QuickTip

To apply a new color scheme to only selected slides, switch to Slide Sorter view, select the slides you want to change, then click Apply instead of Apply to All in the dialog box.

QuickTip

Note that if you click the Preset option button, you can choose from a variety of predesigned backgrounds. To add a textured background to a slide, click the Texture tab, select any texture, read its name below the texture icons, click OK, then click Apply or Apply to All.

FIGURE C-20: Color Scheme dialog box

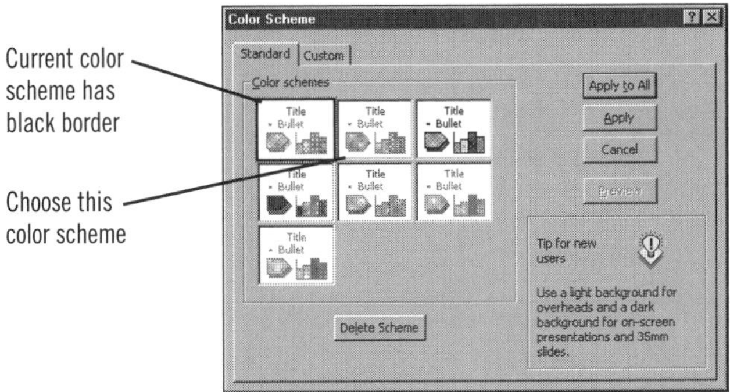

FIGURE C-21: Gradient tab of Fill Effects dialog box

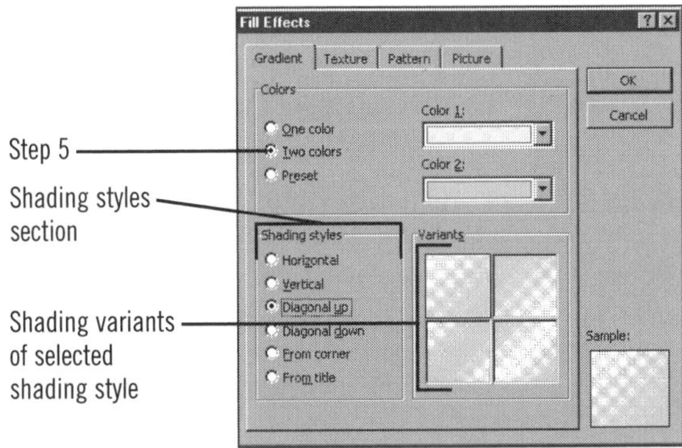

FIGURE C-22: Standard tab in the Accent and Hyperlink Color dialog box

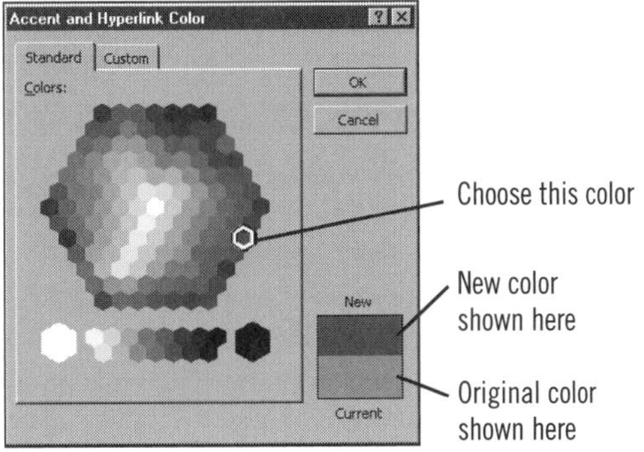

TABLE C-1: Color scheme elements

scheme element	description
Background color	Color of the slide's canvas, or background
Text and lines color	Used for text and drawn lines; contrasts with the background color
Shadows color	Color of the shadow of the text or other object; generally a darker shade of the background color
Title text color	Used for slide title; like the text and line colors, contrasts with the background color
Fills color	Contrasts with both the background and the text and line colors
Accent color	Colors used for other objects on slides, such as bullets
Accent and hyperlink colors	Colors used for accent objects and for hyperlinks you insert
Accent and followed hyperlink color	Color used for accent objects and for hyperlinks after they have been clicked

PowerPoint 2000

Correcting Text Automatically

As you enter text into your presentation, the AutoCorrect feature in PowerPoint automatically replaces misspelled words and corrects some capitalization mistakes, whether on slides or in speaker notes, without bringing up a dialog box or a menu. For example, if you type "THursday" instead of "Thursday," PowerPoint corrects it as soon as you type it. If there is a word you often type incorrectly, for example, if you type "tehm" instead of "them," you can create an AutoCorrect entry that corrects that misspelled word whenever you type it in a presentation. Scenario After reviewing the presentation, Maria uses the AutoCorrect feature as she adds one more slide, thanking the employees for their support.

Steps 1 2 3 4

1. Click the **slide icon** for slide 5 in the Outline pane, hold down **[Shift]**, then click the **New Slide button** on the Standard toolbar
   A new slide 6 with the bulleted list AutoLayout appears.
2. Click **Tools** on the menu bar, then click **AutoCorrect**
   The AutoCorrect dialog box opens, as shown in Figure C-23. The top part of the dialog box contains check boxes that have PowerPoint automatically change two capital letters at the beginning of a word to a single capital letter, capitalize the first letter of a sentence and the names of days, and correct capitalization errors caused by accidental use of the Caps Lock key. The fifth check box, Replace text as you type, tells PowerPoint to change any of the mistyped words listed on the left in the scroll box in the lower part of the dialog box with the correct word listed on the right. The scroll box contains customized entries. For example, if you type (c), PowerPoint will automatically change it to ©, the copyright symbol. See Table C-2 for a summary of AutoCorrect options.
3. Click any check boxes that are not selected
4. In the Replace text as you type section, click the **down scroll arrow** to view all the current text replacement entries, noticing that there is already an entry to automatically replace cafe with café, then click **OK**
   To test the AutoCorrect feature, you decide to enter incorrect text on the sixth slide. As you type text in the following step, watch what happens to that word when you press [Spacebar].
5. Click the **title placeholder**, then type **THank You**
   As soon as you pressed [Spacebar] after typing the word "THank," PowerPoint automatically corrected it to read "Thank." You'll make another intentional error in the next step.
6. Click the **main text placeholder**, type **Sales reps adn managers**, then press **[Enter]**
   As soon as you pressed [Spacebar] after typing the word "adn," PowerPoint automatically corrected it to read "and."
7. Type **CDVision(tm) advisors**, then click outside the main text object
   As soon as you typed the closing parenthesis, PowerPoint automatically changed the (tm) to the trademark symbol ™.
8. Click the **Slide Sorter View button**, then compare your screen to Figure C-24
9. Click **View** on the menu bar, click **Header and Footer**, click the **Notes and Handouts tab**, click in the **Footer text box**, type your name, then click **Apply to All**
   Now your name appears in the slide footer when you print the presentation, making it easier to find your printout if you are sharing the printer.
10. Save your presentation, print the slides as handouts, six slides to a page, then exit PowerPoint

QuickTip

In order for most automatic corrections to take effect, you must first press [Spacebar], [Enter], or [Tab] after the word. The exceptions are the three symbols that end in parentheses, which take effect immediately.

FIGURE C-23: AutoCorrect dialog box

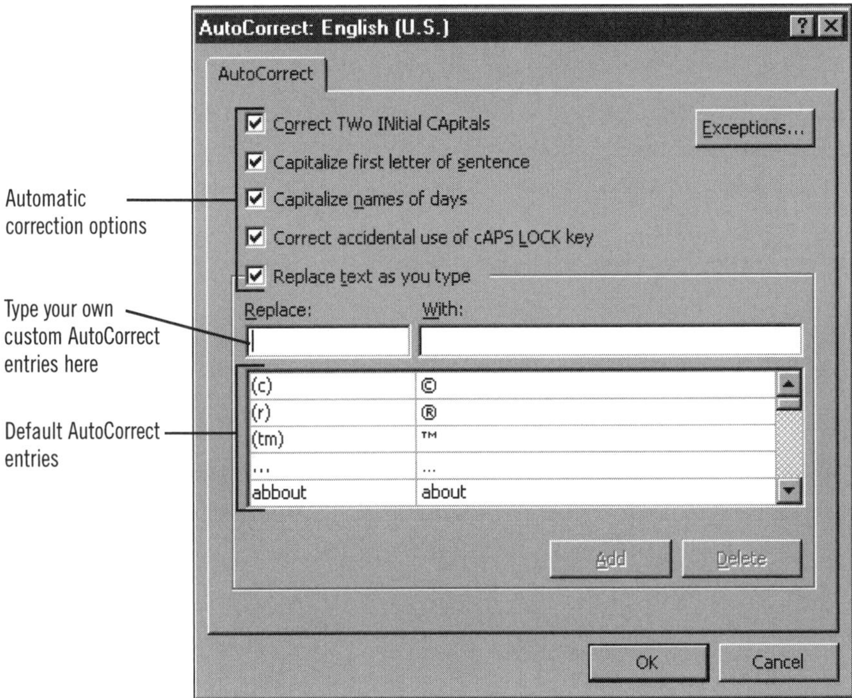

FIGURE C-24: The final presentation

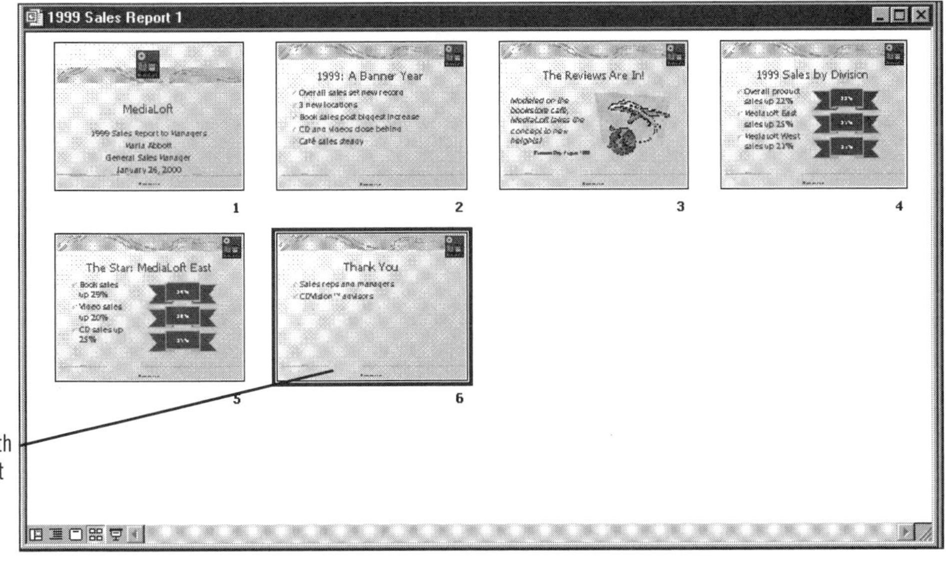

TABLE C-2: AutoCorrect options

option	action
Turn off AutoCorrect	Click to remove all the check marks in the AutoCorrect dialog box
Edit an AutoCorrect entry	Select the entry in the list, click in the With text box, correct the entry, and click Replace
Delete an AutoCorrect entry	Highlight the entry in the scroll box and click Delete
Rename an AutoCorrect entry	Select the entry in the list, click in the Replace text box, click Delete, type a new name in the Replace box, and click Add

PowerPoint 2000

Practice

Concepts Review

Label the elements of the PowerPoint window shown in Figure C-25.

FIGURE C-25

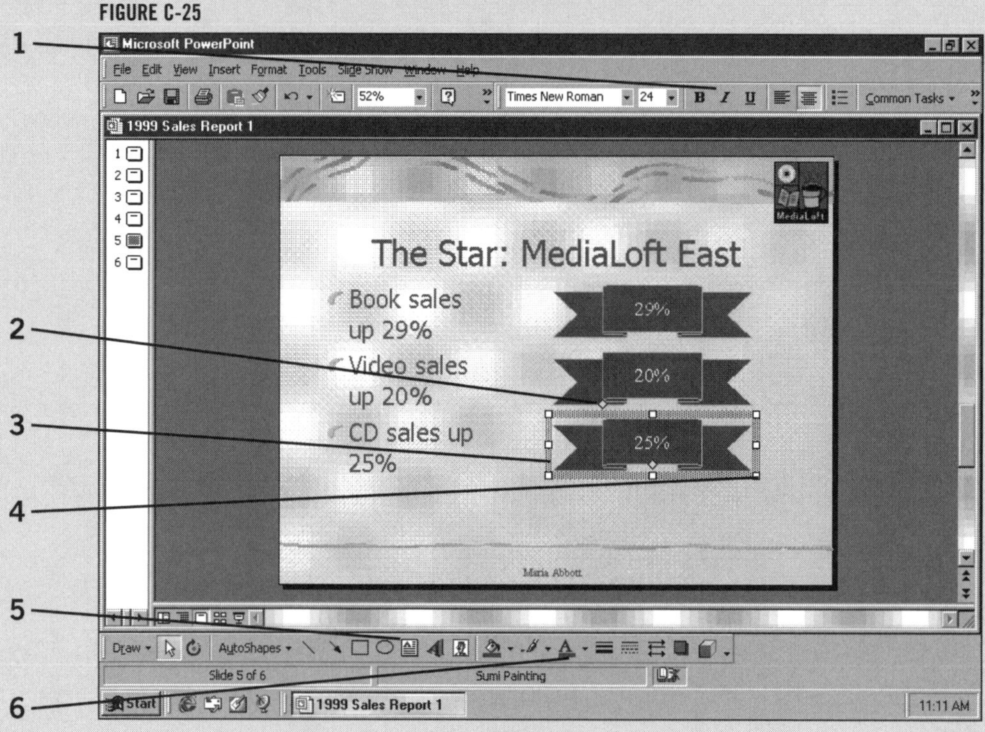

Match each term or button with the statement that describes it.

7. **Word-processing box**
8. **Text label**
9. [Text Box button]
10. [Font Color button]
11. **Sizing handles**

a. A text object that does not word wrap
b. Creates a text object on a slide
c. Small boxes that surround an object when it is selected
d. Button that changes the text color
e. A text object made by dragging to create a box after clicking the Text Box button

Select the best answer from the list of choices.

12. **How do you change the size of a PowerPoint object?**
  a. You can't change the size of a PowerPoint object
  b. Click the Resize button
  c. Drag the adjustment handle
  d. Drag a sizing handle

13. **What would you use to position objects at a specific place on a slide?**
  a. PowerPoint anchor lines
  b. PowerPoint guides and rulers
  c. PowerPoint grid lines
  d. PowerPoint placeholders

Skills Review

1. **Open an existing presentation.**
   a. Open the file PPT C-2 from your Project Disk.
   b. Save it as "Cafe Report."

2. **Draw and modify an object.**
   a. On slide 3, add the AutoShape Lightning Bolt from the Basic Shapes category on the AutoShapes menu. Make it as large as possible from the upper-left corner of the slide. It should partially cover the text.
   b. On the Line Color pop-up menu, click No Line.
   c. Change the fill color to the dark pink color named Follow Accent and Hyperlink Scheme Color.
   d. Click the Shadow button on the Drawing toolbar, then click the Shadow Style 2 button.
   e. Use the appropriate Flip command from the Draw menu on the Drawing toolbar to change the direction of the bolt so it points from the upper-right to the lower-left.
   f. Send the object to the back, then deselect the object and save the document.

3. **Edit drawing objects.**
   a. On slide 6, resize the arrow object so it is about ½" shorter.
   b. Make two copies of the arrow and arrange them to the right of the first one so that they are pointing in succession to the purple box.
   c. Insert the text "Products" on the left arrow object, "Satisfaction" on the middle arrow, and on the right arrow, insert "Growth." Enlarge the arrows so that all the text fits and then reposition them as necessary.

4. **Align and group objects.**
   a. On slide 6, place a text box on the cube, enter "Success" in it, center the text box on the cube, then group the text box and the cube.
   b. Select the four graphics on slide 6 and align their middles.
   c. Change the objects' text font to Arial italic. Enlarge the cube as necessary so the word "Success" fits in it.
   d. Select only the three arrow objects, click the Draw menu button on the Drawing toolbar, then point to Align or Distribute, and click Distribute Horizontally.
   e. Group the three arrow objects and the cube.
   f. Display the guides, then move the vertical guide left to about 4.17, and the horizontal guide down to about 2.50.
   g. Align the grouped object so its bottom-left resize handle snaps to where the guides intersect. If your object does not snap to the guides, click the Draw menu button, point to Snap, and make sure the To Grid command on the Snap menu is selected (it should look indented).
   h. Right-click in an empty area of the slide, then hide the guides.

5. **Add and arrange text.**
   a. Add a fourth item to slide 2 that reads "Next steps."
   b. Near the bottom of the slide, below the graphic, create a word-processing box about 3" wide, and in it enter the text "A relaxing café is a reading haven."
   c. Drag the word "relaxing" in front of the word "reading."
   d. Open the presentation PPT C-3 in Slide Sorter view and copy slide 3 ("The Reviews Are In!") to the Clipboard, then close the PPT C-3 presentation. In the Cafe Report presentation, switch to Slide Sorter view, then paste the copied slide after slide 5.
   e. Use the Slides from Files command on the Insert menu to insert slide 2 ("1999: A Banner Year") from the PPT C-3 presentation after slide 6 ("The Reviews Are In!") in the Cafe Report presentation.

f. Switch to Outline view, import the Word file PPT C-4 to the end of the presentation. Check each slide's formatting. (*Hint:* If the program tells you that you need to install this feature, insert your Office 2000 CD and click OK.)

6. Format text.

a. Go to slide 2 in Slide view and select the entire word-processing box so that formatting commands will apply to all the text in the box.
b. Change the font color to the purple color in the current color scheme, then increase its size once.
c. Select the entire main text object.
d. Click the Bullets button on the Formatting toolbar to add bullets to the list.
e. Go to slide 8, drag to select all the text on the cube, then change the text color to light blue.
f. Go to slide 2, select the entire main text object, then click the Center alignment button.
g. Use the Replace command on the Edit menu to replace all occurrences of "sellers" with "performers." Make sure you capitalize the second occurrence.
h. On slide 2, replace the font of the main text object and the word-processing box with Arial.
i. Use the Replace Fonts command on the Format menu to change all instances of the Times New Roman font in the presentation to Arial.
j. Go to slide 1 and change the title text font to Arial Black, 48 points.
k. Deselect the text object, then save your changes.

7. Customize the color scheme and background.

a. Open the Color Scheme dialog box.
b. Click the upper-left color scheme then apply it to all the slides.
c. Open the Background dialog box, then the Fill Effects dialog box.
d. On the Gradient tab, select a two-color gradient, picking the light brown that represents Follow Accent and Followed Hyperlink Scheme color as the first color, and the off-white that represents the Follow Background Scheme color as the second color. Select the Diagonal up option and the first variant. Apply this background to all slides.
e. Open the Color Scheme dialog box.
f. On the Custom tab, change the color of the Title text on all slides to a brighter shade of purple.
g. Add the new scheme as a Standard Scheme, and check that it is available on the Standard tab.
h. Add the Canvas texture to the background of slide 1.

8. Correct text automatically.

a. Go to slide 5 and turn on Caps Lock.
b. After the third bullet, add a fourth bullet that reads "Herbal teas." Notice how PowerPoint reverses the capitalization as soon as you press [Spacebar].
c. For the next bullet, enter the text "Give additional suggestions by thursday." and press [Spacebar]. Notice that PowerPoint automatically capitalizes the word "Thursday" for you.
d. Check the spelling in the presentation and make any necessary changes.
e. Go to slide 1, view the final slide show, and evaluate your presentation.
f. Add your name to the footer of all notes and handouts.
g. Save your changes, print the slides as handouts, six slides per page, and then close the presentation and exit PowerPoint.

Visual Workshop

Create a one-slide presentation that looks like the one shown in Figures C-26. Use a text box for each bullet. Add your name as a footer on the slide. Group the objects in each logo. Save the presentation as "Bowman Logos" to your Project Disk, then print the slide in Slide view. (*Hint:* The top design uses the 3-D menu.) If you don't have the exact fonts, use something similar.

FIGURE C-26

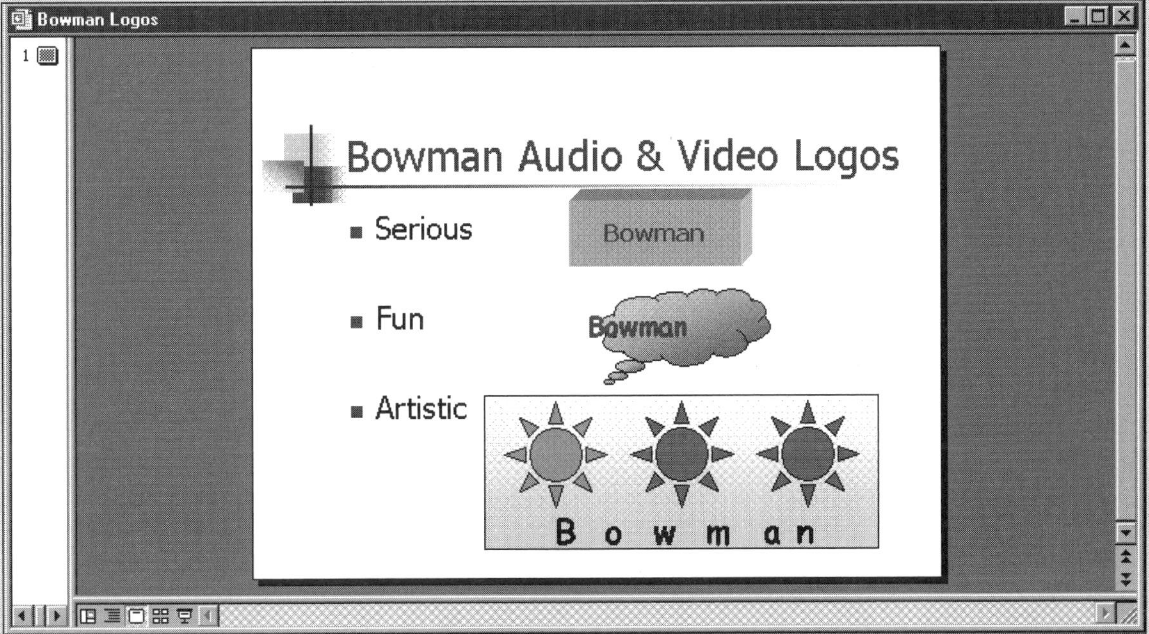

Enhancing a Presentation

Objectives

- MOUS ► Insert clip art
- MOUS ► Insert, crop, and scale a picture
- MOUS ► Embed a chart
- MOUS ► Enter and edit data in the datasheet
- MOUS ► Format a chart
- MOUS ► Use slide show commands
- MOUS ► Create tables in PowerPoint
- MOUS ► Set slide show timings and transitions
- MOUS ► Set slide animation effects

After completing the content of your presentation, you can supplement your slide text with clip art or graphics, charts, and other visuals that help communicate your content and keep your slide show visually interesting. In this unit, you learn how to insert three of the most common visual enhancements: a clip art image, a picture, and a chart. These objects are created in other programs. After you add the visuals, you rehearse the slide show and add special effects. Scenario ► Maria Abbot has changed her presentation based on feedback from her colleagues. Now she wants to revise the sales presentation to make it easier to understand and more interesting to watch.

PowerPoint 2000

Inserting Clip Art

PowerPoint has more than 1000 professionally designed images, called **clip art**, that you can place in your presentation. Using clip art is the easiest and fastest way to enhance your presentations. In Microsoft Office, clip art is stored in a file index system called a **gallery** that sorts the clip art into categories. You can open the Clip Gallery in one of three ways: double-click a clip art placeholder from an AutoLayout; use the Insert Clip Art button on the Drawing toolbar; or choose Picture, then Clip Art on the Insert menu. As with drawing objects, you can modify clip art images by changing their shape, size, fill, or shading. Clip art is the most widely used method of enhancing presentations, and it is available from many sources outside the Clip Gallery, including the World Wide Web (WWW) and collections on CD-ROMs. Scenario Maria wants to add a picture from the Clip Gallery to one of the slides and then adjust its size and placement.

Steps 1 2 3 4

1. Start PowerPoint, open the presentation **PPT D-1** from your Project Disk, save it as **1999 Sales Presentation 2**, click **Window** on the menu bar, click **Arrange All**, then click the **slide icon** for slide 2 in the outline pane
   The 1999: A Banner Year slide appears.
2. Click **Tools** on the menu bar, click **Customize**, click the **Options tab** in the Customize dialog box, click **Reset my usage data** to restore the default settings, click **Yes** in the alert box or dialog balloon, then click **Close**
3. Click the **Common Tasks menu button** on the Formatting toolbar, then click **Slide Layout**
   The Slide Layout dialog box opens with the Bulleted List AutoLayout selected.
4. Click the **Text & Clip Art AutoLayout** (third row, first column), then click **Apply**
   PowerPoint applies the Text and Clip Art AutoLayout to the slide, which makes the existing text object narrower, automatically reduces its font size from 32 points to 28 points, and inserts a clip art placeholder, where you will place the clip art object.
5. Double-click the **clip art placeholder**
   The Microsoft Clip Gallery dialog box opens with the Pictures tab visible, similar to Figure D-1.
6. Scroll down to and click the **Flags category**
   If the Flags category doesn't appear, select a different category.
7. Position the mouse pointer over the **Mountains graphic** whose ScreenTip says "mountains", click the **graphic**, then on the pop-up menu, click the **Insert Clip icon** (the top icon)
   The picture of the mountain with a flag on it appears on the right side of the slide. In addition, the Picture toolbar might open automatically. If you don't have the Mountains picture in your Clip Gallery, select a similar picture. If you use the Insert Clip Art button on the Drawing toolbar or the Picture command on the Insert menu to insert a clip art image, the Clip Gallery stays open, which is useful in situations where you want to insert more than one picture at a time.
8. Place the pointer over the lower-right sizing handle and drag the handle up and to the left about ½"
9. With the clip art object still selected, hold down **[Shift]**, click the **bulleted list**, click the **Draw menu button** on the Drawing toolbar, point to **Align or Distribute**, click **Align Middle**, then click in a blank area to deselect the objects
   The text object and the clip art object align vertically. Compare your screen to Figure D-2, and make any necessary corrections.

Trouble?

Click the More Buttons button to locate buttons that are not visible on your toolbar.

QuickTip

If you open the Clip Gallery via the icon in the Drawing toolbar or the Picture command on the Insert menu, you will see three tabs: Pictures, Sounds, and Motion Clips.

QuickTip

You can also use the keyboard arrow keys to reposition any selected object by small increments.

FIGURE D-1: Microsoft Clip Gallery dialog box

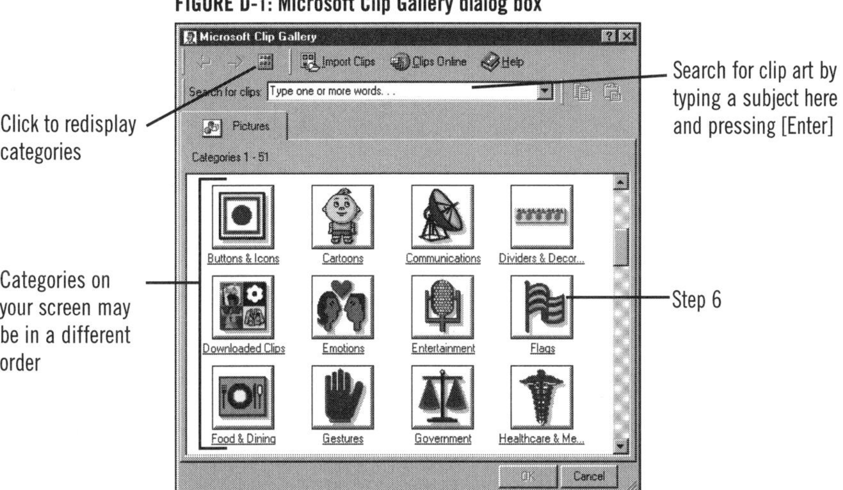

FIGURE D-2: Slide with graphic resized and repositioned

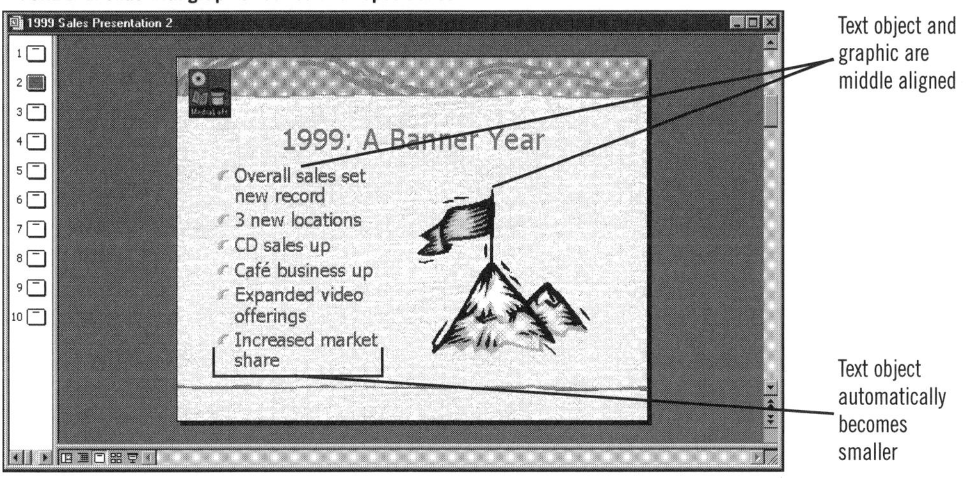

Find more clips online

CLUES TO USE

If you can't find the clips you need in the Clip Gallery, you can easily use clips from the Clip Gallery Live Web site. To get clips from the Microsoft Clip Gallery Live Web site, click Clips Online in the Insert ClipArt dialog box, then click OK. This will launch your Web browser and automatically connect you to the site. Read carefully and accept the License Agreement, which specifies how you are permitted to use clips from this site. The Clip Gallery Live window opens. You can preview and download (import) clips from four tabs: Clip Art, Pictures (photographs), Sounds, and Motion (animated graphics). You can search the site by keyword or browse by category. Each clip you download is automatically inserted into the Clip Gallery. Figure D-3 shows some of the clip art in the Transportation category.

FIGURE D-3: Microsoft Clip Gallery Live Web site

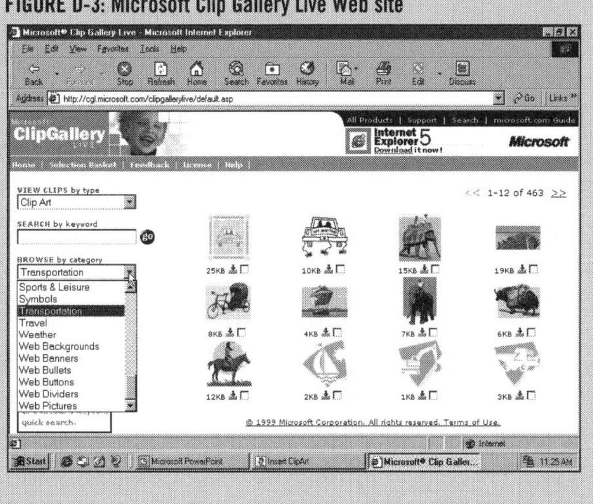

PowerPoint 2000

PowerPoint 2000

Inserting, Cropping, and Scaling a Picture

A picture in PowerPoint is a scanned photograph, a piece of line art, clip art, or other artwork that is created in another program and inserted into a PowerPoint presentation. You can insert 20 types of pictures using the Insert Picture command. As with other PowerPoint objects, you can move or crop an inserted picture. **Cropping** a picture means to hide a portion of the picture if you don't want to include all of the original. Although you can easily change a picture's size by dragging a corner resize handle, you can also **scale** it to change its size by a specific percentage. Scenario Maria inserts a picture that has previously been saved to a file, crops and scales it, and then adjusts its background.

Steps

1. Go to **slide 6**, titled "Reasons for Our Growth," click the **Common Tasks menu button** on the Formatting toolbar, click **Slide Layout**, click the **Text & Object AutoLayout** (fourth row, first column), then click **Apply**
2. Double-click the **object placeholder**
   The Insert Object dialog box opens.
3. Click the **Create from file option button** to select it
   The dialog box changes to include a text box that will contain the file name of the object you will insert.
4. Click **Browse**, click the **Look in list arrow**, click the drive containing your Project Disk, click **PPT D-2** in the Look in list, click **OK**, then click **OK** in the Insert Object dialog box
   The picture appears on the slide, and the Picture toolbar automatically opens. See Figure D-4. The slide would have more impact without the sun image.
5. Click the **Crop button** on the Picture toolbar, then place the cursor over the top, middle sizing handle of the tree picture
   The pointer changes to .
6. Drag the top edge downward until the dotted line indicating the top edge of the picture is below the sun image, as shown in Figure D-5
   As you drag with the cropping tool, the pointer changes to ⊥. But now the picture needs to be larger to fill the space.
7. Click a blank area of the slide to deselect the cropping tool and leave the picture selected
8. Click the **Format Picture button** on the Picture toolbar, click the **Size tab**, under Scale, make sure the **Lock aspect ratio check box** is selected, click and hold the **Height up arrow** until the Height and Width percentages reach **275%**, then click **OK**
   When you are scaling a picture and Lock aspect ratio is checked, the ratio of height to width remains the same. Although you cannot change the colors in this bitmapped (.bmp) object in PowerPoint, you can change its background.
9. With the image still selected, click the **Set Transparent Color button** on the Picture toolbar, then click the **white background** in the image with the pointer
   The white background is no longer visible, and the tree contrasts well with the background.
10. Drag the graphic to center it in the blank space, deselect it, then save your changes
   See Figure D-6.

QuickTip

If you want to go to a particular slide but aren't sure what the number is, drag the vertical scroll box in the Slide pane to see both the slide number and the slide title.

Trouble?

If the Picture toolbar does not appear, right-click the picture, then click Show Picture Toolbar on the pop-up menu.

QuickTip

You can change the colors of a bitmapped graphic by double-clicking it, which will open Microsoft Paint. Use the Fill Color tool in Paint to recolor portions of the graphic.

FIGURE D-4: Inserted picture object and Picture toolbar

Picture toolbar may appear in a different position on your screen

Inserted picture object

Crop button

Set Transparent Color button

FIGURE D-5: Using the cropping pointer to crop out the sun image

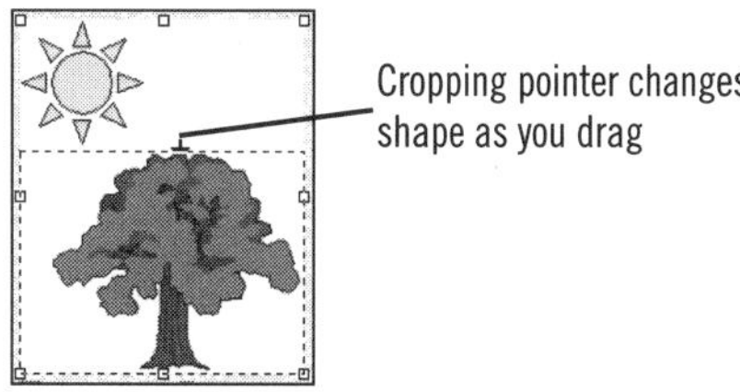

Cropping pointer changes shape as you drag

FIGURE D-6: Completed slide with the cropped and resized graphic

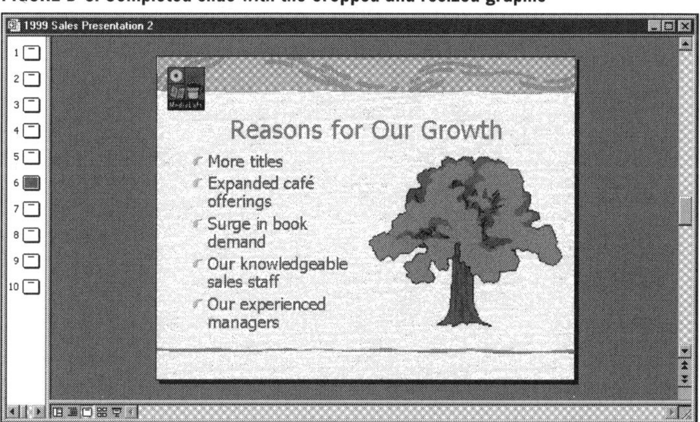

Graphics in PowerPoint

You can insert pictures with a variety of graphics file **formats**, or file types, in PowerPoint. Most of the clip art that comes with PowerPoint is in **Windows metafile** format and has a **.wmf** file extension. A graphic in .wmf format can be ungrouped into its separate PowerPoint objects and then edited with PowerPoint drawing tools. You can recolor a .wmf graphic by selecting it and clicking the Recolor picture icon on the Picture toolbar, which lets you replace each color in the graphic with another color. You can also recolor any portion of an ungrouped .wmf graphic by selecting it and using the Fill Color drawing tool. If you ungroup a .wmf graphic and find that it has too many parts, you can regroup them using the Group command on the Draw menu. The clip art you inserted in the last lesson is in .wmf format, and the tree picture you inserted in this lesson is in .bmp format.

You can also save PowerPoint slides as graphics and then use them in other presentations, in graphics programs, and on Web pages. Display the slide you want to save, then click Save As from the File menu. In the Save As dialog box, click the Save As type list arrow, and scroll to the desired graphics format. Name the file, click OK, then click the desired option when the alert box appears asking if you want to save all the slides or only the current slide.

PowerPoint 2000

Embedding a Chart

Often, the best way to communicate information is with a visual aid such as a chart. PowerPoint comes with a program called **Microsoft Graph** (often called **Graph**) that you use to create graph charts for your slides. A **graph object** is made up of two components: a **datasheet**, containing the numbers you want to chart, and a **chart**, which is the graphical representation of the datasheet. Table D-1 lists the Graph chart types. When you insert a Graph object into PowerPoint, you are actually embedding it. **Embedding** an object means that the object copy becomes part of the PowerPoint file, but you can double-click on the embedded object to display the tools of the program in which the object was created. You can use these tools to modify the object. If you modify the embedded object, the original object file does not change. Scenario Maria wants to embed a Graph object in the slide containing the 1999 revenue by quarter.

1. Go to **slide 5**, titled "1999 Revenue by Quarter," click the **Common Tasks menu button** on the Formatting toolbar, then click **Slide Layout**
   The Slide Layout dialog box opens with the Title only Layout selected.
2. Click the **Chart AutoLayout** (second row, far right), then click **Apply**
   The Chart AutoLayout, which contains a chart placeholder, appears on the slide.
3. Double-click the **chart placeholder**
   Microsoft Graph opens and embeds a default datasheet and chart into the slide, as shown in Figure D-7. The Graph datasheet consists of rows and columns. The intersection of a row and a column is called a **cell**. Cells are referred to by their row and column location; for example, the cell at the intersection of column A and row 1 is called cell A1. Cells along the left column and top row of the datasheet typically contain **data labels** that identify the data in a column or row; for example, "East" and "1st Qtr" are data labels. Cells below and to the right of the data labels contain the data values that are represented in the Graph chart. Each column and row of data in the datasheet is called a **data series**. Each data series has corresponding **data series markers** in the chart, which are graphical representations such as bars, columns, or pie wedges. The PowerPoint Standard and Formatting toolbars have been replaced with the Microsoft Graph Standard and Formatting toolbars, and the menu bar has changed to include Microsoft Graph commands.
4. Move the pointer over the datasheet
   The pointer changes to ✚. Cell A1 is the **active cell**, which means that it is selected. The active cell has a heavy black border around it.
5. Click cell **B3**, which currently has the value 46.9 in it
   Cell B3 is now the active cell.
6. Click a blank area of the Presentation window to exit Graph and deselect the chart object
   Compare your slide to Figure D-8.

Trouble?

If the Graph Formatting toolbar doesn't appear, click View on the menu bar, point to Toolbars, and click the Formatting check box.

QuickTip

When the Data and Chart menus are present, you are working in Graph. Clicking outside the Graph object returns you to PowerPoint.

FIGURE D-7: Datasheet and chart in the PowerPoint window

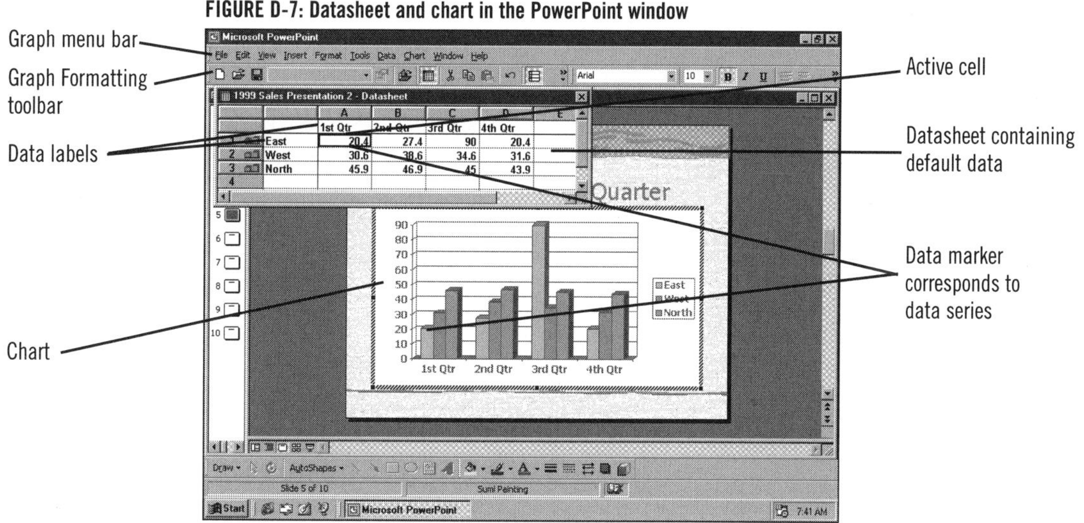

FIGURE D-8: Chart object on a slide

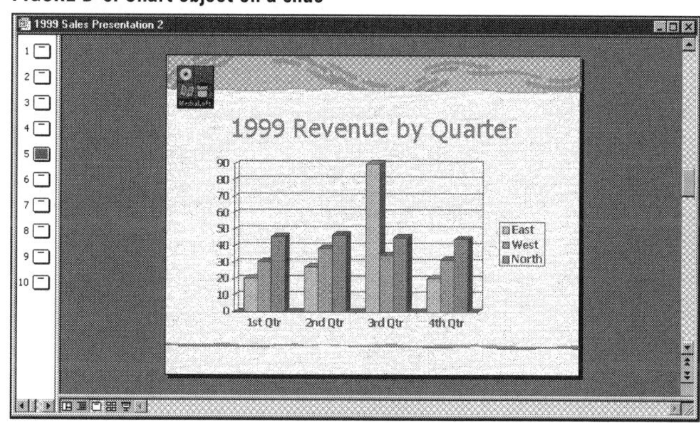

TABLE D-1: Microsoft Graph chart types

chart type	looks like	use to
Column		Track values over time or across categories
Bar		Compare values in categories or over time
Line		Track values over time
Pie		Compare individual values to the whole
XY (Scatter)		Compare pairs of values
Area		Show contribution of each data series to the total over time
Doughnut		Compare individual values to the whole with multiple series
Radar		Show changes in values in relation to a center point
Surface		Show value trends across two dimensions
Bubble		Indicate relative size of data points
Stock		Show stock market information or scientific data
Cylinder, cone, pyramid		Track values over time or across categories

PowerPoint 2000

Entering and Editing Data in the Datasheet

After you embed the default datasheet and chart into your presentation, you need to change the data label and cell information in the sample datasheet to create the chart you need. Although you can import information from a spreadsheet, it is often easier to use Graph and type in the information. As you enter data or make changes to the datasheet, the chart automatically changes to reflect your alterations. Scenario Maria enters the 1999 quarterly sales figures by division that she wants to show to the employees. She first changes the data labels and then the series information in the cells.

1. Double-click the **chart** on slide 5
   The graph is selected and the datasheet appears. The labels representing the quarters across the top are correct, but the row labels need adjusting, and the data needs to be replaced with MediaLoft's quarterly sales figures for each division.
2. Click the **East row label**, type **MediaLoft East**, then press **[Enter]**
   After you press [Enter], the first data label changes from East to MediaLoft East (although you cannot see all of it right now), and the data label in row 2, the cell directly below the active cell, becomes selected. Don't worry that the column is not wide enough to accommodate the label; you'll fix that after you enter all the labels.
3. Type **MediaLoft West**, press **[Tab]**, then press **[↑]**
   Pressing [Tab] moves the active cell one column to the right and pressing [↑] moves it up one row—cell A1 is the active cell. Notice that in the chart itself, below the datasheet, the data labels you typed are now in the legend to the right of the chart.
4. Position the pointer on top of the column divider to the left of the letter A so that ✚ changes to ↔ and double-click
   The data label column automatically widens to accommodate all the column label text.
5. With cell A1 selected, type **600,000**, press **[Enter]**, type **300,000**, press **[Tab]**, then press **[↑]** to move to cell B1, to the top of the second data series column
   Notice that the heights of the columns in the chart change to reflect the numbers you typed.
6. Enter the rest of the numbers shown in Figure D-9 to complete the datasheet
7. Click the **row 3 row number**, then press **[Delete]**
   The chart columns adjust to reflect the new information, and the default information in row 3 no longer appears. The chart currently shows the columns grouped by quarter (the legend represents the rows in the datasheet). It would be more effective if the columns were grouped by division (with the legend representing the columns in the datasheet).
8. Click **Data** on the menu bar, then click **Series in Columns**
   The division labels are now on the horizontal axis, and the quarters are listed in the legend. The groups of data markers (the columns) now represent the sales for each division by quarter. Notice that the small column chart graphics that used to be in the row labels have now moved to the column labels, indicating that the series are now in columns.
9. Click in the Presentation window outside the chart area, compare your chart to Figure D-10, then save the presentation
   The datasheet closes, allowing you to see your entire chart. This chart layout clearly shows MediaLoft East's sales have exceeded MediaLoft West's, but that MediaLoft West's sales are increasing steadily.

Trouble?

The datasheet window can be manipulated in the same ways other windows are. If you can't see a column or a row, use the scroll bars to move another part of the datasheet into view, or resize the datasheet window so you can see all the data.

FIGURE D-9: Datasheet showing MediaLoft's revenue for each quarter

1999 Sales Presentation 2 - Datasheet

		A	B	C	D
		1st Qtr	2nd Qtr	3rd Qtr	4th Qtr
1	MediaLoft East	600,000	900,000	800,000	900,000
2	MediaLoft West	300,000	500,000	700,000	800,000
3					
4					

Graphic shows that series are currently in rows

Step 7

Bars automatically show the new values

FIGURE D-10: Chart showing data grouped by division

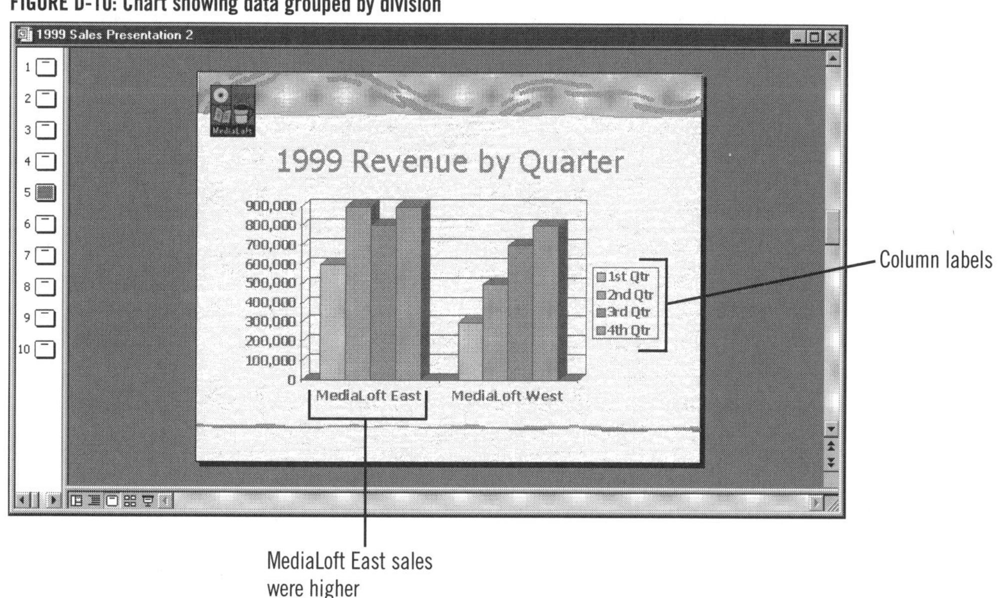

Series in Rows vs. Series in Columns

If you have difficulty visualizing the difference between the Series in Rows and the Series in Columns commands on the Data menu, think about the legend. **Series in Rows** means that the information in the rows will become the legend in the chart (and the column labels will be on the horizontal axis). **Series in Columns** means that the information in the columns will become the legend in the chart (and the row labels will be on the horizontal axis). Microsoft Graph places a small graphic representing the chart type on the axis items that are currently represented by the chart series items (bars, etc.).

PowerPoint 2000

PowerPoint 2000

Formatting a Chart

Graph lets you change the appearance of the chart to emphasize certain aspects of the information you are presenting. You can change the chart type, create titles, format the chart labels, move the legend, or add arrows. Scenario Maria wants to improve the appearance of her chart by formatting the vertical and horizontal axes and by inserting a title.

1. Double-click the **chart** to reopen Microsoft Graph, then click the **Close button** in the Datasheet window to close the datasheet
   The Microsoft Graph menu and toolbar remain at the top of the window.
2. Click the **sales numbers** on the vertical axis to select the axis, then click **the Currency Style button** on the Chart Formatting toolbar
   The numbers on the vertical axis appear with dollar signs and two decimal places. You don't need to show the two decimal places, because all the values are whole numbers.
3. Click the **Decrease Decimal button** on the Chart Formatting toolbar twice
   The numbers on the vertical axis now have dollar signs and show only whole numbers. The division names on the horizontal axis would be easier to see if they were larger.
4. Click either of the **division names** on the horizontal axis, click the **Font Size list arrow** on the Chart Formatting toolbar, then click **20**
   The font size changes from 18 points to 20 points for both labels on the horizontal axis. Viewers would understand the chart more readily if it had a title and axis labels.
5. Click **Chart** on the menu bar, click **Chart Options**, then click the **Titles tab**
   The Chart Options dialog box opens, in which you can change the chart title, axes, gridlines, legend, data labels, and the table.
6. Click in the **Chart title text box**, then type **MediaLoft 1999 Sales by Division**
   The preview box changes to show you the chart with the title.
7. Press **[Tab]** twice to move the cursor to the Value (Z) axis text box, then type **Sales**
   In a 3-D chart, the vertical axis is called the Z-axis, and the depth axis, which you don't usually work with, is the Y-axis. See Figure D-11 for the completed Titles tab.
8. Click the **Legend tab**, click the **Bottom option button**, then click **OK**
9. Double-click the border of the **"Sales" label** on the vertical axis, click the **Alignment tab**, drag the **red diamond** in the Orientation section up to a vertical position so the spin box reads 90 degrees, click **OK**, then click a blank area of the Presentation window
   Graph closes and the PowerPoint toolbars and menu bar appear. See Figure D-12.

Trouble?

Click the More Buttons button to locate buttons that are not visible on your toolbar.

Trouble?

If the Office Assistant appears with a tip in the balloon-shaped dialog box, drag it out of the way or click OK in the Office Assistant dialog balloon.

Customizing charts

You can easily customize the look of any chart in Microsoft Graph. Click the chart to select it, then double-click any data series element (a column, for example) to open the Format Data Series dialog box. Use the tabs to change the element's fill color, border, shape, or data label. You can even use the same fill effects you apply to a presentation background. In 3-D charts, you can change the chart depth as well as the distances between series.

FIGURE D-11: Titles tab in the Chart Options dialog box

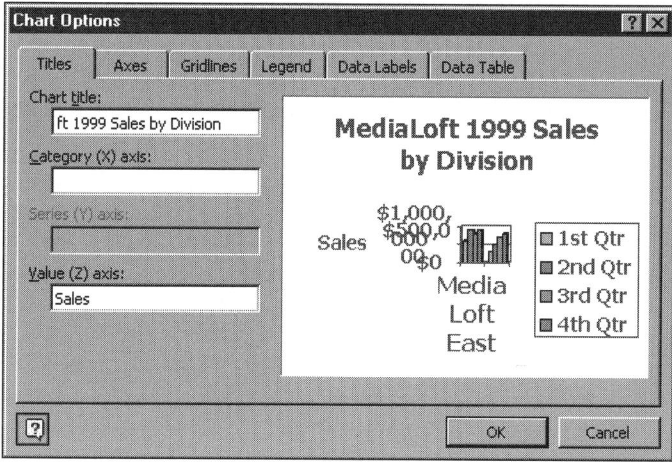

FIGURE D-12: Slide showing formatted chart

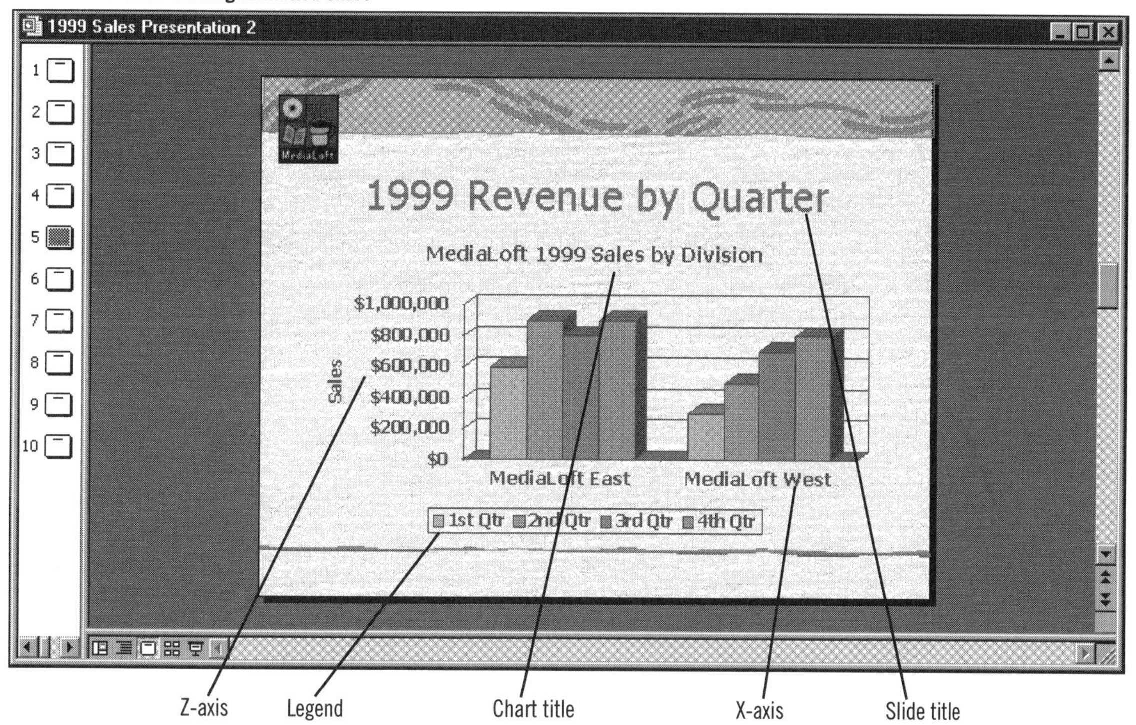

PowerPoint 2000

PowerPoint 2000

Using Slide Show Commands

With PowerPoint, you can show a presentation on any compatible computer using Slide Show view. As you've seen, Slide Show view fills your computer screen with the slides of your presentation, showing them one at a time—similar to how a slide projector shows slides. Once your presentation is in Slide Show view, you can use a number of slide show options to tailor the show. For example, you can draw on, or **annotate**, slides or jump to a specific slide. Scenario Maria runs a slide show of her presentation and practices using some of the custom slide show options to make her presentation more effective.

Steps

1. Go to **slide 1**, then click the **Slide Show button**
   The first slide of the presentation fills the screen.
2. Press **[Spacebar]**
   Slide 2 appears on the screen. Pressing [Spacebar] or clicking the left mouse button is the easiest way to move through a slide show. You can also use the keys listed in Table D-2. You can also use the Slide Show pop-up menu for on-screen navigation during a slide show.
3. Right-click anywhere on the screen, point to **Go** on the pop-up menu, then click **Slide Navigator**
   The Slide Navigator dialog box opens and displays a list of the presentation slides.
4. Click **6. Reasons for Our Growth** in the Slide titles list box, then click **Go To**
   The slide show jumps to slide 6. You can emphasize major points in your presentation by annotating the slide during a slide show using the Pen.
5. Right-click the slide, point to **Pointer Options** on the pop-up menu, then click **Pen**
   The pointer changes to .
6. Press and hold **[Shift]** and drag to draw a line under each of the bulleted points on the slide
   Holding down [Shift] constrains the Pen tool to straight horizontal or vertical lines. Compare your screen to Figure D-13. While the annotation pen is visible, mouse clicks do not advance the slide show. However, you can still move to the next slide by pressing [Spacebar] or [Enter].
7. Right-click to view the Slide Show pop-up menu, point to **Screen**, click **Erase Pen**, then press **[Ctrl][A]**
   The annotations on slide 6 are erased and the pointer returns to .
8. Right-click anywhere on the screen to view the Slide Show pop-up menu, point to **Go**, point to **By Title**, then click **4 1999 Sales by Division** on the pop-up menu
   Slide 4 appears.
9. Press **[Home]**, then click the mouse, press **[Spacebar]**, or press **[Enter]** to advance through the slide show
   After the black slide that indicates the end of the slide show appears, the next click ends the slide show and returns you to Slide view.

QuickTip

You can also access the Slide Show menu by moving the mouse pointer, then clicking the Slide Show menu icon that appears in the lower-left corner of the screen.

QuickTip

If you know the slide number of the slide you want to jump to, type the number, then press [Enter].

FIGURE D-13: Slide 6 in Slide Show view with annotations

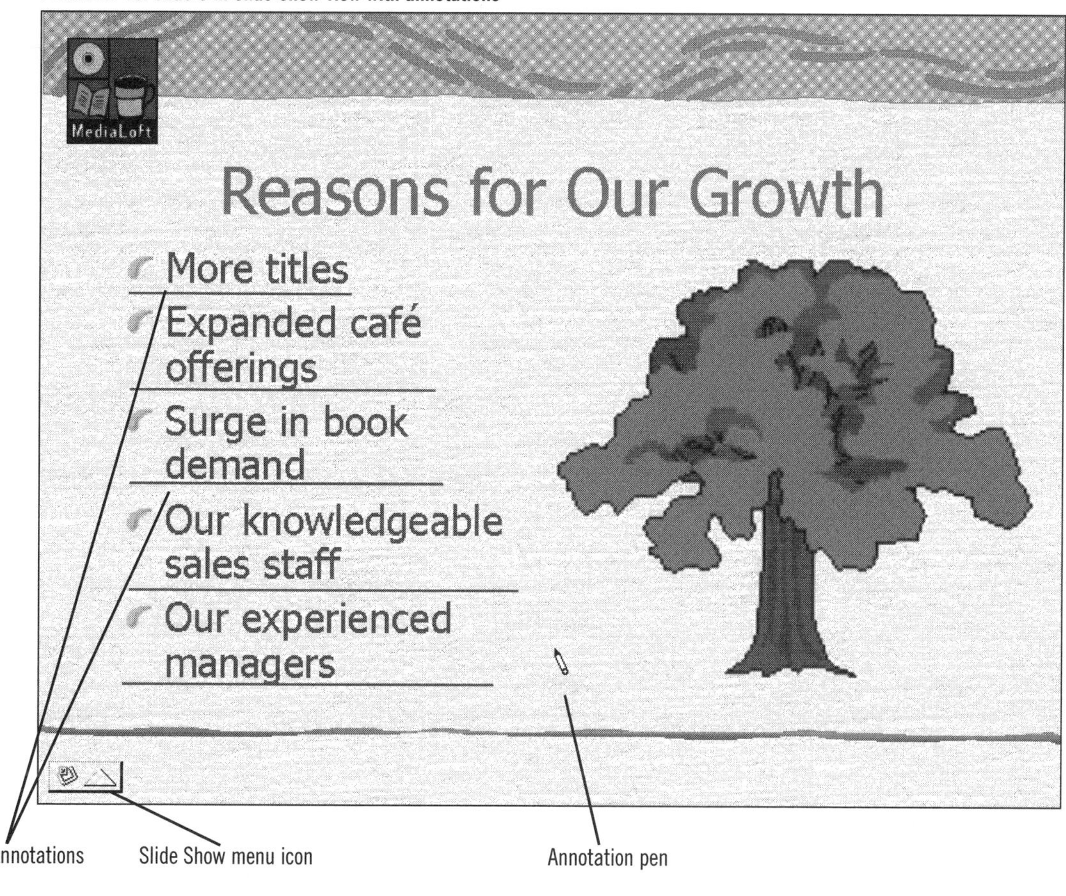

TABLE D-2: Slide show keyboard controls

control	description
[E]	Erases the annotation drawing
[Enter], [Spacebar], [PgDn], [N], [↓] or [→]	Advances to the next slide
[H]	Displays a hidden slide
[↑] or [PgUp]	Returns to the previous slide
[W]	Changes the screen to white; press again to return
[S]	Pauses the slide show; press again to continue
[B]	Changes the screen to black; press again to return
[Ctrl][P]	Changes pointer to ✎
[CTRL][A]	Changes pointer to ↖
[Esc]	Stops the slide show

PowerPoint 2000

PowerPoint 2000

Creating Tables in PowerPoint

As you create your PowerPoint presentations, you may need to insert information in a row and column format. A table you create in PowerPoint is ideal for this type of information layout. There are two ways to create a table in PowerPoint: the Table command on the Insert menu and the Table slide layout. Once you have created a table, you can use the buttons on the Tables and Borders toolbar to format it, as well as the buttons on the Formatting toolbar. Scenario Maria uses the Table command on the Insert menu to create a table describing MediaLoft's competition.

Steps

1. Go to **slide 7**, click **Insert** on the menu bar, then click **Table**
   The Insert Table dialog box opens, allowing you to specify the number of columns and rows you want in your table. The default of 2 columns is correct but you want 4 rows.
2. Press **[Tab]**, type **4**, then click **OK**
   A table with 2 columns and 4 rows appears on the slide, and the Tables and Borders toolbar opens. See Table D-3 to learn about the buttons on this toolbar.
3. Type **Seller**, press **[Tab]**, type **# of Titles**, then press **[Tab]**
4. Enter the rest of the table information shown in Figure D-14, pressing **[Tab]** after each entry except the last one
5. Drag the table by its border down below the slide title
   See Figure D-14. The table would look better if it were formatted.
6. Drag to select the column headings in the top row of the table
   The column headings row becomes highlighted.
7. Click the **Center Vertically button** on the Tables and Borders toolbar, click the **Fill Color list arrow** on the Tables and Borders toolbar, then click the **light purple color** in the second row
8. With the column headings still selected, click the **Center button** on the Formatting toolbar, then click in a blank area of the presentation window
   The column headings are centered horizontally and vertically and the row is filled with purple.
9. Vertically center the text in the other three rows, then fill these three rows with the **light orange color** in the second row
   The table would look better if the last three rows were a little farther away from the cell edges.
10. With the bottom three rows still selected, click **Format** on the menu bar, click **Table**, click the **Text Box tab**, click the **Left up scroll arrow** twice so it reads **.2**, click **OK**, click outside the table, then save the presentation
   The Tables and Borders toolbar closes and the table is no longer selected. Compare your screen with Figure D-15.

Trouble?

If the Tables and Borders toolbar does not open, click View on the menu bar, click Toolbars, then click Tables and Borders. If the toolbar obscures part of the table, drag it out of the way.

QuickTip

You can change the height or width of any table cell by dragging its top or side borders.

QuickTip

You can use the Format Table dialog box to apply a diagonal line through any table cell. Click the Borders tab, then click the diagonal line button.

FIGURE D-14: The new table before formatting

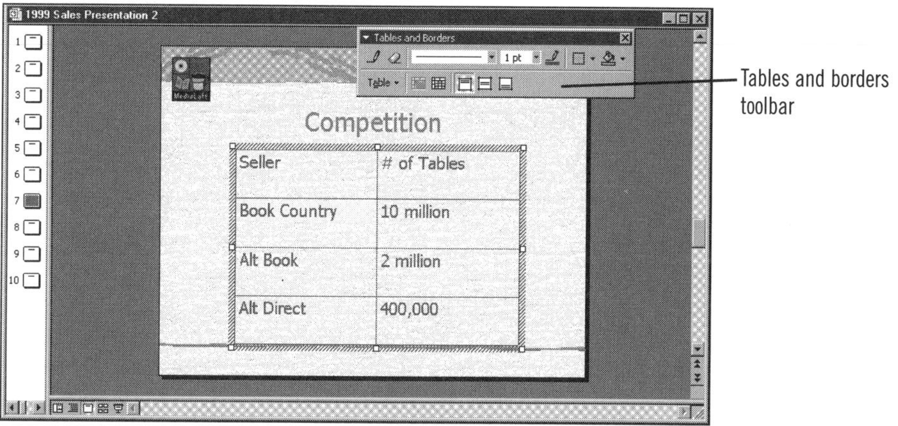

FIGURE D-15: The formatted table

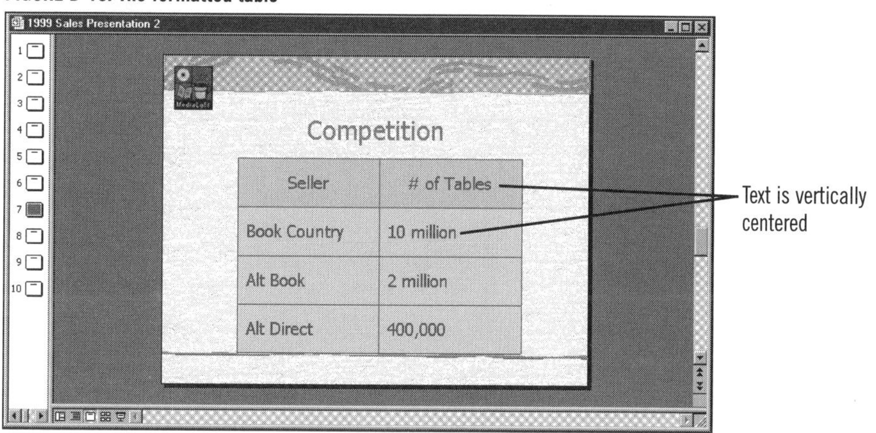

TABLE D-3: The buttons on the Tables and Borders toolbar

button	name	What it does
	Draw Table	Changes the pointer to ✎, which lets you drag to create a table or draw lines in an existing table
	Eraser	Changes the pointer to the eraser pointer, which lets you click any line in a drawn table to erase the line
	Border Style	Lets you change the border style of the next line you draw with the Pencil pointer
1 pt	**Border Width**	Lets you change the width of the next line you draw with the Pencil pointer
	Border Color	Changes the color of any table border
	Outside Border	Lets you choose a border, horizontal, or vertical line for any selected table cell(s)
	Fill Color	Lets you change the fill color of any selected table cell(s)
Table	**Table Menu**	Lets you insert a table, insert or delete rows or columns, merge or split cells, select parts of a table, or modify borders and fills
	Merge Cells	Lets you merge two selected table cells into one
	Split Cells	Lets you split a selected table cell into two cells
, ,	**Align top, center vertically, align bottom**	Let you change the vertical alignment of selected cell text

PowerPoint 2000

Setting Slide Show Timings and Transitions

In a slide show, you can preset when and how each slide appears on the screen. You can set the **slide timing**, which is the amount of time a slide is visible on the screen. Each slide can have the same or different timing. Setting the right slide timing is important because it determines the amount of time you have to discuss the material on each slide. You can also set slide transitions, the special visual and audio effects you apply to a slide that determine how it moves in and out of view during the slide show. Scenario Maria decides to set her slide timings for 10 seconds per slide and to set the transitions for all slides but the last one to fade to black before the next slide appears.

1. Click the **Slide Sorter View button**
   Slide Sorter view shows a miniature image of the slides in your presentation. The number of slides you see on your screen depends on the current zoom setting. Notice that the Slide Sorter toolbar appears below the Standard and Formatting toolbars.
2. Right-click one of the slides, then click **Slide Transition** on the pop-up menu
   The Slide Transition dialog box, shown in Figure D-16, opens.
3. In the Advance section, make sure the **On mouse click check box** is selected, click the **Automatically after check box** to select it, type **10** in the Automatically after text box, then click **Apply to All**
   The timing between slides is 10 seconds, which appears under each slide. When you run the slide show, each slide will remain on the screen for 10 seconds. If you finish talking in less time and want to advance more quickly, press [Spacebar] or click the mouse button.
4. Right-click one of the slides, click **Slide Transition** on the pop-up menu, then click the **Effect list arrow** in the top section
   A drop-down menu appears, showing all the transition effects.
5. Scroll down the list, click **Fade Through Black**, note that the Preview picture in the Effect section demonstrates the selected effect, click **Apply to All**, then click in a blank area of the Presentation window to deselect the slide
   As shown in Figure D-17, each slide in Slide Sorter view now has a small transition icon under it, indicating there is a transition effect set for the slides.
6. Click the **transition icon** under any slide
   The previous slide appears briefly, then the transition effect appears; in this case the image fades then the current slide appears.
7. Scroll down the Presentation window, right-click the **last slide**, click **Slide Transition** on the pop-up menu, click the **Effect list arrow**, then click **Split Vertical Out**
   As the preview shows, the last slide will now appear with a split from the center of the screen.
8. Click the **Sound list arrow**, scroll down the list, click **Drum Roll** or choose another sound effect, then click **Apply**
   Make sure you did not click Apply to All this time. The last slide now has a different visual effect and a drum roll transition applied to it.
9. Press **[Home]**, click the **Slide Show button** and watch the slide show advance
   To move more quickly, press [Spacebar] or [Enter].
10. When you see the black slide at the end of the slide show, press **[Enter]**
    The slide show ends.

QuickTip

You also can click Slide Show on the menu bar, then click Slide Transition.

QuickTip

You also can click Edit on the menu bar, click Select All, then click the Transition list arrow on the Slide Sorter toolbar to apply a transition effect to all the slides.

FIGURE D-16: Slide Transition dialog box

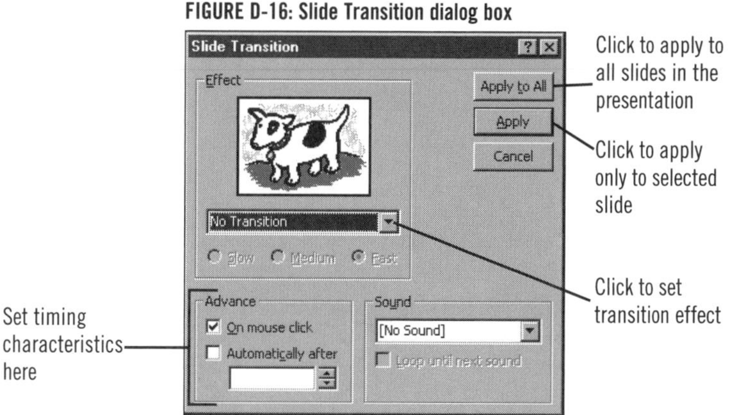

FIGURE D-17: Slide Sorter view showing transition effects and timing

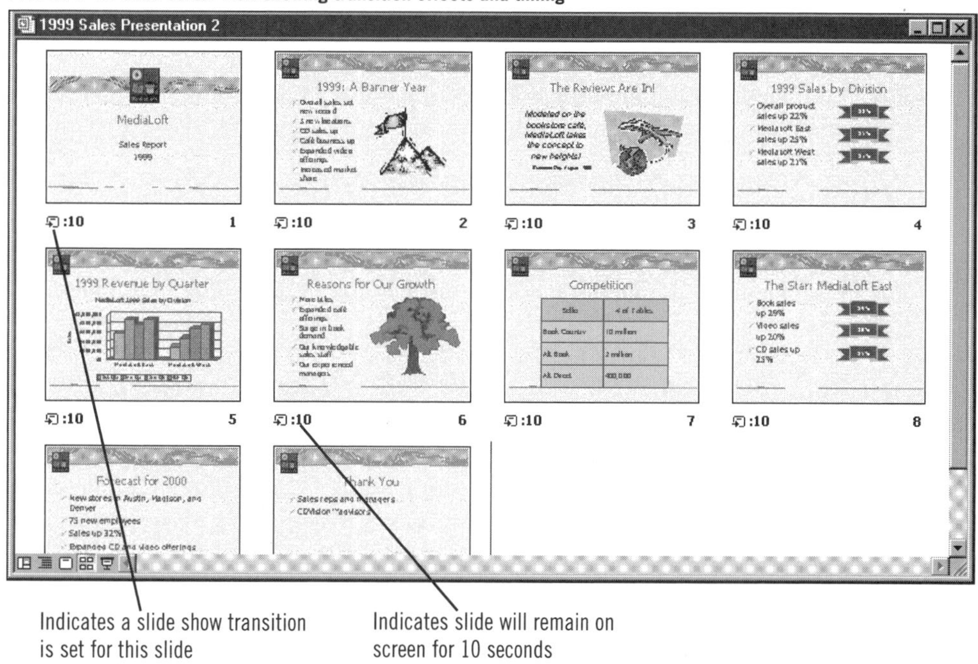

Rehearsing slide show timing

You can set different slide timings for each slide. For example, you can have the title slide appear for 20 seconds, the second slide for 3 minutes, and so on. You also can set timings by clicking the Rehearse Timings button on the Slide Sorter toolbar or by choosing the Rehearse Timings command on the Slide Show menu. The Rehearsal dialog box shown in Figure D-18 opens. It contains buttons to pause between slides and to advance to the next slide. After opening the Rehearsal dialog box, practice giving your presentation. PowerPoint keeps track of how long each slide appears and sets the timing accordingly. You can view your rehearsed timings in Slide Sorter view. The next time you run the slide show, you can use the timings you rehearsed.

FIGURE D-18: Rehearsal dialog box

PowerPoint 2000

Setting Slide Animation Effects

Animation effects let you control how the graphics and main points in your presentation appear on the screen during a slide show. You can animate text, images, or even individual chart elements, or you can add sound effects. Keep in mind that the animation effects you choose give a certain "flavor" to your presentation. They can be serious and businesslike or humorous. Choose appropriate effects for your presentation content and audience. Scenario ▸ Maria wants to animate the text and graphics of several slides in her presentation.

Steps 1 2 3 4

1. Click **slide 2**, press and hold down **[Ctrl]**, then click **slides 4**, **6**, **8**, **9**, and **10**
   The selected slides have bullets on them. The bullets can be animated to appear on the slide individually when you click the mouse during the slide show.

2. On the Slide Sorter toolbar, click the **Preset Animation list arrow**, then click **Fly From Left**
   Slide 10 previews the bullets flying in from the left side of the slide, and because this slide has a custom animation applied to it, you also hear the drum roll. When you run the slide show, instead of appearing all at once, the bullets of the selected slides will appear one at a time, "flying" in from the left each time you click the mouse button.

3. Click **slide 1**, then run the slide show
   The bullets fly in from the left. (Some of the graphics on these slides may also fly in from the left.) To set custom animation effects, the target slide must be in Slide view.

4. Double-click **slide 6** to view it in the previous view, which in this case is Slide view, click **Slide Show** on the menu bar, then click **Custom Animation**
   The Custom Animation dialog box opens. Objects that are already animated appear in the Animation Order section in the order in which they will be animated.

5. In the Check to animate slide objects list box, click **Object 3**
   Make sure you do not click the Object 3 check box and remove its checkmark. Object 3 represents the tree, which becomes highlighted in the preview. See Figure D-19.

6. Click the **Effects tab**, click the **top left list arrow** in the Entry animation and sound section, click **Dissolve**, click **Preview** in the upper-right corner of the dialog box to see the new animation effect, then click **OK**

7. Change the animation effect to **Dissolve** for the mountain graphic on slide 2 and the airplane graphic on slide 3

8. Run the Slide Show again from slide 1, then return to Slide Sorter view
   The special effects make the presentation easier to understand and more interesting.

9. Click the **Zoom text box** on the Standard toolbar, type **50**, press **[Enter]**, click **Window** on the menu bar, then click **Fit to Page**
   Figure D-20 shows the completed presentation in Slide Sorter view at 50% zoom.

10. Click **View** on the menu bar, click **Header and Footer**, click the **Notes and Handouts** tab, type your name in the Footer text box, click **Apply to All**, save your presentation, print it as handouts, six slides per page, then exit PowerPoint

QuickTip

Use the ScreenTips to see the names of the Slide Sorter toolbar buttons.

QuickTip

If you want a grouped object, like the ribbons on slides 4 and 8, to fly in individually, then you must ungroup them first.

QuickTip

To preview animation in Normal view, Slide Sorter view, or Slide view, click Slide Show on the menu bar, then click Animation Preview.

FIGURE D-19: Custom Animation dialog box

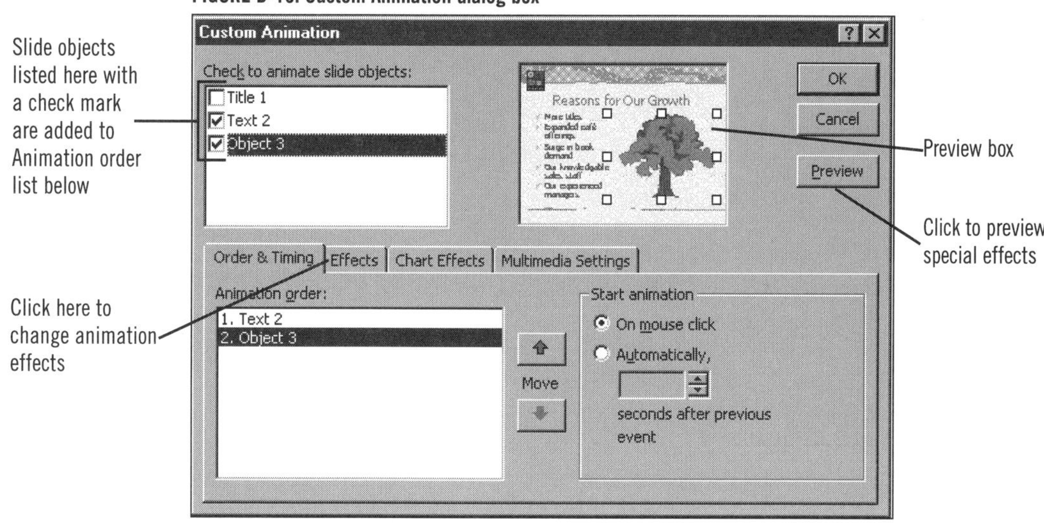

FIGURE D-20: Completed presentation in Slide Sorter view

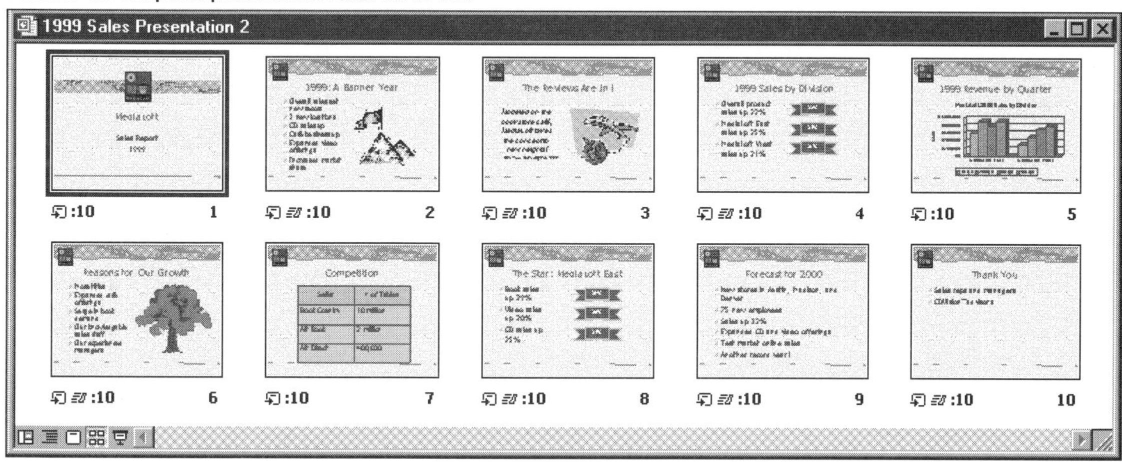

Presentation checklist

You should always rehearse your slide show. If possible, rehearse your presentation in the room and with the computer that you will use. Use the following checklist to prepare for the slide show.

✔ Is **PowerPoint** or **PowerPoint Viewer** installed on the computer?

✔ Is your **presentation file** on the hard drive of the computer you will be using? Try putting a shortcut for the file on the desktop. Do you have a backup copy of your presentation file on a floppy disk?

✔ Is the **projection device** working correctly? Can the slides be seen from the back of the room?

✔ Do you know how to control **room lighting** so that the audience can both see your slides and their handouts and notes? You may want to designate someone to control the lights if the controls are not close to you.

✔ Will the **computer** be situated so you can advance and annotate the slides yourself? If not, designate someone to advance them for you.

✔ Do you have enough copies of your **handouts**? Bring extras. Decide when to hand them out, or whether you prefer to have them waiting at the audience members' places when they enter.

PowerPoint 2000

PowerPoint 2000

Practice

Concepts Review

Label each element of the PowerPoint window shown in Figure D-21.

FIGURE D-21

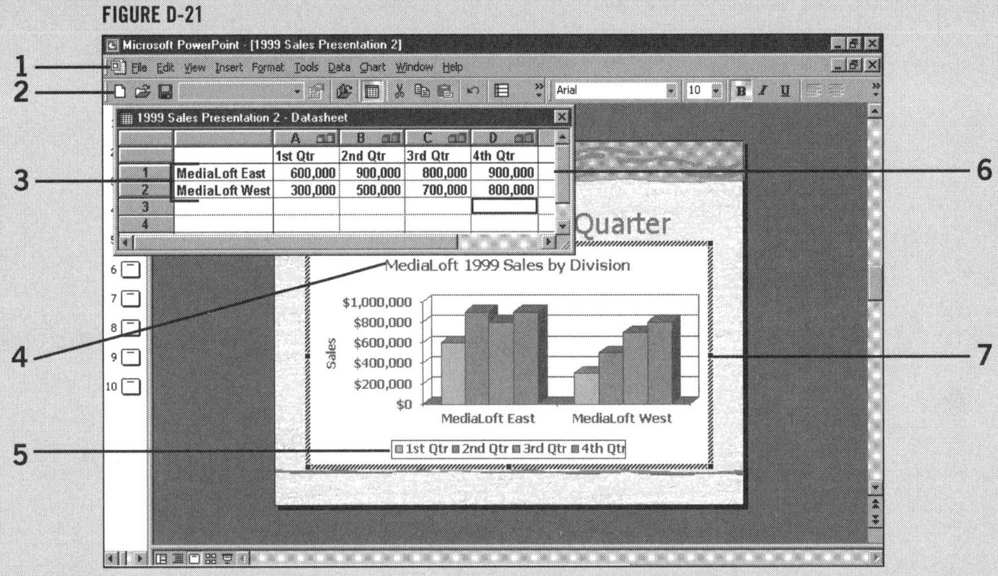

Match each term with the statement that describes it.

8. **Chart**
9. **Embedded object**
10. **Animation effect**
11. **Data series markers**
12. **Clip Gallery**
13. **Scaling**

a. The way bulleted items and images appear on a slide
b. A graphic representation of a datasheet
c. Graphic representations of data series
d. Resizing an object by a specific percentage
e. A copy of an object from which you can access another program's tools
f. A file index system that organizes images

Select the best answer from the list of choices.

14. PowerPoint animation effects let you control

a. Which text and images are animated.
b. The direction from which animated objects appear.
c. The order in which text and objects are animated.
d. All of the above.

15. Which of the following is *not* true of a Microsoft Graph chart?

a. You cannot import data from other programs into a datasheet.
b. You can double-click a chart to view its corresponding datasheet.
c. An active cell has a black selection rectangle around it.
d. A graph is made up of a datasheet and chart.

Skills Review

1. **Insert clip art.**
   a. Open the presentation PPT D-3 on your Project Disk, save it as "CD Product Report" to your Project Disk.
   b. Go to slide 2 and insert the musical notes graphic from the Music category in the Clip Gallery.
   c. On the Size tab of the Format Picture dialog box, deselect Relative to original picture size, scale the graphic to 125% of its current size, and center it in the blank space.
   d. Align the top of the main text placeholder with the top of the graphic, and adjust their position as necessary.
2. **Insert, crop, and scale a picture.**
   a. Change the layout of slide 6 to the Text & Object layout, and insert PPT D-4 into the object placeholder.
   b. Crop about ¾" off the left side of the picture.
   c. Align the tops of the text box and the graphic.
   d. Scale the graphic to an appropriate percentage of its original size so it is approximately the same size as the main text box.
   e. Reposition the graphic, then make the background of the graphic transparent.
3. **Embed a chart.**
   a. Go to slide 3, "1999 CD Sales by Quarter," and apply the Chart AutoLayout.
   b. Start Microsoft Graph.
   c. Move the mouse pointer around on the datasheet and note the different pointer shapes.
   d. Deselect the chart object.
4. **Enter and edit data in the datasheet.**
   a. Open Graph again, and for the row 1 datasheet label, enter "MediaLoft East."
   b. Enter the information shown in Table D-4 into the datasheet and widen the column to fit all the data.
   c. Delete any unused rows of default data.
   d. Place the Data Series in Columns.

TABLE D-4

	1st Qtr	2nd Qtr	3rd Qtr	4th Qtr
MediaLoft East	36	40	45	43
MediaLoft West	44	50	52	53

5. **Format a chart.**
   a. Close the datasheet but leave Graph running.
   b. Change the region names on the X-axis to 20 points.
   c. Apply the Currency Style with no decimals to the values on the vertical axis.
   d. Insert the chart title "1999 CD Sales."
   e. Add the text "Sales in 000s" to the Z-axis, then change the orientation of the Z-axis to vertical.
   f. Place the legend below the graphic.
   g. Exit Graph.
6. **Use slide show commands.**
   a. Begin the slide show at slide 1, then proceed through the slide show to slide 3.
   b. On slide 3, use the Pen to draw straight-line annotations under the labels on the horizontal axis.
   c. Erase the pen annotations, then change the pointer back to an arrow.
   d. Go to slide 2 using the Go command on the slide show pop-up menu.
   e. Use [End] to move to the last slide.
   f. Return to Slide view.
7. **Create a table.**
   a. Add a slide using the title only format after slide 2.
   b. Add the slide title "CD Sales by Type."
   c. Insert a PowerPoint table with 2 columns and 5 rows.

- **d.** For the header row, enter Type and Sales.
- **e.** In the left column, add the following types: Rock, Folk, Classical, and Jazz/Blues.
- **f.** In the right column, add realistic sales figures for each CD type.
- **g.** Reposition the table so it doesn't obscure the slide title.
- **h.** Format the table using fills, horizontal and vertical alignment, or any other features.

8. Set slide show timings and transitions.

- **a.** Switch to Slide Sorter view.
- **b.** Open the Slide Transition dialog box using the pop-up menu.
- **c.** Specify that all slides should advance after 15 seconds, unless the mouse is clicked first.
- **d.** Apply the Box Out transition effect to all slides.
- **e.** In Slide Sorter view, preview the transition effect on two slides.
- **f.** Apply the Cover Down transition effect to the last slide in the presentation.
- **g.** View the slide show to verify the transitions are correct.

9. Set slide animation effects.

- **a.** In Slide Sorter view, apply the Peek from Right animation effect to the bulleted list on slide 5.
- **b.** Go to slide 2 in Slide or Normal view, and using the Custom Animation dialog box, apply the Dissolve effect to the Music graphic and preview the effect in the dialog box.
- **c.** Specify that the bulleted list text object should spiral in after the musical notes graphic appears, and preview the effect. (*Hint:* Check the Order & Timing tab to make sure the musical notes graphic is first in the list.)
- **d.** Run the slide show from the beginning to check the animation effects.
- **e.** Save the presentation.
- **f.** Add your name as a footer to the notes and handouts, then print the presentation as handouts, six slides per page.
- **g.** Close the presentation and exit PowerPoint.

Visual Workshop

Create a slide that looks like the example in Figure D-22. Add your name as a footer on the slide. Save the presentation as "Costs" to your Project Disk.

FIGURE D-22

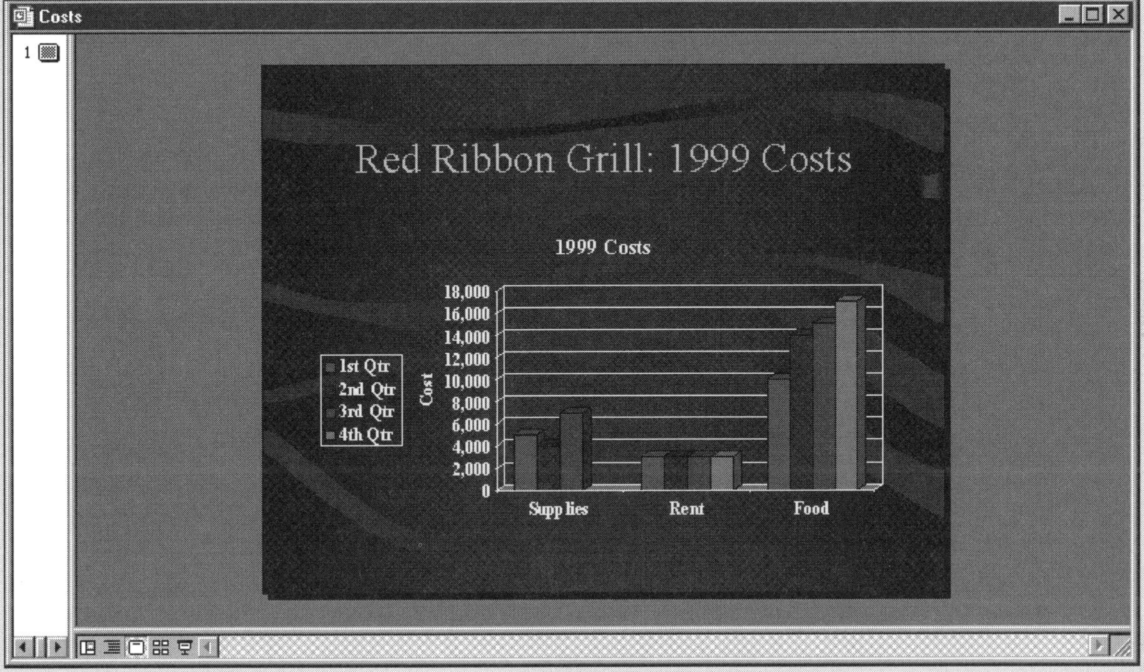

PowerPoint 2000

Customizing Your Presentation

Objectives

- Understand PowerPoint masters
- MOUS Format master text
- MOUS Change master text indents
- Adjust text objects
- Use advanced drawing tools
- MOUS Use advanced formatting tools
- Use the Style Checker
- MOUS Create and customize a Toolbar

Design features such as text spacing and color are some of the most important qualities of a professional-looking presentation. It is important, however, to make design elements consistent throughout a presentation to hold the reader's attention and to avoid confusion. PowerPoint helps you achieve the look you want by providing ways to customize and enhance your slides, notes pages, and handouts. Scenario Maria Abbott, the general sales manager of MediaLoft, is working on a presentation that she will give at a meeting of store managers. After receiving feedback from the co-workers, she revises her presentation by customizing the format of her slides and enhancing the graphics.

PowerPoint 2000

Understanding PowerPoint Masters

Presentations in PowerPoint use **Slide Masters**, templates for all of the slides in the presentation. Three of the PowerPoint views have a corresponding master view—Slide Master view for Slide view, Notes Master view for Notes Page view, and Handout Master view for Slide Sorter view. Slide view actually has two masters; the second, called the Title Master, allows you to customize just the title slide of your presentation. Design elements that you place on the Slide Master appear on every slide in the presentation. When you insert an object or change text formatting in one of the text placeholders on the Slide Master, the change appears in all the slides of the presentation. For example, you could insert a company logo in the upper-right corner of the Slide Master and that logo would then appear on every slide in your presentation. When you apply a template from another presentation, the Slide Masters from that presentation automatically replace the existing ones. You can always override the settings on the Slide Master by changing the background, text formats, and color scheme in the Slide pane or Slide view, then clicking Apply in the dialog box. As long as you click Apply, not Apply All, the changes will affect only the displayed slide. Scenario Maria wants to make a few changes to the presentation design, so she opens her presentation and examines the Slide Master.

Steps 1 2 3 4

QuickTip

To return personalized toolbars and menus to the default state, click Tools on the menu bar, click Customize, click Reset my usage data on the Options tab, click Yes, then click Close.

QuickTip

You can also hold down [Shift] and click the Slide View button to display the slide master.

QuickTip

In Slide Master view, click New Title Master on the Common Tasks menu button to add a Title Master to a presentation that does not have one.

1. Start PowerPoint, open the presentation **PPT E-1**, then save it as **1999 Sales Presentation 3**

   The title slide of the presentation appears.

2. Click **Window** on the menu bar, then click **Arrange All**

   This ensures that your screen will match the figures in this book.

3. Click **View**, point to **Master**, then click **Title Master**

   The presentation's Title Master appears, showing the master elements along with the Master toolbar. A slide miniature may also appear.

4. Drag the **vertical scroll box** to the top of the scroll bar, then, if the slide miniature is visible, click the **Close box** on the slide miniature

   The Slide Master appears. It contains a **Master title placeholder**, and a **Master text placeholder** as shown in Figure E-1. These placeholders control the format for each title text object and main text object for each slide in the presentation after slide 1. Figure E-2 shows slide 2 of the presentation. Examine Figures E-1 and E-2 to better understand the relationship between the Slide Master and the slide.

   - The Master title placeholder, labeled "Title Area for AutoLayouts," indicates the position of the title text object and its font size, style, and color. Compare this to the slide title shown in Figure E-2.
   - The Master text placeholder, labeled "Object Area for AutoLayouts" determines the characteristics of the main text objects on all the slides in the presentation. Notice how the bullet levels in the main text object of Figure E-2 compare to the corresponding bullet levels of the Master text placeholder in Figure E-1.
   - You can resize and move master title and text placeholders as you would any placeholder in PowerPoint.
   - Slide Masters can also contain background objects, such AutoShapes, clip art, or pictures that will appear on every slide in the presentation behind the text and objects you place on the slides. In Maria's presentation, the company logo appears on both the Title Master and the Slide Master, so that it shows on every slide in the presentation.

FIGURE E-1: Slide Master

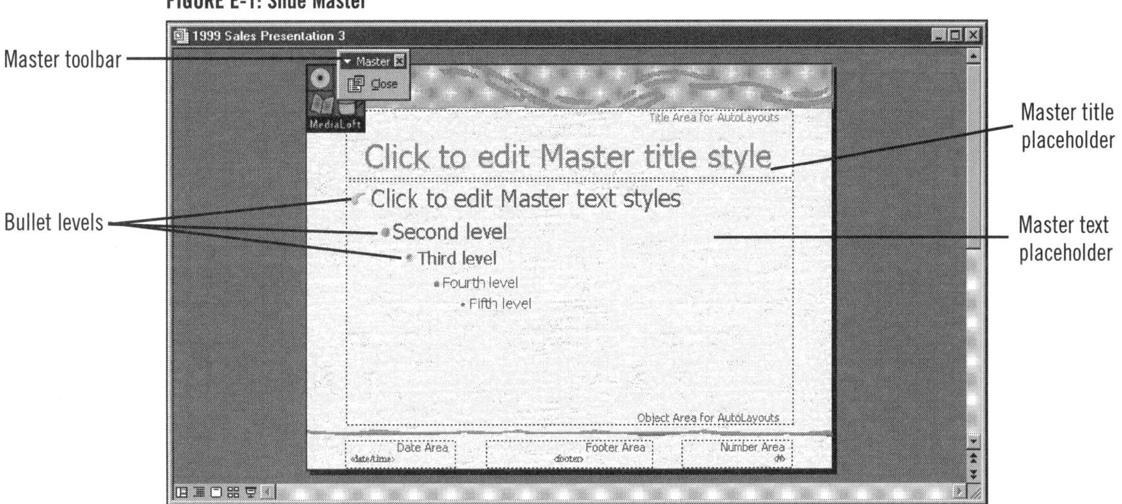

FIGURE E-2: Slide 2 in Slide view

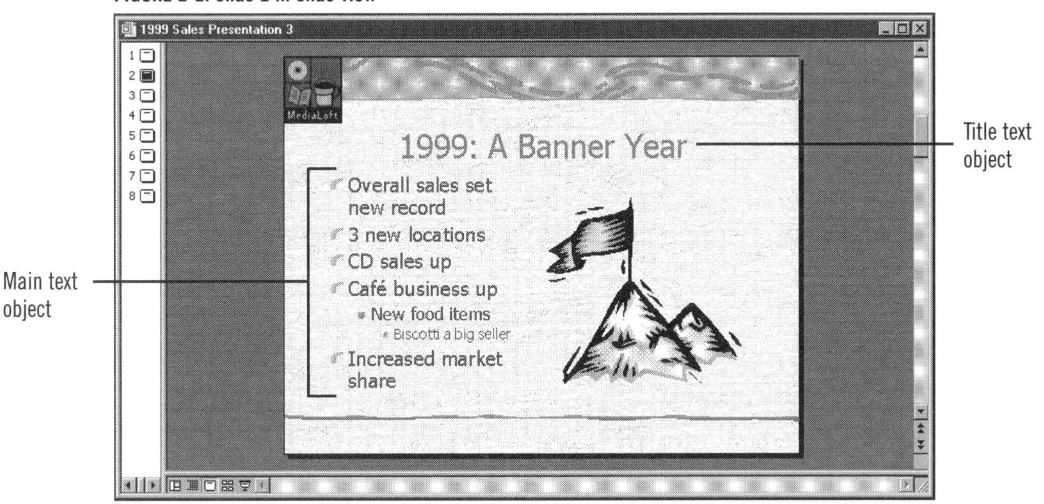

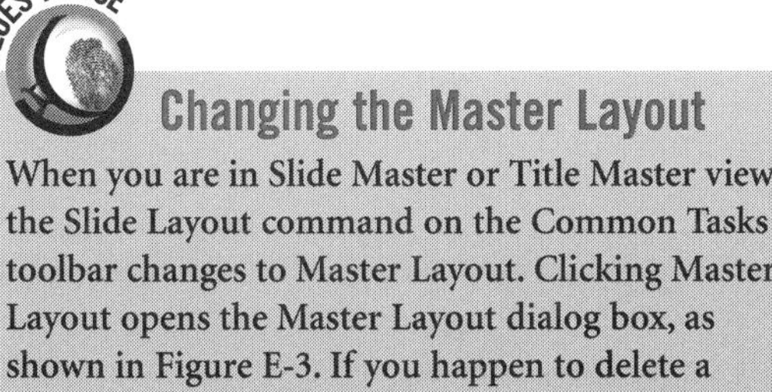

Changing the Master Layout

When you are in Slide Master or Title Master view, the Slide Layout command on the Common Tasks toolbar changes to Master Layout. Clicking Master Layout opens the Master Layout dialog box, as shown in Figure E-3. If you happen to delete a master placeholder or if one doesn't appear in a master view, use the Master Layout dialog box to reapply a master placeholder. Each master view has its own Master Layout dialog box.

FIGURE E-3: Master Layout dialog box

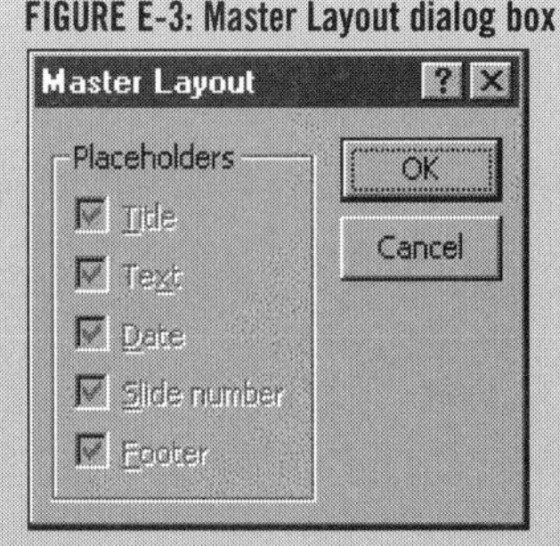

PowerPoint 2000

PowerPoint 2000

Formatting Master Text

Formatting text in a master view works the same as it does in other views, but PowerPoint applies the changes you make to the whole presentation. This ensures that you don't use a mixture of fonts and styles throughout the presentation. For example, if your presentation is part of a marketing campaign for a travel tour to the Middle East, you may decide to switch the title text font of the entire presentation from the standard Times New Roman font to a script font. You can change text color, style, size, and bullet type in the master view. When you change a bullet type, you can use a character bullet symbol from a font, a picture bullet from the Clip Gallery, or an image that you scan in. Scenario Maria decides to make a few formatting changes to the text of her Slide Master.

1. Make sure the Slide Master is still visible
2. Move I anywhere in the first line of text in the Master text placeholder, then click
   The insertion point appears. To make the formatting changes to the whole line of text, you don't have to select the line; just click to insert the insertion point. The first line of text could be more prominent.
3. Click the **Bold button** on the Formatting toolbar, then click the **Text Shadow button** on the Formatting toolbar
   The first line of text becomes bold with a shadow. The third level bullet would be more visible if it were darker.
4. Right-click anywhere in the third line of text in the Master text placeholder, then click **Bullets and Numbering** on the pop-up menu
   The Bullets and Numbering dialog box opens. Notice that there is also a Numbered tab that you can use to create sequentially numbered or lettered bullets.
5. Click **Character**, click the **Bullets from list arrow**, then click **Wingdings**
   The available bullet choices change.
6. Click the **airplane** in the second row, as shown in Figure E-4, click the **Color list arrow**, then click the **blue-gray square** (labeled Follow Shadows Scheme Color)
7. Click **OK**, then click a blank area of the slide
   A blue-gray airplane replaces the third level bullet.
8. Click the **Slide View button**, then click the **slide icon** for slide 2 in the Outline pane
   Compare your screen to Figure E-5.
9. Click the **Save button** on the Standard toolbar to save your changes

Trouble?

If you don't see the Text Shadow button, click the More Buttons button on the Formatting toolbar.

QuickTip

A bullet looks best if it is the same size or smaller than the text it identifies. Use the Size spin arrows to specify the percentage of the text size you want the bullet to be.

QuickTip

The first level bullet is a picture bullet. To insert a picture bullet, click Picture in the Bullets and Numbering dialog box, then click the desired bullet. You may need access to the Office 2000 CD to use picture bullets.

FIGURE E-4: Bullet dialog box

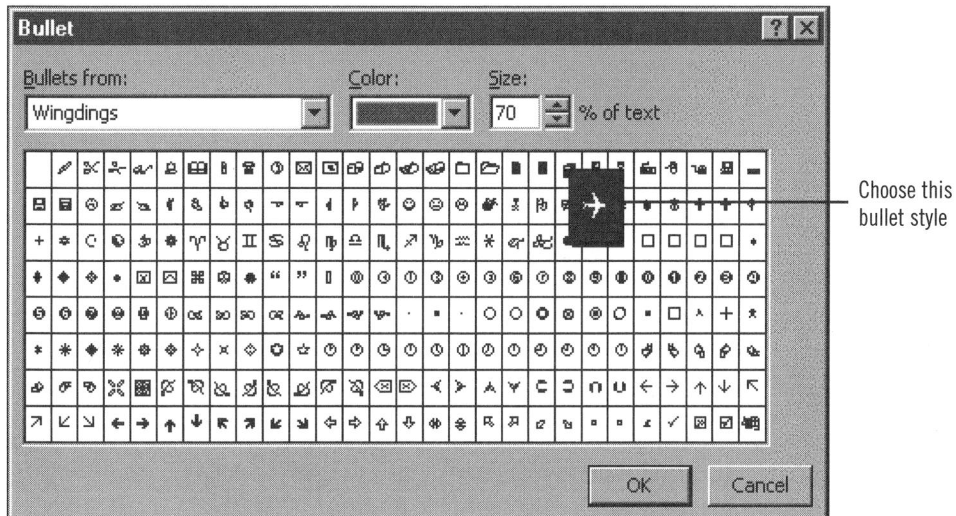

FIGURE E-5: Slide 2 with modified text style and bullet type

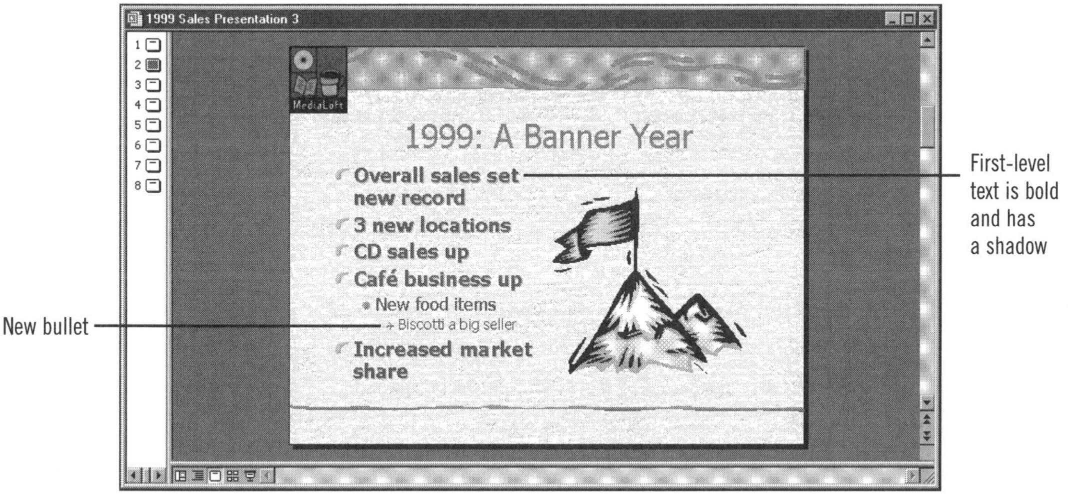

Applying a template from another presentation

When you apply a template from another presentation, you automatically apply the master layouts, fonts, and colors to the new presentation. To apply a template from another presentation, click the Common Tasks menu button on the Formatting toolbar and click Apply Design template. In the Apply Design Template dialog box, click All Files in the Files of type list box, then use the Look in list arrow to navigate to the presentation whose design you want to apply. (It does not have to be a template.) Click the presentation or template name, then click Apply.

PowerPoint 2000

Changing Master Text Indents

The master text placeholder in every presentation has five levels of text, called **indent levels.** You can use the horizontal slide ruler to control the space between the bullets and the text or to change the position of the whole indent level. Each indent level is represented by two small triangles called **indent markers** on the ruler that identify the position of each indent level in the master text placeholder. You can also set tabs on the horizontal ruler by clicking the tab indicator to the left of the horizontal ruler. Table E-1 describes the indent and tab markers on the ruler. Scenario Maria decides to change the distance between the bullet symbols and the text in the first two indent levels of her presentation to emphasize the bullets.

1. Click **View** on the menu bar, point to **Master**, then click **Slide Master**
   The Slide Master appears.
2. Click anywhere in the master text placeholder to place the insertion point, click **View** on the menu bar, then click **Ruler**
   The rulers and indent markers for the Master text placeholder appear. The indent markers are set so that the first line of text in each level, in this case the bullet, begins to the left of subsequent lines of text. This is a **hanging indent**.
3. Position the pointer over the left indent marker of the first indent level, then drag to the right to the ½" mark
   Compare your screen to Figure E-6.
4. Position the pointer over the left indent marker of the second indent level, then drag to the right to the 1⅛" mark
   See Figure E-7. The rulers take up valuable screen area.
5. Click the right mouse button in a blank area of the Presentation window, then click **Ruler** on the pop-up menu
   The rulers are no longer visible.
6. Click **Close** on the Master toolbar
   Slide Master view closes and slide 2 appears, showing the increased indents in the main text object.
7. Click the **Save button** on the Standard toolbar

Trouble?

If your rulers are already visible skip step 2.

Trouble?

If you accidentally drag an indent marker into another marker. Click the Undo button to restore the indent levels to their original position.

QuickTip

You can add tabs to any level text by clicking on the ruler where you want the tab. Click the tab indicator to the left of the ruler to cycle through the different tab alignment options.

TABLE E-1: Indent and tab markers

symbol	name	function
	First line indent marker	Controls the position of the first line of text in an indent level
	Left indent marker	Controls the position of subsequent lines of text in an indent level
	Margin marker	Moves both indent markers of an indent level at the same time
	Left aligned tab	Aligns tab text on the left
	Right aligned tab	Aligns tab text on the right
	Center aligned tab	Aligns tab text in the center
	Decimal aligned tab	Aligns tab text on a decimal point

FIGURE E-6: Slide Master with first-level, left, indent marker moved

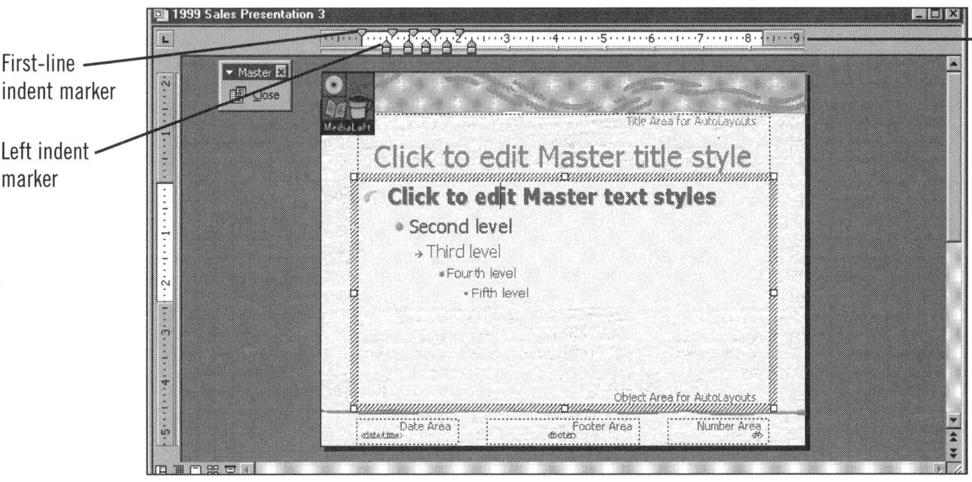

FIGURE E-7: Slide Master with second-level, left, indent marker moved

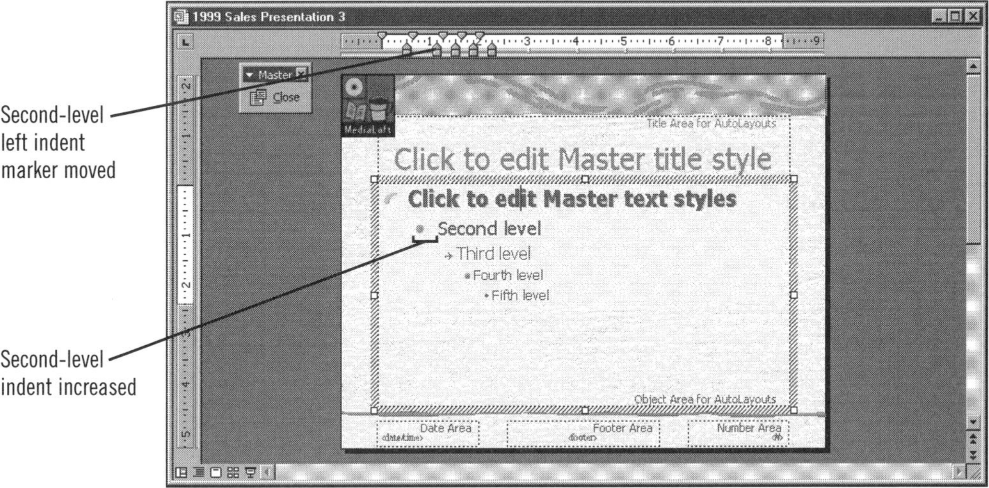

PowerPoint 2000

CLUES TO USE

Exceptions to the Slide Master

If you change the format of text on a slide and then apply a different template to the presentation, the slide that you formatted retains the text formatting changes you made. These format changes that differ from the Slide Master are known as **exceptions**. Exceptions can only be changed on the individual slides where they occur. For example, you might change the font and size of a particular piece of text on a slide to make it stand out and then decide later to add a different template to your presentation. The text you formatted before you applied the template is an exception, and it is unaffected by the new template. Another way to override the Slide Master is to remove the master graphics on one or more slides. You might want to do this to get a clearer view of your slide text. Click Format on the menu bar, click Background, then click the Omit background graphics from master check box to select it.

PowerPoint 2000

Adjusting Text Objects

You have complete control over the placement of your text in PowerPoint. With the **text anchor** feature, you can adjust text position within text objects or shapes to achieve the best look. If you want your text to fill more or less of the slide, you can adjust the spacing between lines of text, called **leading** (rhymes with "wedding"). Scenario Maria decides that the graphic on the last slide in her presentation makes it look cluttered. She decides to delete it and adjust the text position and line spacing to give the slide a more open and polished look.

Steps

1. Drag the **vertical scroll box** down to view slide 8
2. Click the **graphic**, then press **[Delete]**
3. Click the **Common Tasks menu button** on the Formatting toolbar, click **Slide Layout**, select the **Bulleted List AutoLayout**, then click **Apply**
4. Press **[Shift]**, right-click the **main text object,** click **Format Placeholder** on the pop-up menu, then click the **Text Box tab**
   The Format AutoShape dialog box opens, similar to Figure E-8. The text would look better centered in the text box.
5. Click the **Text anchor point list arrow**, click **Top Centered**, then click **OK**
   The text moves to the center of the text object. The bullets are a little too close together.
6. Click **Format** on the menu bar, then click **Line Spacing**
   The Line Spacing dialog box opens, similar to Figure E-9.
7. In the After paragraph section, click the **up spin arrow** three times so that 0.15 appears, click **Preview**, then drag the dialog box out of the way
   The space, or leading, after each paragraph increases, and the text automatically becomes smaller to make it look less crowded.
8. In the Line spacing section, click the **up spin arrow** twice so that 1.1 appears, then click **Preview**
   The line spacing between the text lines increases and the text shrinks again. Because each bulleted item is considered to be a separate paragraph, the Line Spacing and the After Paragraph commands have similar effects.
9. Click **OK**, then click in a blank area of the Presentation window to deselect the main text object
   Compare your screen to Figure E-10.

FIGURE E-8: Format AutoShape dialog box

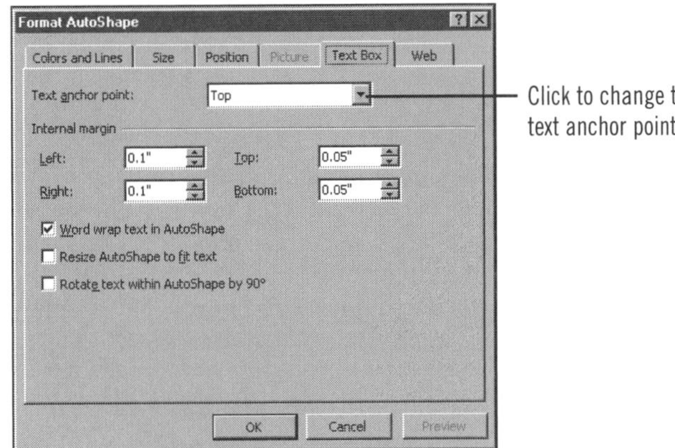

Click to change the text anchor point

FIGURE E-9: Line Spacing dialog box

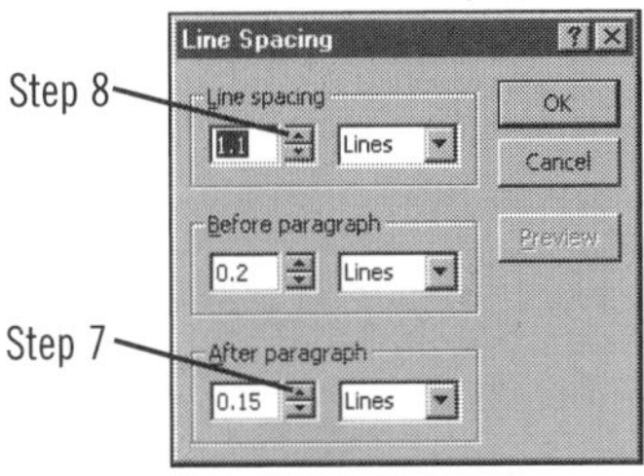

Step 8

Step 7

FIGURE E-10: Slide showing formatted main text object

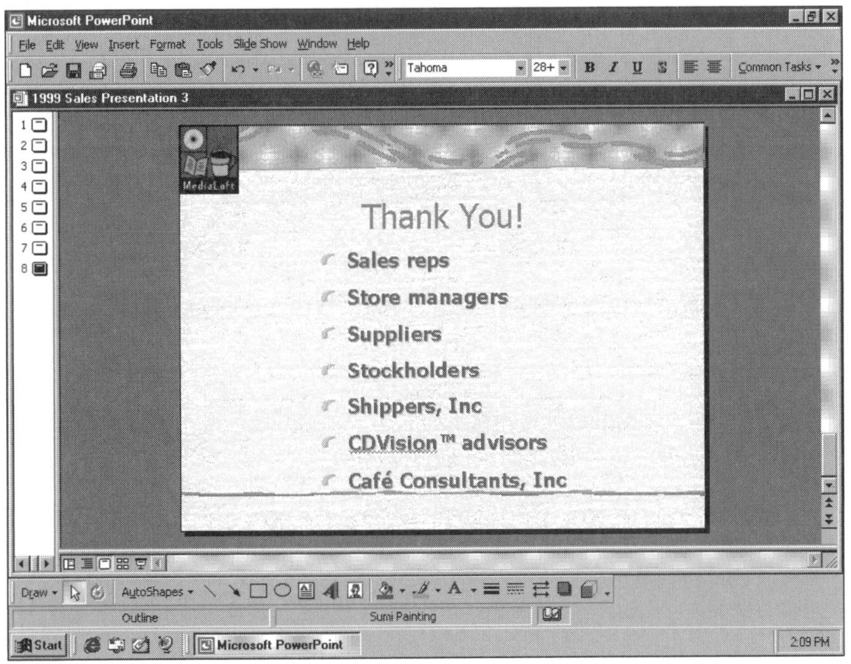

PowerPoint 2000

CLUES TO USE

Changing margins around text in shapes

You can also use the Text Anchor Point command to change the margins around a text object to form a shape that suits the text better. Right-click the shape, click Format Placeholder, click the Text Box tab, then adjust the Internal margin settings. Click Preview to see your changes before you apply them to the shape.

PowerPoint 2000

Using Advanced Drawing Tools

PowerPoint has a number of powerful drawing tools on the AutoShapes menu to help you draw all types of shapes. For example, the Curve drawing tool allows you to create a freeform curved line, the Arc tool helps you draw smooth, curved lines and pie-shaped wedges, and the Connector line tool allows you to connect slide objects with a line. Once you have drawn a shape, you can format and rearrange it to create the effect you want. Scenario Maria uses the Arc tool and a Connector line tool to complete the diagram on slide 7.

Steps

1. Click the **slide icon** for slide 7, click the **AutoShapes menu button** on the Drawing toolbar, point to **Basic Shapes**, then click the **Arc button**
   The pointer changes to +.
2. Position + on the center of the left edge of the **CDs object**, then drag down to the top, center edge of the **Videos object**
   See Figure E-11. The direction in which you drag the arc determines whether the arc opens up or down and the distance you drag the arc determines its size.
3. Drag the arc's **bottom adjustment handle** down and to the right so the arc becomes a half circle, then drag the lower middle sizing handle down so that the end of the arc touches the middle of the Books object
   The adjustment handle determines the length of the arc; the sizing handle changes its size.
4. Click the **Line Style button** on the Drawing toolbar, then click the **4½ pt** line style
   The line style of the arc changes to a thicker weight.
5. Click the **Arrow Style button** on the Drawing toolbar, then click **Arrow Style 5**
   An arrowhead appears on the arc. The direction in which you dragged the arc determines the direction of the arrowhead. The arrow is in front of the Videos object.
6. Click the **Draw menu button** on the Drawing toolbar, point to **Order**, click **Send to Back**, then click a blank area of the slide
   There needs to be a connector between the Videos and the Café objects.
7. Click the **AutoShapes menu button** on the Drawing toolbar, point to **Connectors**, then click the **Straight Double-Arrow Connector button**
8. Move + to the right side of the **Videos object** until it changes to ⌖ and blue dots appear around the object, then click the blue dot on the right side of the Videos object
   The blue dots are anchor points for the connector line.
9. Move the pointer to the **Café object**, then when you see the blue dot inside the pointer, click the button again to place the right side of the connector line
   A red square appears at either end of the connector line, indicating that the line connects the two objects.
10. Click , click **4½ pt**, click in a blank area of the Presentation window, then save the presentation.
    Compare your screen to Figure E-12.

QuickTip

To constrain the arc to a proportional size, press and hold edge down [Shift] while you drag.

QuickTip

To change the default attributes of a particular AutoShape, format the AutoShape, select it, click Draw on the Drawing toolbar, then click Set AutoShape Defaults.

Trouble?

If a green box appears at either end of the line, drag the green square until the blue connection point on the object appears.

FIGURE E-11: Slide showing drawn arc object

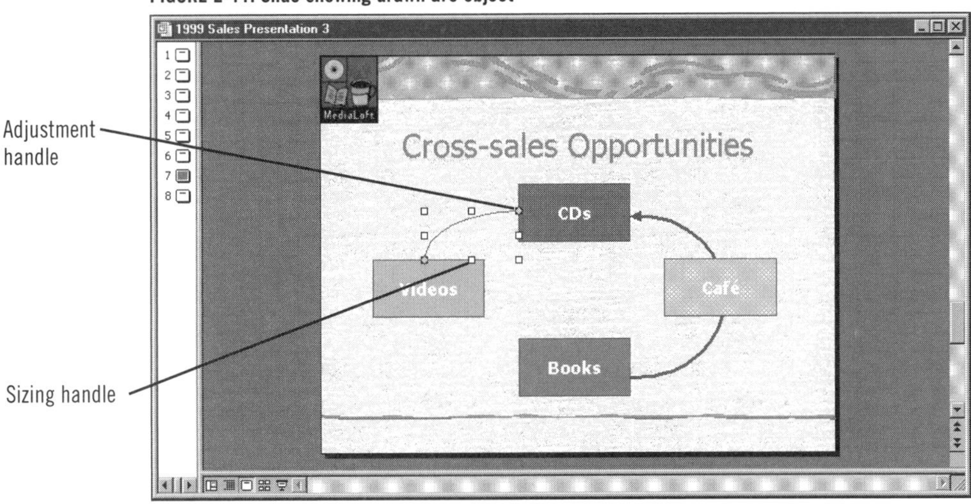

FIGURE E-12: Slide showing formatted arc and connector line

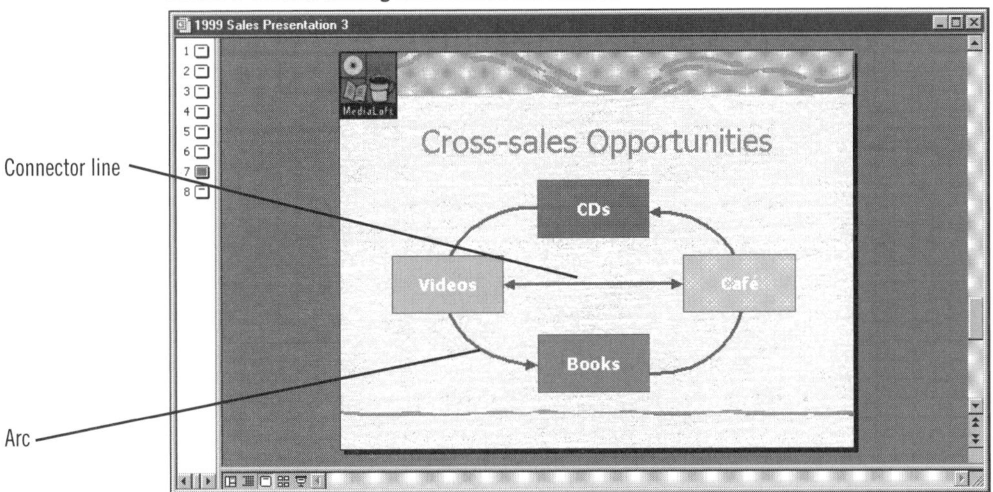

PowerPoint 2000

Drawing a freeform shape

A **freeform** shape can consist of straight lines, freehand (or curved) lines, or a combination of the two. To draw a freeform shape, click the AutoShapes menu button, point to Lines, then click the Freeform button. Drag the mouse to draw the desired shape (the cursor changes to a pencil as you draw), then double-click when you are done. To draw a straight line with the Freeform tool, click where you want to begin the line, move the mouse, then double-click to deactivate the Freeform tool. To edit a freeform object, right-click the object, then click Edit Points on the pop-up menu.

PowerPoint 2000

Using Advanced Formatting Tools

With PowerPoint's advanced formatting tools, you can change formatting attributes such as fill texture, 3-D effects, and shadow for text and shapes. If you like the attributes of an object, you can use the Format Painter button to pick up the attributes and apply them to another object. Scenario Maria wants to use the advanced formatting tools to enhance the diagram on the slide.

Steps 1 2 3 4

1. Right-click the Videos object, click **Format AutoShape** on the pop-up menu, click the **Colors and Lines tab**, click the **Color list arrow** in the Fill section, then click **Fill Effects**
   The Fill Effects dialog box opens.
2. Click the **Texture tab**, click the **down scroll arrow** once, click the **Papyrus square** (first square in the bottom row), click **OK**, then click **OK** again
   The papyrus pattern fills the shape.
3. Click the **3-D button** on the Drawing toolbar, then click **3-D Settings**
   The 3-D Settings toolbar appears.
4. Click the **Depth button** on the 3-D Settings toolbar, then click **72 pt**.
   A 3-D effect is applied and the depth of the 3-D effect lengthens from the default of 36 points.
5. Click the **Direction button** on the 3-D Settings toolbar, click the right effect in the bottom row, then click the **Close button** on the 3-D Settings toolbar
   The 3-D effect changes to the left side of the object.
6. With the cube still selected, click the **Font Color list arrow** on the Drawing toolbar, then click the **blue square** (third from the left) labeled Follow Shadows Scheme Color
   The other three cube objects would look better if they matched the one you just formatted.
7. Double-click the **Format Painter button** on the Standard toolbar, click each of the other three boxes, then click again to turn off the Format Painter
   Now all the objects on the slide have the same fill effect. When you use the Format Painter tool, it "picks up" the attributes of the object that is selected and copies them to the next object that you click. If you click the Format Painter button only once, it pastes the attributes of the selected object to the next object you select, then turns off automatically. The Books cube is now on top of the arrowhead.
8. Click the **Books cube**, click the **Draw menu button** on the Drawing toolbar, point to **Order**, click **Send to Back**, then click in a blank area of the slide
   Compare your screen to Figure E-13.
9. Press **[Ctrl][Home]** to move to slide 1, click the **Slide Show button**, press **[Spacebar]** or click the left mouse button to run through the presentation, then click the **Slide Sorter View button**
   Compare your screen to Figure E-14.

QuickTip

When you click the 3-D button on the Drawing toolbar, you can click one of the 3-D styles on the pop-up menu. The default 3-D style is Style 1, the first style in the first row.

QuickTip

If you don't see the Format Painter button, try clicking the More Buttons button on the Standard toolbar.

FIGURE E-13: Slide showing formatted objects

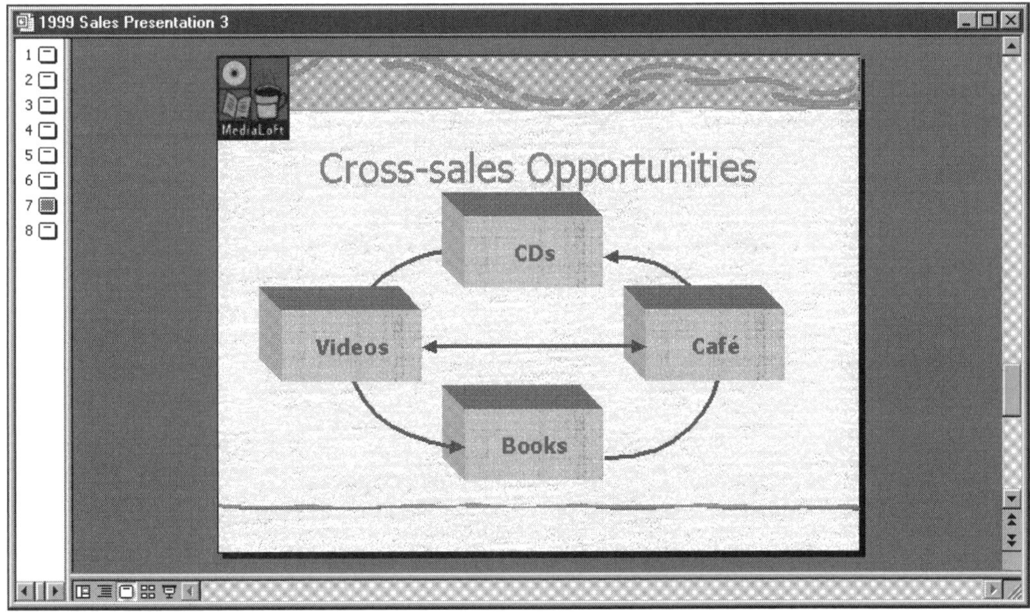

FIGURE E-14: Final presentation in Slide Sorter view

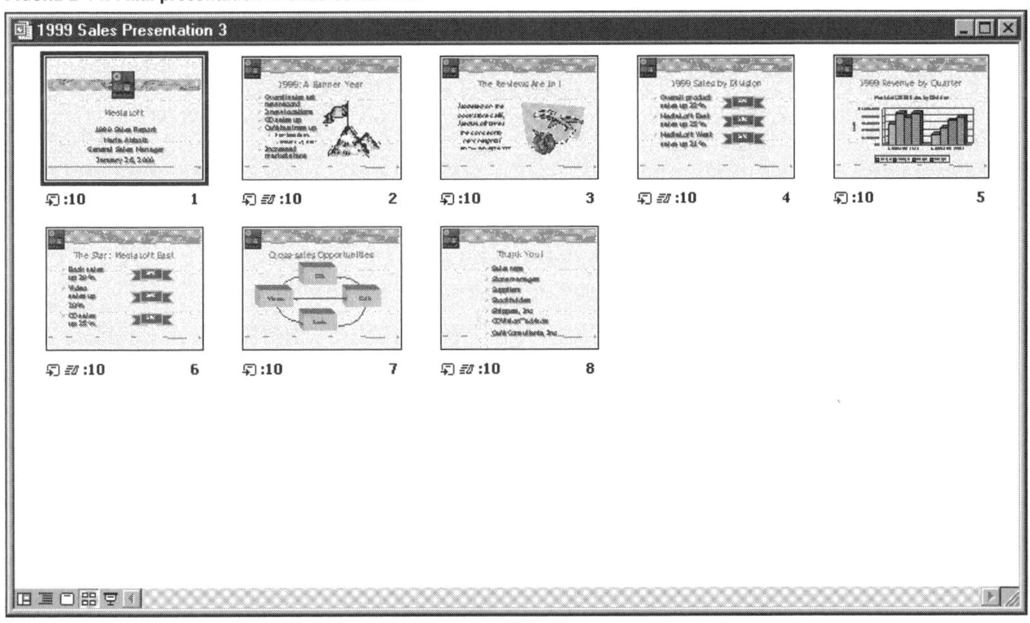

Applying a color scheme to another presentation

If you develop a custom color scheme that you like, you can use the Format Painter tool to apply it to another presentation. To apply a color scheme from one presentation to another, open each presentation in Slide Sorter view, then use the Arrange All command on the Windows menu to arrange the Presentation windows side by side. Select a slide in the presentation with the color scheme you want to copy, double-click the Format Painter button on the Standard toolbar, then click each slide that you want to change in the other presentation.

PowerPoint 2000

Using the Style Checker

To help you correct common design mistakes, the Style Checker feature in PowerPoint reviews your presentation for typical errors such as incorrect font sizes, use of too many fonts, extra words, errors in punctuation, and other readability problems. The Style Checker then suggests ways to improve your presentation. By default, PowerPoint checks your presentation for style inconsistencies and flags potential problem areas with a lightbulb. If you see the lightbulb, click it to see a list of options for handling the problem. Scenario Maria knows it's easy to overlook mistakes while preparing a presentation, so she reviews the Style Checker settings, then looks for errors she may have missed.

Steps 1 2 3 4

1. Click **Tools** on the menu bar, click **Options**, click the **Spelling and Style tab** in the Options dialog box, then click **Style Options**
   The Style Options dialog box opens, similar to Figure E-15.
2. Click check boxes as necessary so that your screen matches the dialog box shown in Figure E-15
3. Click the **Visual Clarity tab**, click **Defaults**, then review the options
   The Style Checker Options dialog box indicates the current option settings for visual clarity.
4. Click **OK** twice
5. Click **Help** on the menu bar, then click **Show the Office Assistant**
   The Office Assistant appears. It may display several tips for working with your presentation.
6. Click **slide 8**, click the **Slide View button**, then click the **lightbulb** on slide 8
   The Office Assistant tells you that the text in the main text placeholder should use sentence case capitalization, in other words, that only the first letter in each bulleted item should be capital. See Figure E-16. You know this is not a problem.
7. Click **OK** to ignore this message, then click the **lightbulb** that appears at the bottom of the slide
   Now the Office Assistant tells you that you have too much text on this slide. This layout is fine for the Thank You slide.
8. Click **OK**
9. Go to **slide 4**, click the **lightbulb** on the slide, then click **OK** to ignore the capitalization suggestions
10. Hide the Office Assistant again, then save your changes

FIGURE E-15: Case and End Punctuation tab in the Style Options dialog box

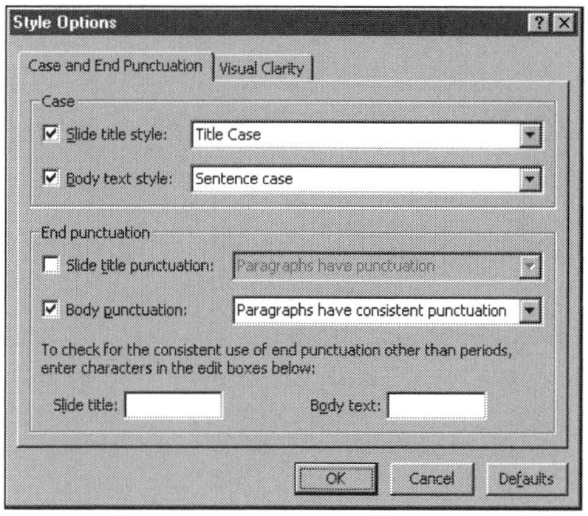

FIGURE E-16: Capitalization tip displayed by the Office Assistant

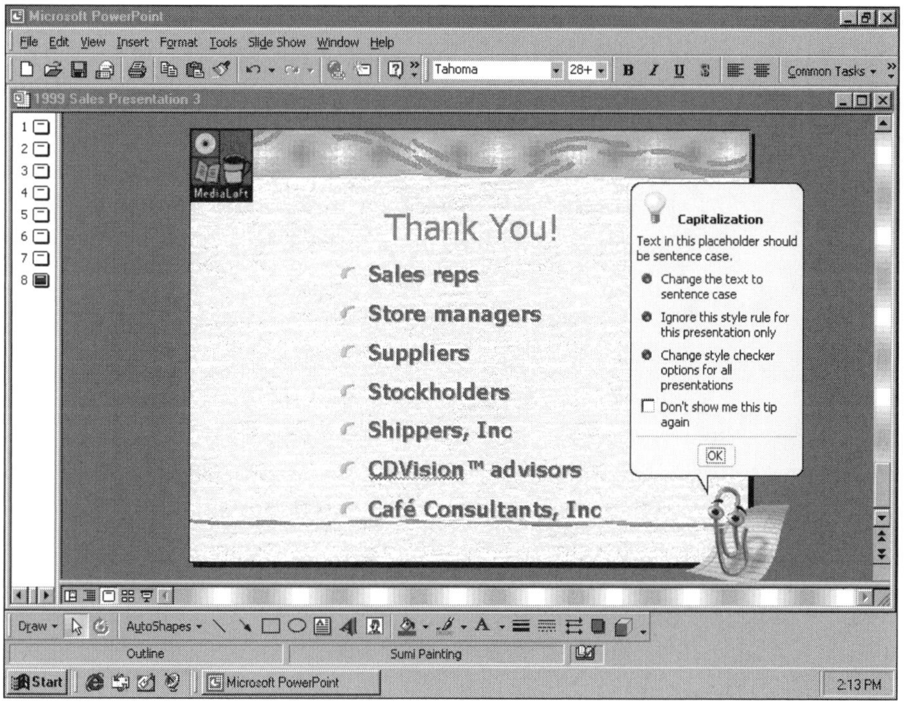

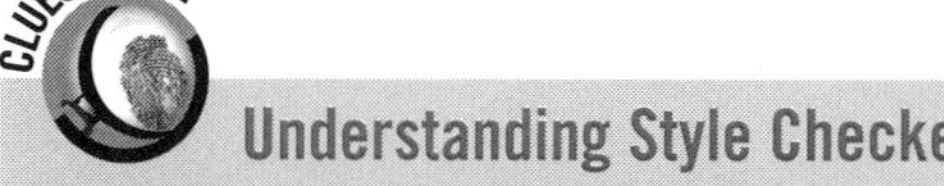

Understanding Style Checker options

The Style Checker is helpful, but before you accept its suggestions, be careful that it doesn't make changes you don't expect. In the Capitalization tip, for example, if you had selected the "Change the text to sentence case" option, all the uppercase letters in the middle of each bullet would become lowercase. In the "Too much text" warning shown in Figure E-17, the first two options would add slides to your presentation.

FIGURE E-17: "Too much text" warning

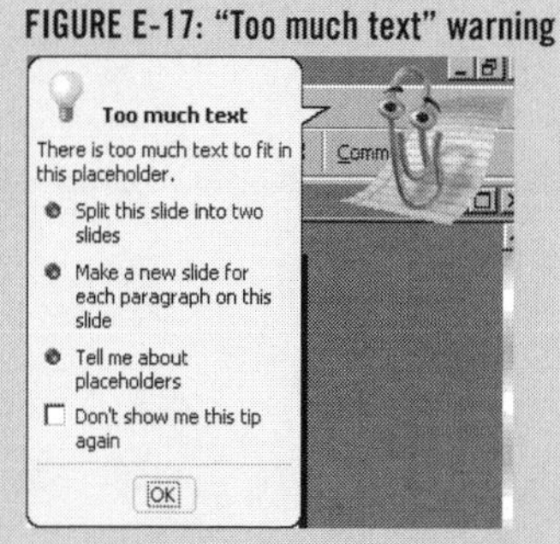

PowerPoint 2000

PowerPoint 2000

Creating and Customizing a Toolbar

As you know from working with PowerPoint, the program automatically customizes toolbars based on how often you use the buttons. You can use the Customize command on the Tools menu to add and remove buttons so they contain only the buttons you want. You can also create your own toolbars that contain only the menu commands and images you select, giving you easy access to program features you use frequently in your particular work situation. Scenario Maria creates a custom toolbar to help her update and view the links in her presentation and then modifies it by adding buttons and images to suit her needs.

QuickTip
You can also right-click any toolbar, then click Customize on the pop-up menu.

1. Click **Tools** on the menu bar, then click **Customize**.
   The Customize dialog box opens.
2. Click the **Toolbars tab**, then click **New**
   The New Toolbar dialog box opens, asking you to name your new toolbar.
3. Type **Links**, then click **OK**
   The name of your new toolbar, Links, appears at the bottom of the toolbars list. It has a check mark next to it, indicating that it is displayed on the screen. A small, empty toolbar appears on the presentation screen next to the dialog box, as shown in Figure E-18.
4. Click the **Commands tab**, click **Edit** in the Categories list, then scroll down the Commands list until you see Update Link

QuickTip
You can drag any command from the Commands list to *any* toolbar displayed on your screen.

5. Drag the **Update Link command** over your new menu until you see I on the Links toolbar, as shown in Figure E-19, then release the mouse button
   The Update Link command appears in your new toolbar. For commands that don't have an icon already associated with them, such as the Links commands, you can add a graphic to the command name.
6. Click **Modify Selection** in the Customize dialog box, point to **Change Button Image**, then click the image of the **bell** in the second row
   The bell image is added to the left of the command name on the toolbar.

QuickTip
To remove a button from a toolbar, open the Customize dialog box, then drag the button off the toolbar.

7. Drag the **Links command** from the Commands list in the Customize dialog box to the right of the Update Link command on the Links toolbar, then change the button image to include the **telephone image**
   See Figure E-20.
8. Click the **Toolbars** tab
   If you are working in a lab, you may not be able to create new toolbars, so it's best to delete them.
9. Make sure the **Links toolbar** is selected (not just the check box next to it), click **Delete**, click **OK** in the alert box, then click **Close** in the Customize dialog box
   The new toolbar disappears from the screen.
10. Add your name in the notes and handouts footer, save your changes, print the presentation as **Handouts (6 per page)** in pure black and white, close the presentation, and exit PowerPoint

FIGURE E-18: New custom toolbar

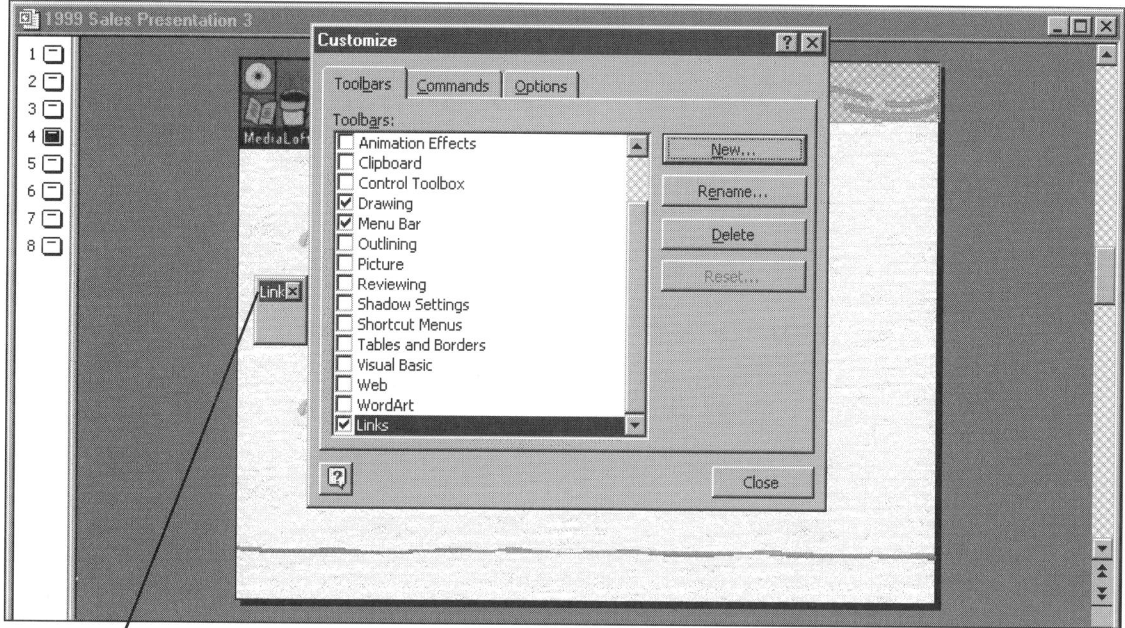

FIGURE E-19: Dragging the Update Link command to the custom toolbar

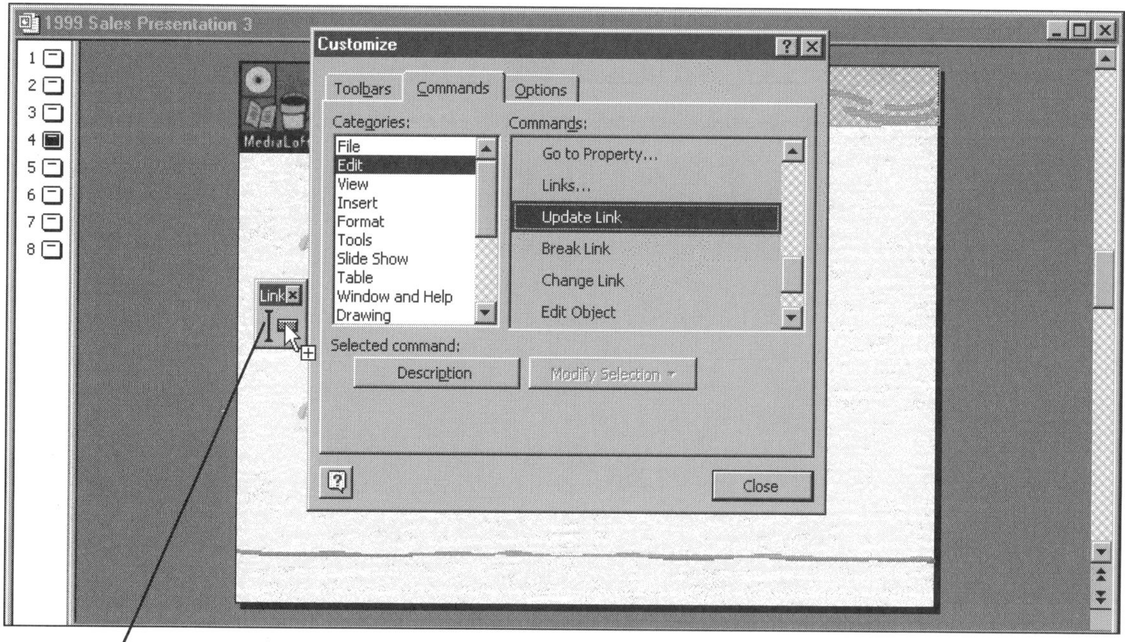

FIGURE E-20: Completed toolbar with commands and images

PowerPoint 2000

Practice

► Concepts Review

Label each of the elements of the PowerPoint window shown in Figure E-21.

FIGURE E-21

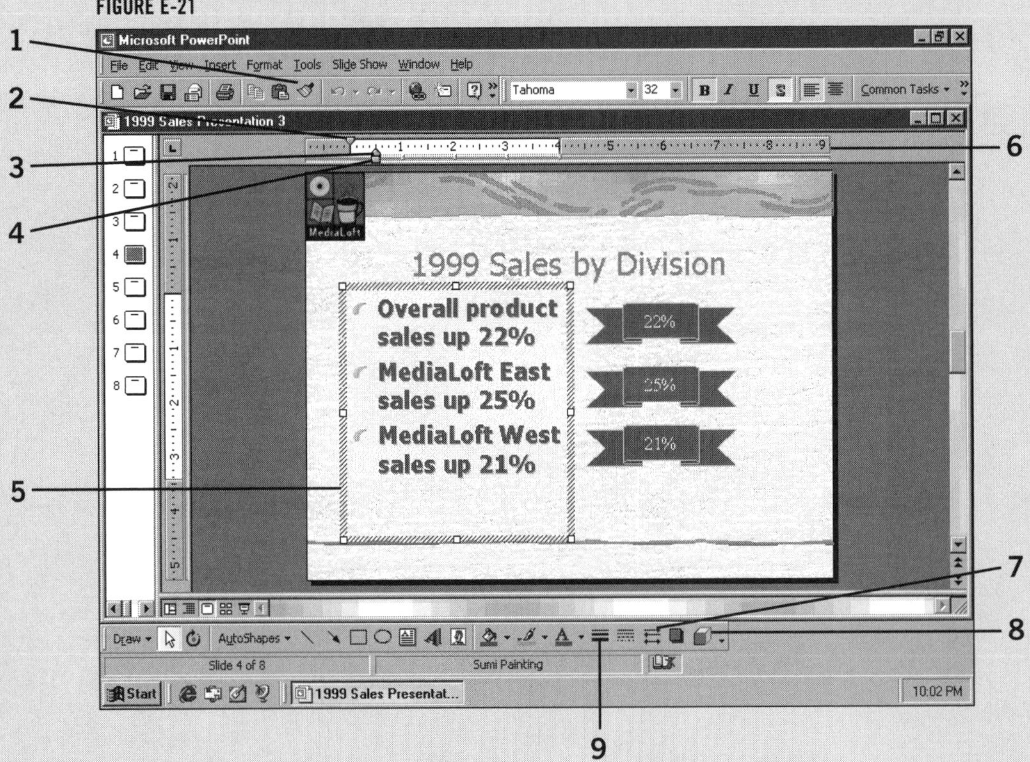

Match each of the terms with the statement that describes its function.

10. Line spacing
11. Indent levels
12. Text anchor
13. Margin marker
14. Master
15. Bottom indent marker

a. A template for all the slides in a presentation.
b. Moves the whole indent level
c. Controls subsequent lines of text in an indent level
d. The five levels of text in a master text placeholder
e. Adjusts the distance between text lines
f. Adjusts the position of text in a text object

Select the best answer from the list of choices.

16. A hanging indent is an indent in which the
- **a.** The bullet symbol is to the right of the first line of text.
- **b.** First line of text begins to the left of subsequent lines of text.
- **c.** The bullet symbol is to the left of the first line of text.
- **d.** First line of text begins to the right of subsequent lines of text.

17. A background item on the Title Master
- **a.** Does not affect the slides of your presentation.
- **b.** Is only visible on the title slide.
- **c.** Is a simple way to place an object on every slide of your presentation.
- **d.** Changes all views of your presentation.

18. The Style Checker checks for all of the following *except*:
- **a.** Incorrect color scheme colors
- **b.** The number of fonts in a presentation
- **c.** The number of bullets in a presentation
- **d.** Case and punctuation

19. What is leading?
- **a.** Space between graphics on the slide master
- **b.** Horizontal space between letters
- **c.** Diagonal space between letters
- **d.** Vertical space between lines of text

20. In PowerPoint, tabs
- **a.** Can be only left or center aligned.
- **b.** Determine the location of margins.
- **c.** Have symbols for top and bottom tabs.
- **d.** Can be aligned on the left, right, or center of a character or on a decimal

21. When you create a custom toolbar,
- **a.** You can delete it by dragging it off the screen.
- **b.** All commands you place there have default graphics.
- **c.** You can add commands and choose images that represent them.
- **d.** You can only have one button on it.

Skills Review

1. Format master text.
- **a.** Start PowerPoint and open the presentation PPT E-2, then save it as "Book Presentation."
- **b.** Apply the presentation design from PPT E-3. (*Hint:* Remember to select All Files in the Files of type list box and select the folder containing your Project Files in the Look in list box.)
- **c.** Go to slide 2, switch to Slide Master view, then make the highest level bulleted item in the Master text placeholder bold.
- **d.** Change the bullet symbol of the highest level bullet to a character bullet in Wingdings 3, the third bullet from the right in the third row, at 75% the size of the text.

e. Change the bullet color to the dark red color on the far right of the color pop-up menu (named Follow Accent and Followed Hyperlink Scheme Color).
f. Italicize the second-level bulleted item and change its font to Arial.
g. Save the presentation.

2. Change master text indents.

a. Display the rulers.
b. Move the left indent marker of the first-level bullet to ½" and the second level bullet to 1".
c. Hide the rulers, switch to Slide view, then save the presentation.

3. Adjust text objects.

a. Right-click anywhere in the main text object on slide 2, then click Format Placeholder on the pop-up menu.
b. Click the Text Box tab.
c. Set the text anchor point to Top Centered.
d. Adjust the internal margin on all sides to .5 and preview your change.
e. Select the Resize AutoShape to fit text command, preview it, and click OK.
f. Select the entire text object. (*Hint:* Press [Shift] while clicking the object.)
g. Change the line spacing to .75, preview it, then click OK.
h. Move the text object up about ½".
i. Save the changes.

4. Use advanced drawing tools.

a. Go to slide 4.
b. Use the Elbow Connector to connect the left corner of the Warehouse diamond to the top corner of the MediaLoft Regional Warehouse diamond.
c. Use the Straight Connector to connect the right side of the Warehouse diamond to the left side of the Individual Stores diamond.
d. Use the Elbow Arrow Connector to connect the right corner of the Individual Stores diamond to the right corner of the MediaLoft Regional Warehouse diamond.
e. Select all three of the connector lines, make them 3 points wide, then deselect them.
f. Apply Arrow Style 5 to the connector line connecting the Individual Stores diamond to the MediaLoft Regional Warehouse diamond.
g. Deselect all objects, then save your changes.

5. Use advanced formatting tools.

a. Go to slide 1.
b. Select the entire text object in the lower-right corner of the slide.
c. Use the Texture tab in the Fill Effects dialog box to apply the Stationery texture to the object. (*Hint:* Read the description of the selected texture in the box under the textures.)
d. Double-click the Format Painter to pick up the format of the selected text box on the title slide and apply it to each of the diamond objects on slide 4, then deselect the Format Painter and all objects.
e. On the title slide, apply the 3-D Style 2 effect to the 1999 Fiscal Year text box.
f. Use 3-D Settings to change the depth to 72 points and to change the direction so it points in the opposite direction.
g. Move the text box so it is just inside the lower-right corner of the slide, then close the 3-D Settings toolbar.
h. Deselect all objects, then save your changes.

6. Use the Style Checker.

- **a.** Open the Style Options dialog box, and on the Visual Clarity tab, make sure there is a check mark next to the Title text size should be at least, select 48 from the list, then click OK twice.
- **b.** Turn on the Office Assistant, click in the Presentation window if the Office Assistant displays a tip, then click the lightbulb on the title slide. Notice that the title text font is too small based on your adjustment to the style options.
- **c.** In the Office Assistant dialog balloon, click Change text to be at least 48 point.
- **d.** Scroll through the presentation clicking the lightbulbs that appear on the screen. Decide whether to accept the Office Assistant's suggestions or to ignore them. (On slide 5, if the Style Checker offers to find appropriate clip art for the concept of demanding, ignore it by clicking OK.)
- **e.** Hide the Office Assistant.

7. Create and customize a toolbar.

- **a.** Create a custom toolbar called "My Toolbar."
- **b.** Add the Find and Replace commands from the Edit category.
- **c.** Add the right arrow graphic to the Find button and the down arrow graphic to the Replace button. Notice that they replace the existing graphics.
- **d.** Drag the Replace button off My Toolbar.
- **e.** Delete the toolbar named My Toolbar.
- **f.** Add your name to the footer in the notes and handouts, save the presentation, then print the presentation as handouts, 6 slides per page.
- **g.** Close the presentation and exit PowerPoint.

Visual Workshop

Create two slides that look like the examples in Figures E-22 and E-23. Be sure to use connector lines. Add your name to the handout footer, then save the presentation as "New Products." Print the Slide view of the presentation. Submit the final presentation output.

FIGURE E-22

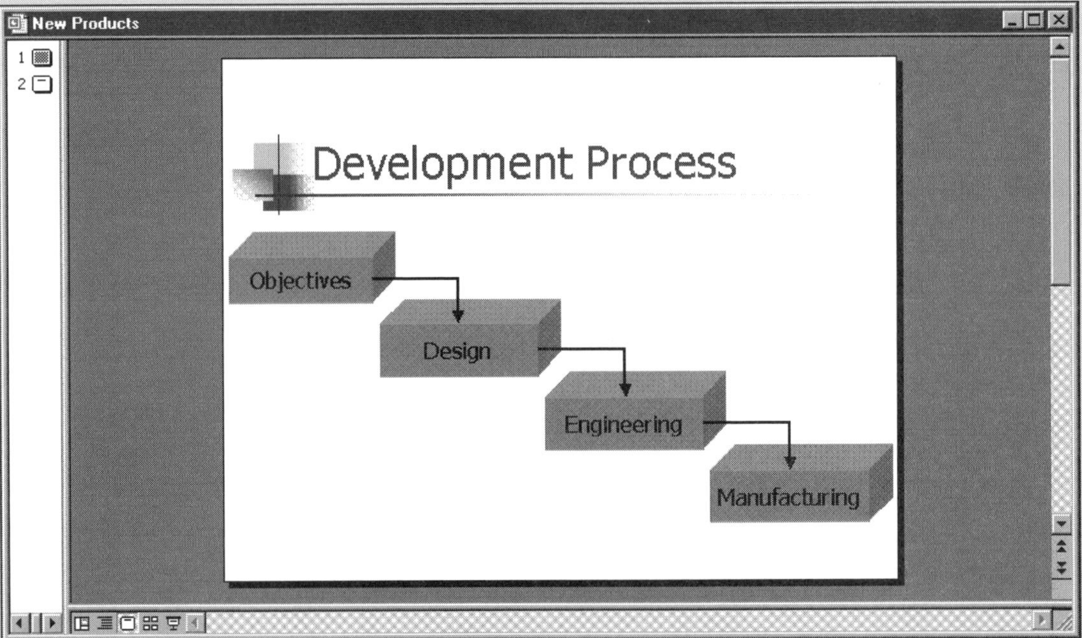

FIGURE E-23

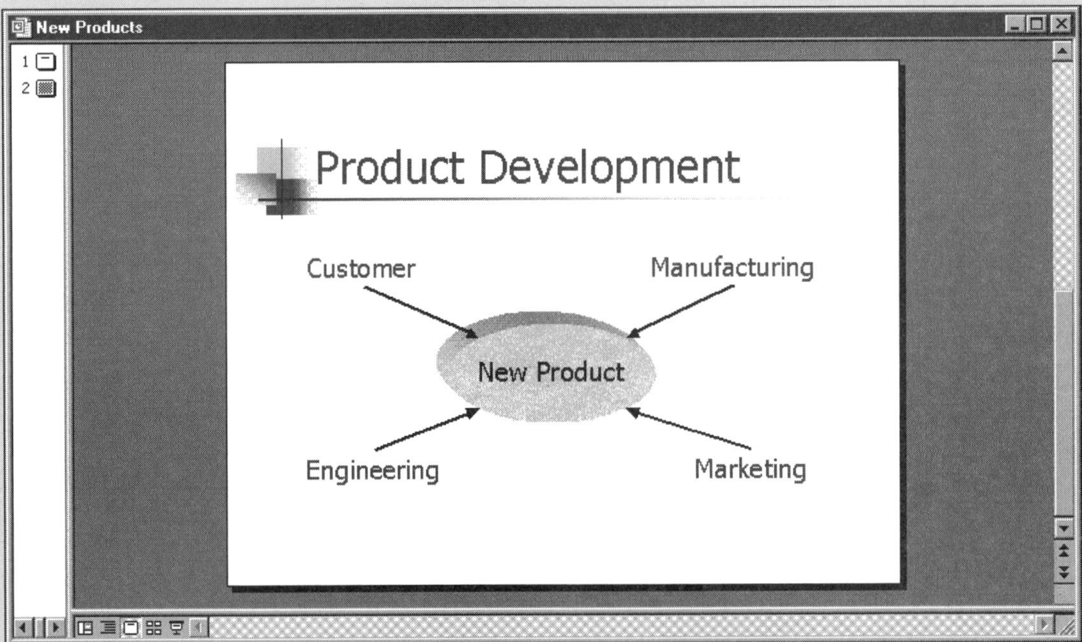

Unit F

Enhancing Charts

Objectives

- MOUS ► Insert data from a file into a datasheet
- ► Format a datasheet
- ► Change a chart's type
- ► Change a chart display
- ► Work with chart elements
- ► Animate charts and sounds
- MOUS ► Embed and format an organizational chart
- MOUS ► Modify an organizational chart

A PowerPoint presentation is a visual communication tool. A slide that delivers information with a relevant graphic object has a more lasting impact than a slide with plain text. Graphs and charts often communicate information more effectively than words. Microsoft Graph and Microsoft Organization Chart are built-in PowerPoint programs that allow you to easily create and embed charts in your presentation. Scenario ► In this unit, Maria Abbott updates the data and enhances the appearance of a Microsoft Graph chart and then creates and formats an organizational chart showing the top management structure at MediaLoft.

PowerPoint 2000

Inserting Data from a File into a Datasheet

With Microsoft Graph, you can enter your own data into a datasheet using the keyboard, or you can import existing data from a spreadsheet program like Microsoft Excel. Scenario The accounting department gave Maria sales data in an Excel file. Maria wants to insert this data as a chart on slide 6. To do this, she will open Graph and import the data from Excel.

QuickTip

To return personalized toolbars and menus to the default state, click Tools on the menu bar, click Customize, click Reset my usage data on the Options tab, click Yes, then click Close.

QuickTip

You can change Graph options, such as how empty cells are plotted in the chart or the color of chart fills and lines, by choosing Options from the Tools menu.

QuickTip

To include data that you've previously excluded, double-click the control box again.

1. Start PowerPoint, open the presentation **PPT F-1**, save it as **1999 Sales Presentation 4**, click **Window** on the menu bar, then click **Arrange All**
2. Add your name as a footer to the notes and handouts
3. Drag the **vertical scroll box** to slide 6, then double-click the **chart object**
   The data in the datasheet needs to be replaced with MediaLoft data, which has already been entered in an Excel worksheet.
4. Click the first cell (upper-left corner) in the datasheet
   This indicates where the imported data will appear in the datasheet.
5. Click the **Import File button** on the Graph Standard toolbar
   The Import File dialog box opens.
6. Click the Excel file **PPT F-2**, then click **Open**
   The Import Data Options dialog box opens. Because you want to import the entire sheet and overwrite the existing cells, all the options are correctly marked.
7. Click **OK**
   The chart changes to reflect the new data you inserted into the datasheet. Compare your screen to Figure F-1. Notice the **control boxes**, the gray boxes along the edges of the datasheet. The data in column D does not need to be included in the chart.
8. Double-click the **column D control box**
   The data in column D is grayed out, indicating that it is excluded from the datasheet and will not appear in the chart. See Figure F-2.
9. Click the **Save button** on the Graph Standard toolbar

FIGURE F-1: Datasheet showing imported data

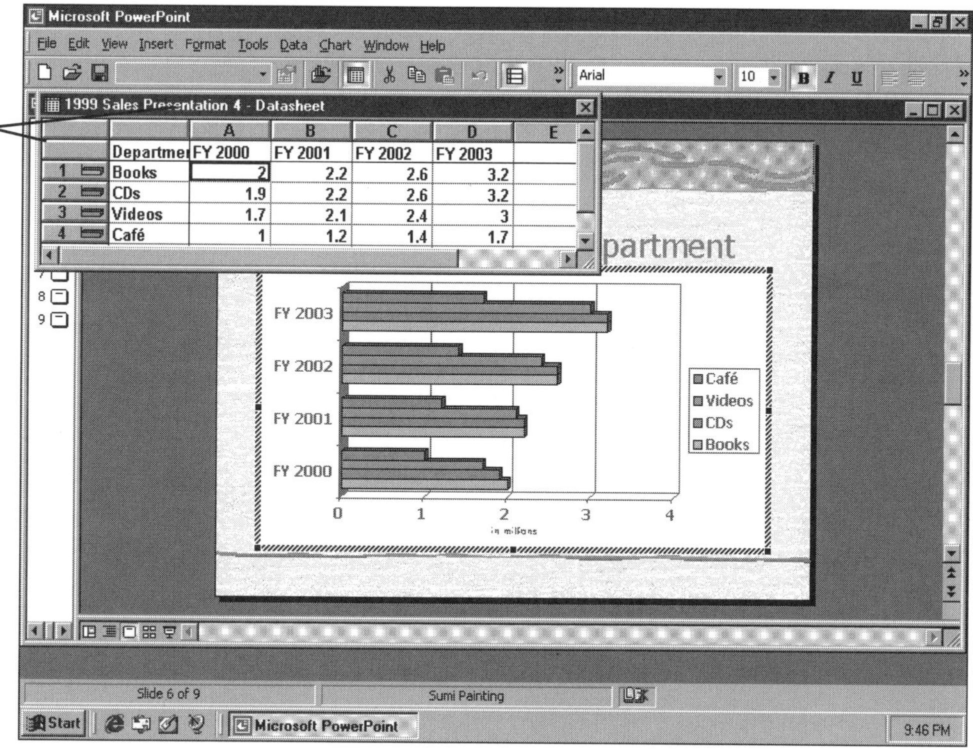

FIGURE F-2: Datasheet showing excluded column

1999 Sales Presentation 4 - Datasheet

		A	B	C	D	E
	Departmer	FY 2000	FY 2001	FY 2002	FY 2003	
1	Books	2	2.2	2.6	3.2	
2	CDs	1.9	2.2	2.6	3.2	
3	Videos	1.7	2.1	2.4	3	
4	Café	1	1.2	1.4	1.7	

CLUES TO USE

Data series and data series markers

Each column or row of data in the datasheet is called a **data series.** Each data series has corresponding **data series markers** in the chart, which are graphical representations such as bars, columns, or pie wedges. Figure F-3 shows how each number in the Café data series (row 4 in the datasheet) appears in the chart.

FIGURE F-3: Graph chart and datasheet

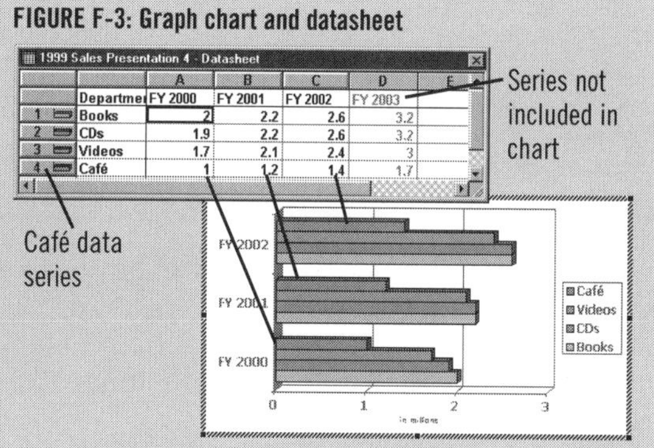

PowerPoint 2000

PowerPoint 2000

Formatting a Datasheet

Once you've imported the data from another file, it can be helpful to modify and format the datasheet to make your data easier to view and use. With Graph, you can make simple formatting changes to the font, number format, and column size in your datasheet. To format the data in the datasheet, you must first select the data. Scenario Maria changes the number format to show the sales numbers correctly, then she changes the chart to show the sales by department rather than by year.

Steps 1 2 3 4

Trouble?

If you can't see all the rows and columns, resize the datasheet window.

1. Click cell **A1** in the datasheet, then drag to cell **D4**
   All the data in this group of continuous cells, or **range**, is selected.

2. Right-click the selection, then click **Number** on the pop-up menu
   The Format number dialog box opens. The Category list on the left side of the dialog box indicates the format categories.

3. In the Category list, click **Currency**
   The sample number format at the top of the dialog box shows you how your data will appear in the selected format. See Figure F-4.

4. Click **OK**
   The data in the datasheet and in the chart change to the currency format. The numbers indicate millions of dollars, so the number of digits after the decimal place needs to be adjusted.

QuickTip

To quickly change the number format to Currency, click the Currency Style button on the Graph Formatting toolbar.

5. Click **Format** on the menu bar, click **Number**, click **Number** in the Format number dialog box, click the **Decimal places down arrow** once to display **1**, click **OK**, then click anywhere in the datasheet
   The datasheet would look better if the columns containing the numbers were not so wide and if the first column were wide enough to accommodate the column head.

QuickTip

To quickly adjust the column width to fit the widest cell of data in a column, double-click the border to the right of the column control box.

6. Drag to select the first cell in each column, click **Format** on the menu bar, click **Column Width**, then click **Best Fit**
   Because you selected the data in the first row, the column widths decrease to fit the labels identifying the years, and the first column increases to accommodate the Department column heading. The icons in the row control boxes indicate that the data appears in a series by row. In other words, the legend indicates the departments listed in the rows in the datasheet. The chart would be more helpful if it showed the sales figures along the vertical axis, in a series by column.

Trouble?

If you don't see the By Column button, click the More Buttons button on the Graph Standard toolbar.

7. Click the **By Column** button on the Graph Standard toolbar
   The icons now appear in the column control boxes in the datasheet to indicate that the fiscal year in the columns is now the legend. Compare your datasheet to Figure F-5.

8. Click the **Close button** in the datasheet
   The datasheet closes, but Graph is still open.

9. Click the **Save button** on the Graph Standard toolbar

FIGURE F-4: Format number dialog box

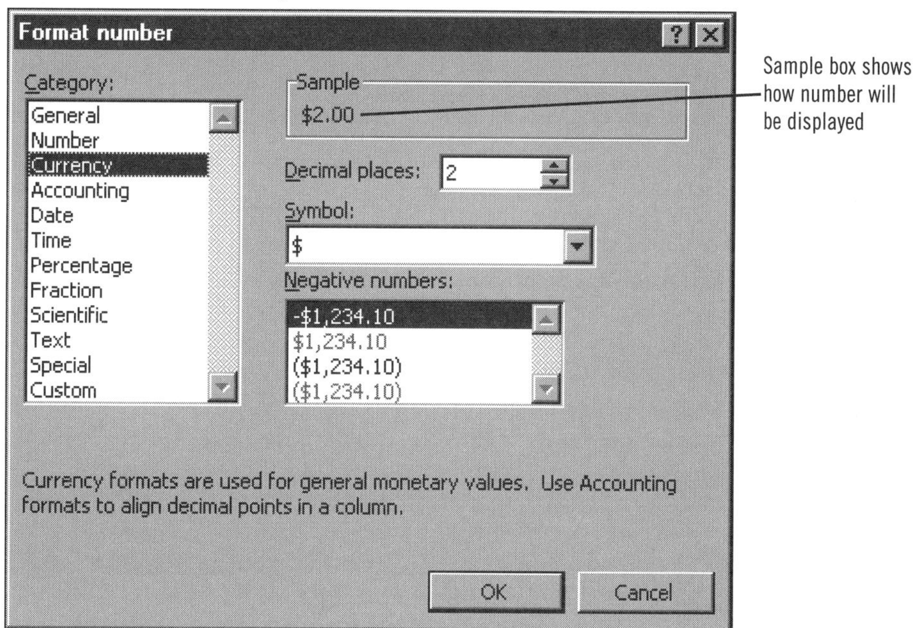

FIGURE F-5: Datasheet showing formatted data

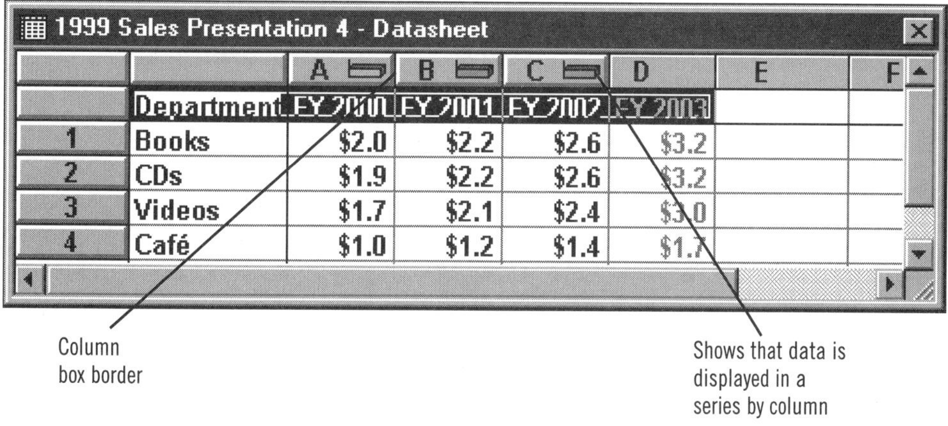

		A	B	C	D	E	F
	Department	FY 2000	FY 2001	FY 2002	FY 2003		
1	Books	$2.0	$2.2	$2.6	$3.2		
2	CDs	$1.9	$2.2	$2.6	$3.2		
3	Videos	$1.7	$2.1	$2.4	$3.0		
4	Café	$1.0	$1.2	$1.4	$1.7		

CLUES TO USE

Formatting datasheets and charts

You can format data in both datasheets and in charts created by Graph. Sometimes it's easier to view the numbers in the datasheet after they have been formatted; other times, you may want to manipulate the numbers after they have been placed into a chart to get a better picture. After you've formatted the data in the datasheet, the formatting changes will be reflected in the chart; however, formatting changes made to the data in the chart will not be reflected in the datasheet.

PowerPoint 2000

Changing a Chart's Type

The type of chart you choose depends on the amount of information you have and how it's best depicted. For example, a chart with more than six or seven data series does not fit well in a pie chart. You can change a chart type quickly and easily by using the Chart Type command on the Chart menu. Scenario Maria decides that a column chart on slide 6 would communicate the information more clearly than a bar chart.

Steps 1 2 3 4

1. With Graph still open, click **Chart** on the menu bar, then click **Chart Type**
   The Chart Type dialog box opens, as shown in Figure F-6. The current chart type is a clustered bar chart with a 3-D effect.
2. In the Chart type list, click **Column**, then in the Chart sub-type section, make sure that the **upper-left sub-type** is selected
   The box below the sub-type section changes to indicate that the selected sub-type is a Clustered Column chart. To see how your data would look in any selected format without closing the dialog box, you can preview it.
3. Click and hold **Press and Hold to View Sample**
   A preview of the chart with your data appears in the area where the sub-types had been listed. This chart would look better if it were 3-D.
4. Release the mouse button, then click the first sub-type in the second row
   The box below the sub-type section shows you have selected a 3-D clustered column.
5. Click **Press and Hold to View Sample**
   The preview shows a 3-D version of the column chart. See Figure F-7.
6. Release the mouse button, then click **OK**
   The chart type changes to the 3-D column chart.
7. Click the **Save button** on the Graph Standard toolbar

QuickTip

To easily change the chart type, click the Chart Type button on the Graph Standard toolbar.

FIGURE F-6: Chart Type dialog box

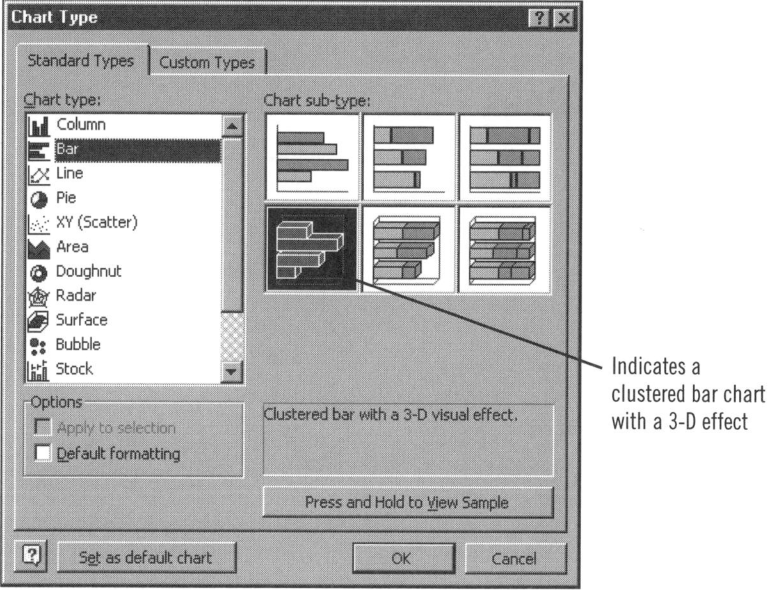

FIGURE F-7: Chart Type dialog box with preview

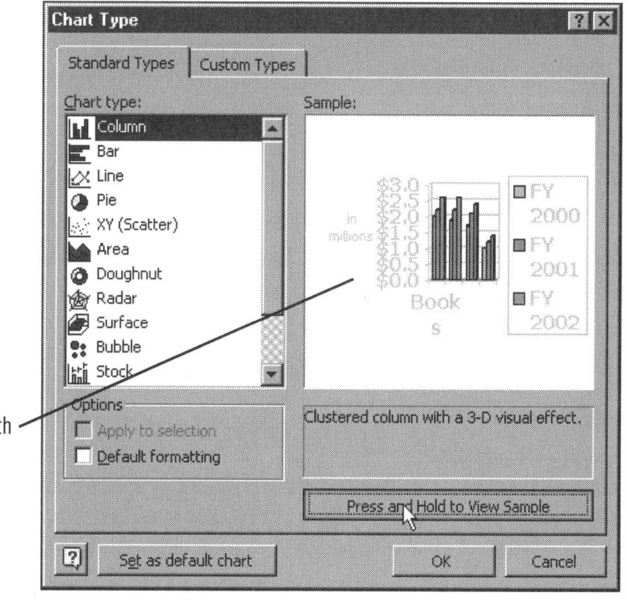

Customized chart types

There are two ways to create customized chart types: You can use PowerPoint custom types or customize your own. To use PowerPoint custom types, click the Custom Types tab in the Chart type dialog box. You will then see more chart types, such as the Floating Bars and the Area Blocks. To define your own custom chart, click any chart series element (such as a bar) in the chart window, click Format on the menu bar, then click the selected series to open the Format Chart dialog box. Use the Patterns, Shape, Data Labels, or Options tabs to customize the color, shape, or appearance of the selected element. To reuse the chart type you have created, make it a type in the Chart type dialog box by clicking the User-defined option button, clicking Add, then assigning a name to it and clicking OK. To use it later, click the name of the type you added.

PowerPoint 2000

Changing a Chart Display

Graph provides many advanced formatting options so that you can customize your chart to emphasize the information you think is important. For example, you can add gridlines to a chart, change the color or pattern of data markers, and format the axes. Scenario Maria wants to improve the appearance of her chart, so she makes several formatting changes.

Steps

1. With Graph still open, click **Chart** on the menu bar, then click **Chart Options**
   The Chart Options dialog box opens. Gridlines will help separate and clarify the data series markers.

2. Click the **Gridlines tab** and in the Category (X) axis section, click the **Major gridlines check box**, click the **Minor gridlines check box**, then click **OK**
   Vertical gridlines appear on the chart. Compare your screen to Figure F-8. Adding minor gridlines increases the number of gridlines in the chart.

3. On the Chart Standard toolbar, click the **Data Table button**
   Adding the data table dramatically decreased the size of the chart, so you decide to return to the previous format.

4. Click again
   The chart returns to its previous format. Adding data labels to one of the data series will make the series easier to identify.

5. Double-click one of the **FY 2002 data markers** in the chart
   The Format Data Series dialog box opens.

6. Click the **Data Labels tab**, click the **Show value option button** to select it, then click **OK**
   The FY 2002 values from the datasheet appear on the data markers, as shown in Figure F-9. Changing the way the numbers appear on the vertical axis will improve the chart's appearance. In a 3-D chart, the vertical axis is the z-axis.

7. Right-click one of the **values** on the vertical axis, click **Format Axis** on the pop-up menu, click the **Scale tab**, double-click in the **Major unit text box**, type **1**, then click **OK**
   After the Format Axis dialog box closes, the values on the z-axis change from increments of .5 to increments of 1, so there are fewer gridlines on the z-axis. The title on the vertical axis would look better if it were oriented vertically.

8. Double-click **in millions** on the vertical axis

9. Click the **Alignment tab**, and under Orientation, drag the **red diamond** up to the top of the semicircle so the scroll box reads **90%**, then click **OK**
   The vertical axis title is now vertical.

10. Click a blank area of the slide, then save your presentation
    Compare your screen to Figure F-10.

QuickTip

To quickly add major gridlines, click the Category Axis Gridlines button on the Graph Standard toolbar.

Trouble?

If the incorrect formatting dialog box opens, you double-clicked the wrong chart element. Close the dialog box, then double-click the correct chart element.

FIGURE F-8: Chart with gridlines

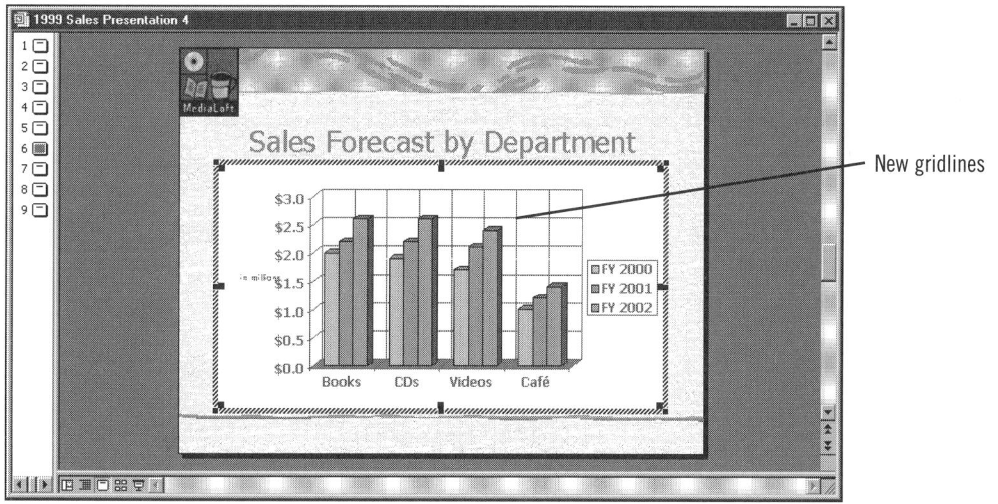

FIGURE F-9: Chart showing data marker labels

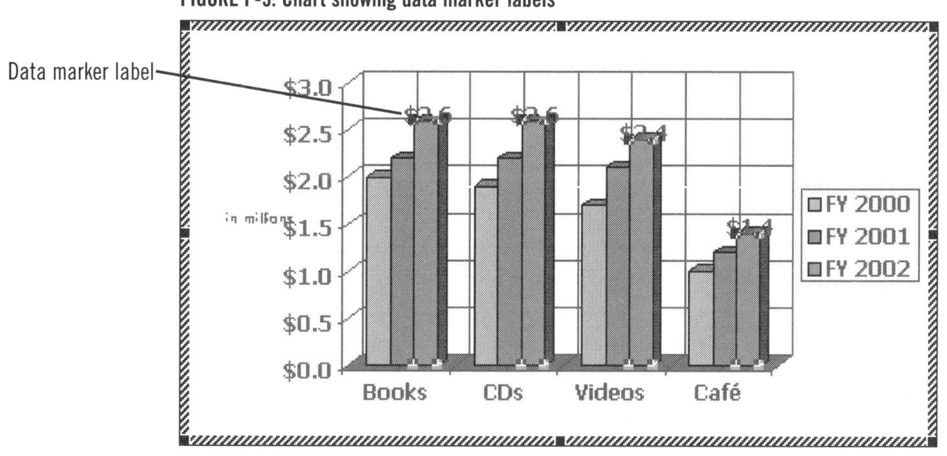

FIGURE F-10: Modified chart

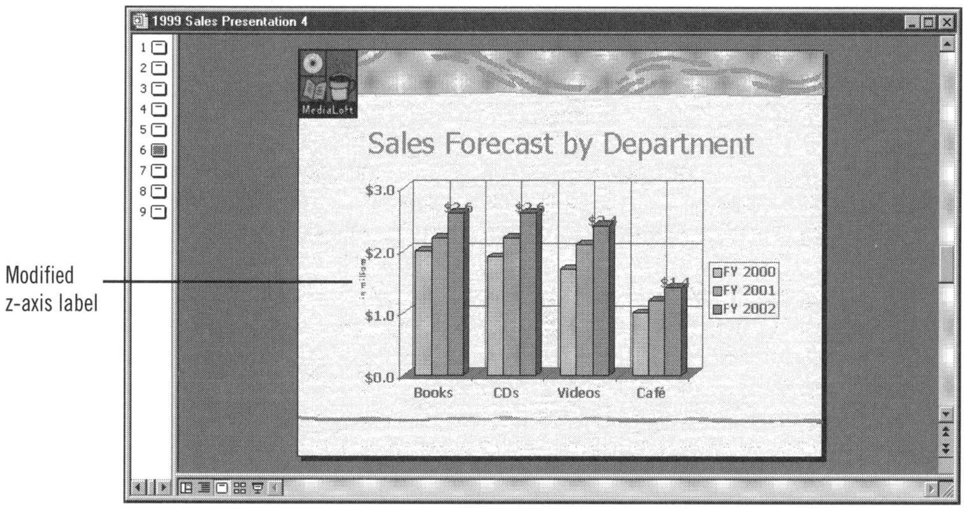

PowerPoint 2000

PowerPoint 2000

Working with Chart Elements

Chart elements are objects you can add and format to help highlight certain information in your chart. Chart elements include legends, arrows, shapes or lines, text objects, and chart titles. Scenario Maria decides to add a text object and an arrow to draw attention to the strong expected sales of CDs in 2002.

Steps

1. Double-click the **Graph chart object**
   Graph opens and the chart appears on the screen.
2. Click the **Text Box button** on the Drawing toolbar
   The pointer changes to +.
3. Position + above the FY 2002 Videos data marker, drag to create a text box, then type **Over Goal**
   Compare your screen to Figure F-11. If the text object is not where you want it, position the pointer over its edge, then drag to reposition the object. Changing the color and size of the text would make it easier to read.
4. Drag I over the text to select it, click the **Font Color button** on the Drawing toolbar, then click the **red box**
5. Click the **Font Size list arrow** on the Graph Formatting toolbar, click **22**, resize the text box if necessary, then click in a blank area of the chart
   An arrow would help connect the new text object to a data marker in the chart.
6. Click the **Arrow button** on the Drawing toolbar, position + to the left of the word "Over," then drag an arrow to the top of the CDs FY 2002 data marker
   The arrow could be more prominent.
7. Click the **Arrow Style button** on the Drawing toolbar, click **More Arrows**, then in the Line section, click the **Color list arrow**
8. Click the **red box**, click the **Weight up arrow** until **2 pt** appears, then click **OK**
9. Click a blank area of the slide, then save your presentation
   Compare your screen to Figure F-12.

QuickTip

If the Drawing toolbar is not visible, right-click the Graph Formatting toolbar, then click Drawing on the pop-up menu.

Trouble?

If the text box no longer accommodates all the text, drag a resizing handle to make it larger.

QuickTip

To quickly change the color of the arrow, click the Line Color button on the Drawing toolbar. To change the weight of the line, click the Line Style button on the Drawing toolbar.

FIGURE F-11: Chart showing new text object

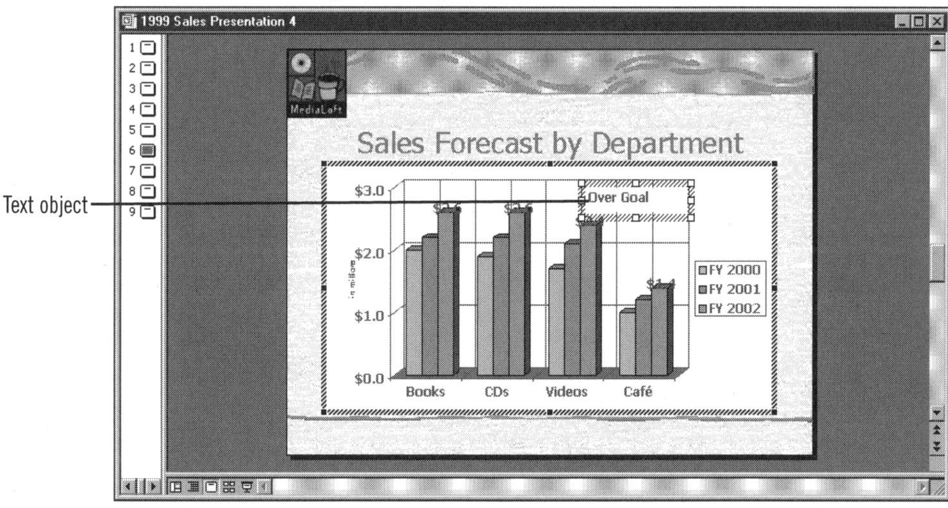

FIGURE F-12: Chart showing added elements

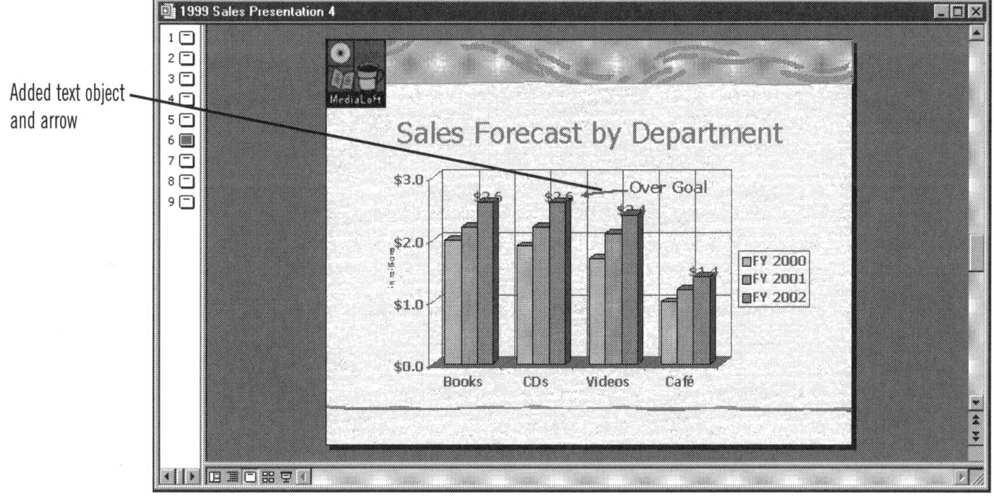

PowerPoint 2000

Moving and sizing chart elements

To move a chart element, such as an arrow or the legend, you must first select the object to view its resizing handles, then drag the object to its new location. Make sure that the pointer is over the object's border when you drag it, not over a resizing handle. To change the size of a chart element, click the object to view its resizing handles, then drag a resizing handle.

PowerPoint 2000

Animating Charts and Sounds

Just as you can animate bullets and graphics on slides, you can animate chart elements. You can have bars appear by series, groups, or individually. You can choose to have the legend and grid animated or not. You can also control the order and timing of the animations. Sound effects can accompany the chart animation, including applause, a drum roll, a typewriter, and an explosion. Be sure to choose sounds that are appropriate for your presentation. For example, you would not use the Screeching Brakes sound in a serious financial presentation. Many presentations are effective with no sound effects to distract from the speaker's message. Scenario Maria decides to animate the elements on her chart and add a sound effect.

1. Make sure **slide 6** is visible, and click the chart once to select it
2. Click **Slide Show** on the menu bar, click **Custom Animation**, then click the **Chart Effects tab**
   The Custom Animation dialog box opens, and the Chart Effects tab provides options for animating your slide display, similar to Figure F-13.
3. In the Check to animate slide objects list, click the check box next to **Chart 2** to select it
4. Under Introduce chart elements, click the **list arrow** and select **by Series**
5. In the Entry animation and sound list boxes, select **Random Bars** in the left list box, and select **Horizontal** in the right list box
6. In the Sound list box, select **Whoosh**
7. Click **Preview**, and watch the preview window
   The grid appears first, then each bar appears in each category, accompanied by the Whoosh sound.
8. Click **OK**, then click the **Slide Show button** and view the animation in Slide Show view
   Each bar appears gradually accompanied by the Whoosh sound effect.
9. When the slide animation is finished, press **[Esc]** to return to Slide view

QuickTip

If you want the animated chart elements to appear automatically, click the Order & Timing tab, click the Automatically option button in the Start Animation section, then type the number of seconds you want between animations.

Trouble?

If you do not hear the Whoosh sound, then your computer might not have a sound card, or if it does, the volume may be turned down. Check with your technical support person.

FIGURE F-13: Custom Animation dialog box with the Chart Effects tab active

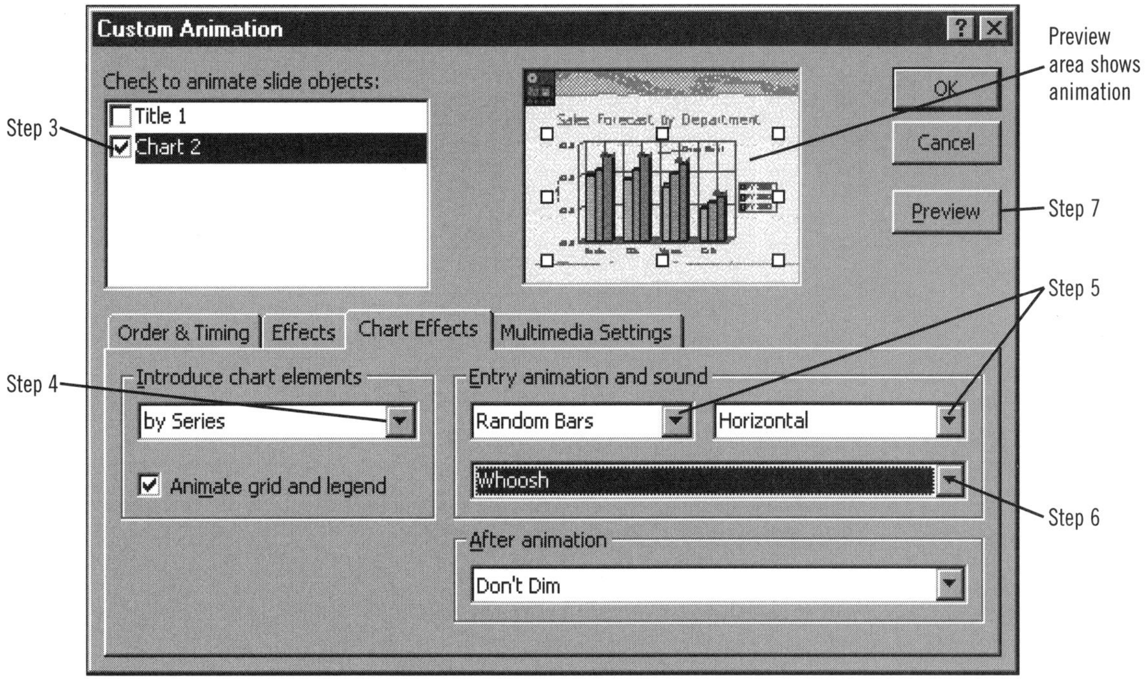

Custom Animation
Check to animate slide objects:
Title 1
Chart 2
OK
Cancel
Preview
Order & Timing | Effects | Chart Effects | Multimedia Settings
Introduce chart elements
by Series
Animate grid and legend
Entry animation and sound
Random Bars
Horizontal
Whoosh
After animation
Don't Dim

Step 3
Step 4
Preview area shows animation
Step 7
Step 5
Step 6

Adding voice narrations

If your computer has a sound card and a microphone, you can record a voice narration that plays with your slide show. To record a voice, click Slide Show on the menu bar, then click Record Narration. If you want the recording to be linked to the presentation, click the Link narrations in check box. If you do not select this option, the recording will be embedded in the presentation. Then start recording. If the Record Narration command is not available, then you do not have the necessary hardware.

PowerPoint 2000

Embedding and Formatting an Organizational Chart

You can create an organizational chart by using the Object command on the Insert menu or by changing the layout of your slide to the Organization Chart slide AutoLayout. Once you open Microsoft Organization Chart, a series of connected boxes called **chart boxes** appears. Each chart box has placeholder text that you replace with the names and titles of people in your organization. Scenario ▶ Maria is satisfied with her graph and now turns her attention to creating an organizational chart showing MediaLoft's top management structure.

Steps 1 2 3 4

1. Go to **slide 8**, click the **Common Tasks menu button** on the Formatting toolbar, click **New Slide**, click the **Organization Chart AutoLayout**, then click **OK**
   A new slide 9 appears showing the org chart placeholder.
2. Type **MediaLoft**, then double-click the **org chart placeholder**
   The text you type is entered into the title placeholder and Microsoft Organization Chart opens with the default organizational chart in a separate window. See Figure F-14. The chart box at the top of the window is a **Manager chart box** and the three chart boxes below it are **Subordinate chart boxes**. The Manager chart box is selected and ready to accept text.
3. Type **Leilani Ho**, press **[Tab]**, type **President**, then click a blank area of the Organization Chart window
   The text is entered into the text box. You can also press [Enter] to move to the next placeholder in a chart box.
4. Click the **left Subordinate chart box**, type **David Dumont**, then press **[Tab]** to move to the next line
5. Enter the rest of the information in the Subordinate chart boxes shown in Figure F-15
   Click each chart box to enter the first line of text, then press [Tab] to move from line to line. The chart boxes would look better with formatting.
6. Click **Edit** on the Organization Chart menu bar, point to **Select**, then click **All**
   All the chart boxes are selected and ready to be formatted.
7. Click **Boxes** on the Organization Chart menu bar, click **Color**, click the **purple box** (the fifth color cell from the left in the top row), then click **OK**
   The chart boxes change to purple. Thicker lines between the boxes would be more visible.
8. Click **Lines** on the Organization Chart menu bar, point to **Thickness**, click the third line in the menu, then click in a blank area of the chart window
   The connector line between the chart boxes is now thicker. The organizational chart you have created exists within the chart program, and is not yet part of your presentation.
9. Click **File** on the Organization Chart menu bar, then click **Exit and Return to 1999 Sales Presentation 4**
   A Microsoft Organization Chart alert box opens to confirm your desire to update your slide with the organizational chart.
10. Click **Yes** to update the presentation, then click a blank area of the Presentation window
    Compare your screen to Figure F-16.

Trouble?

If your PowerPoint installation only includes basic features, the program may ask you to insert the Office CD to install Organization Chart. If you are working in a lab, see your technical support person.

FIGURE F-14: Default organizational chart

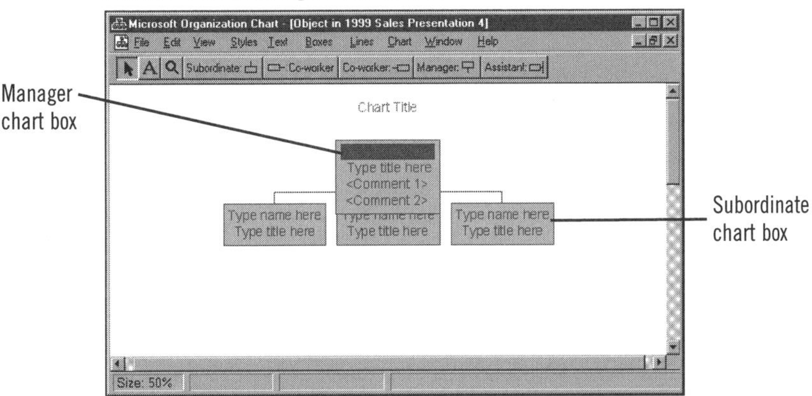

FIGURE F-15: Organizational chart showing completed chart boxes

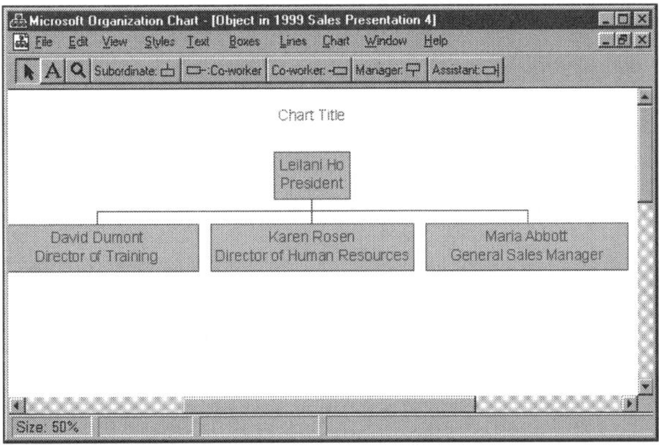

FIGURE F-16: Organizational chart embedded on a slide

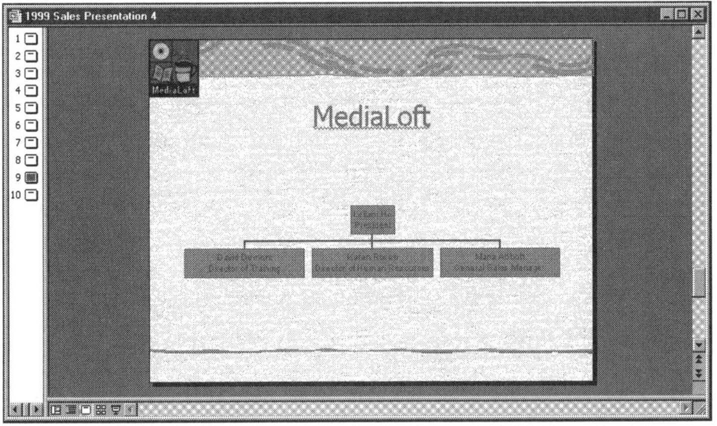

Changing chart styles

In Organization Chart, you can change the way chart boxes are grouped together by clicking a group style on the Styles menu. Figure F-17 illustrates how each Styles button places subordinate chart boxes relative to the Manager chart box.

FIGURE F-17: Styles menu

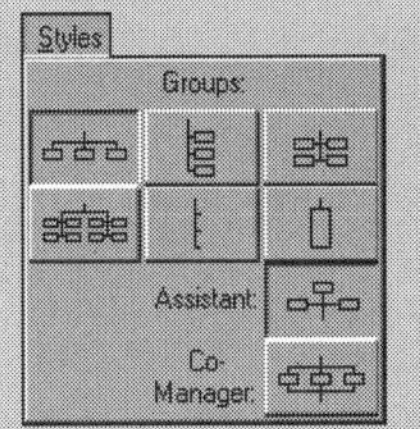

PowerPoint 2000

PowerPoint 2000

Modifying an Organizational Chart

If the organizational chart you want to create requires more than the four default chart boxes, you can add up to nine chart boxes in a row and thirteen chart boxes in a column to accommodate more information. After you add all the chart boxes you need for your chart, you can rearrange them as desired. Scenario Maria needs to add two chart boxes to her organizational chart.

Steps

1. Double-click the **organizational chart**
   The Organization Chart window opens, showing the organizational chart you created in the last lesson.
2. Click the **Right Co-worker button** Co-worker: on the Organization Chart toolbar then move the pointer over the organizational chart
   The pointer changes to -□.
3. Click the **Maria Abbott chart box**, type **Jeff Shimada**, press **[Tab]**, type **Director of Cafe Operations**, then click in a blank area of the Organization Chart window
   Jeff Shimada is added at the same level as Maria Abbott. Compare your screen to Figure F-18.
4. Click the **Subordinate button** Subordinate: on the Organization Chart toolbar, then click the **Maria Abbott chart box**
   A small blank chart box appears under the Maria Abbott chart box.
5. Type **Gary Robbins**, press **[Tab]**, type **Assistant**, then click in a blank area of the Organization Chart window
   Gary is actually Karen Rosen's assistant. It's easy to change the placement of a chart box to another position on the chart.
6. Drag the **Gary Robbins chart box** on top of the Karen Rosen chart box until the pointer changes to the subordinate placement arrow, release the mouse button, then click in a blank area of the Organization Chart window
   You may have to experiment with the placement of the chart box until the pointer changes to the subordinate placement arrow. Compare your organizational chart to Figure F-19. When you move a chart box, all of its subordinate chart boxes move with it, which makes it easy to rearrange the organizational chart. See Table F-1 for an explanation of chart box placement arrows.
7. Click **Edit** on the Organization Chart menu bar, point to **Select**, click **All**, click **Text** on the Chart menu bar, click **Font**, click **Bold** in the Font Style list, click **16 pt** in the Size list, then click **OK**
8. Click **File** on the Organization Chart menu bar, then click **Exit and Return to 1999 Sales Presentation 4**, click **Yes** to update the presentation, drag and reposition the chart so it is as wide as possible, then click in a blank area of the Presentation window
9. Click the **Slide Show button** to view slide 8, press **[Esc]**, then click the **Slide Sorter View button**
   Compare your screen to Figure F-20.
10. Click the **Save button** on the Standard toolbar, then print the presentation as handouts, 6 slides per page

QuickTip
Use Organization Chart Help to find information about keyboard commands you can use to create and edit chart boxes.

QuickTip
Each chart box you add automatically decreases the size of all the chart boxes so that the organizational chart will fit on the slide.

Trouble?
When you move a chart box, make sure the correct placement arrow appears before you release the mouse button.

FIGURE F-18: Organizational chart showing new co-worker chart box

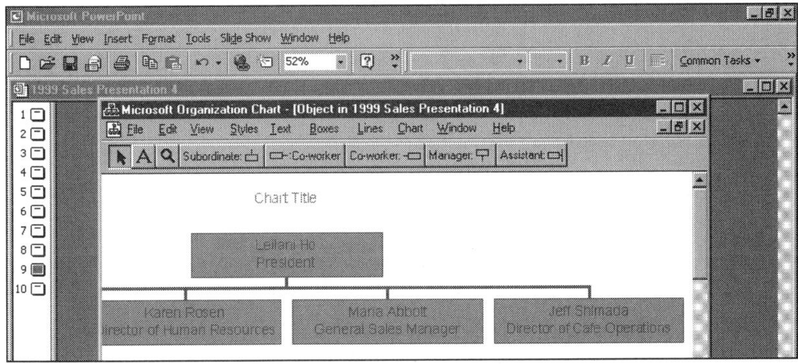

FIGURE F-19: Organizational chart showing rearranged chart boxes

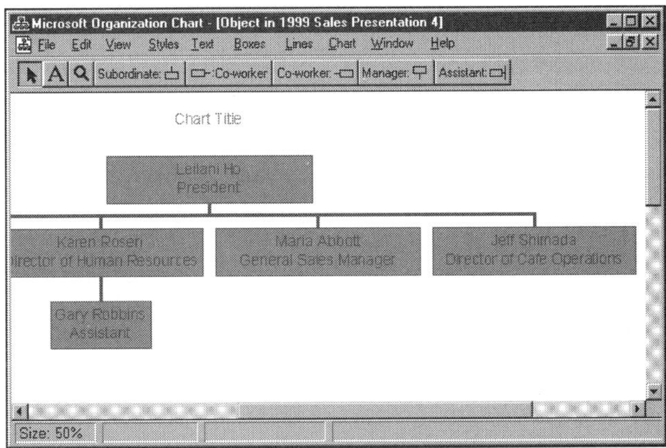

FIGURE F-20: Final presentation in Slide Sorter view

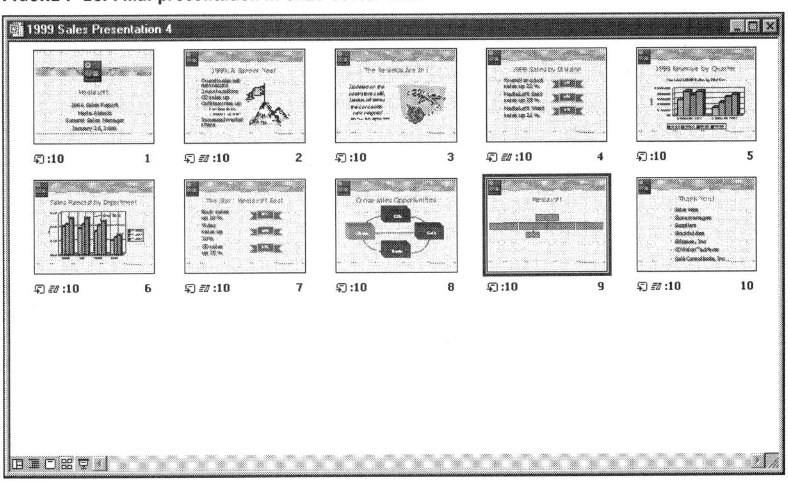

TABLE F-1: Chart box placement arrows

arrow	placement
Co-worker: -▭	Places a chart box to the right of another chart box
▭-:Co-worker	Places a chart box to the left of another chart box
Subordinate: ⏄	Places a chart box below another chart box

Practice

► Concepts Review

Label each of the elements of the PowerPoint window shown in Figure F-21.

FIGURE F-21

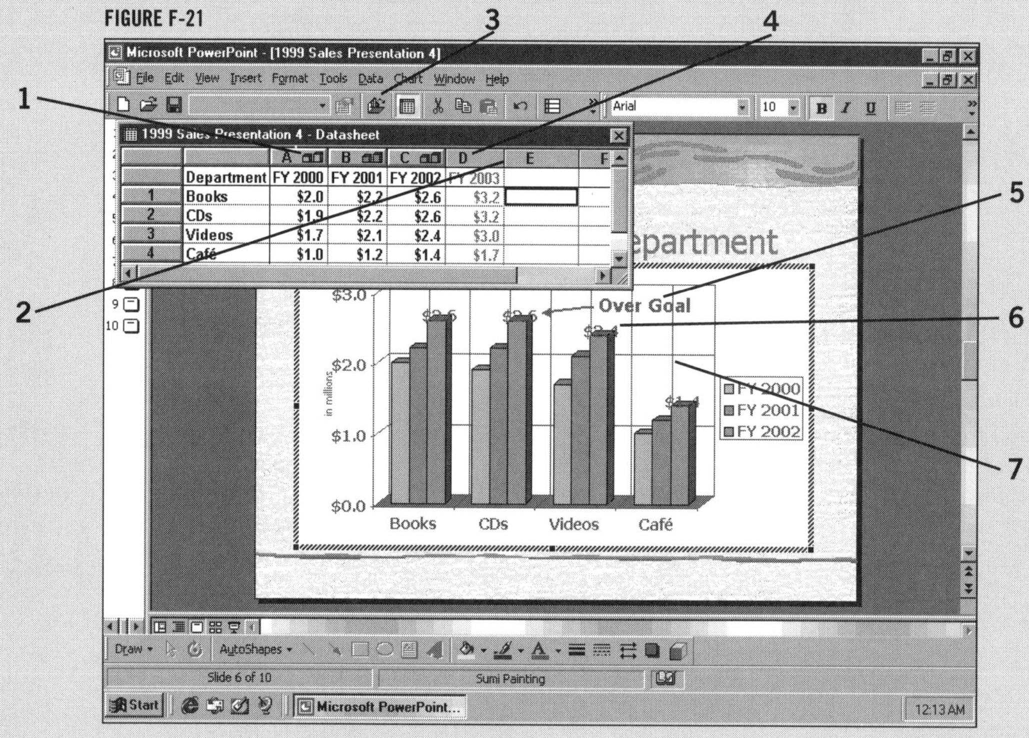

Match each of the terms with the statement that describes its function.

8. Data series markers
9. Range
10. Data series
11. Control box

a. Graphical representation of a data series
b. A box at the edge of a data sheet, usually with a row number or column letter in it
c. A group of connected cells in a datasheet
d. A row or column of data in a datasheet

Select the best answer from the list of choices.

12. **In Graph, clicking a column control box**
    a. Controls the format of the datasheet.
    b. Selects an entire column of data in the datasheet.
    c. Switches the chart format to 3-D column.
    d. Selects all column data markers in a chart.
13. **Which of the following statements about Graph charts is incorrect?**
    a. The type of chart you choose does not depend on the data you have.
    b. You can change the format of data markers.
    c. You can format every element of a chart.
    d. There are 2-D and 3-D chart types.
14. **Which of the following is incorrect about animating charts?**
    a. You don't need to accompany every animation with a sound.
    b. You cannot preview animations before applying them to your presentation.
    c. You can choose to have chart elements appear in a variety of ways.
    d. You can accompany chart animations with a sound.
15. **Which of the following is true about an organizational chart?**
    a. Chart boxes have placeholder text that you type over.
    b. The default organizational chart has two subordinate chart boxes.
    c. Adding chart boxes to your chart increases the size of all the chart boxes.
    d. You can create a chart by using the Organization Chart command on the Insert menu.
16. **Based on what you know of organizational charts, which of the following data would best fit in an organizational chart?**
    a. Spreadsheet data
    b. A company's database mailing list
    c. A company's annual financial numbers
    d. A company's division structure

Skills Review

1. **Insert data from a file into a datasheet.**
    a. Start PowerPoint, open the presentation PPT F-3, then save it as "Book Division Report".
    b. On slide 3, open the Graph chart.
    c. Click the upper-left cell in the datasheet, and import sheet 1 of the Excel file PPT F-4 into the Graph datasheet.
    d. Use the control box to delete Kansas City from the chart.
    e. Save the presentation.
2. **Format a datasheet.**
    a. Select the range of cells from cell A1 to cell D4.
    b. Format the datasheet numbers with Currency format.
    c. Change the format of the datasheet numbers so that they have no decimal places.
    d. Adjust the column width to Best Fit.
    e. Change the data so the series are in columns.
    f. Close the datasheet.
    g. Save the presentation.

3. **Change a chart's type.**
   a. Change the chart type to a clustered 3-D bar chart, preview it, then accept it.
   b. Change the chart to a 3-D column chart.
4. **Change a chart display.**
   a. In the Format Data Series dialog box, use the Shape tab to change each column in each series into a pyramid shape. (*Hint:* Begin by double-clicking a column in each series.)
   b. Use the Gridlines tab in the Chart Options dialog box to show major gridlines on both the x- and the z-axes.
   c. Use the Data Labels tab to add the data values for each data marker.
   d. Change the scale on the z-axis so that the major unit is 100.
   e. Add a label to the z-axis that reads "in 000s".
   f. Save your changes.
5. **Work with chart elements.**
   a. Add a text box to add a label pointing to Dallas fiction sales.
   b. Add the text "A record!" to the text box.
   c. Change the color of the text to blue.
   d. Change the point size of the text to 22-point and the font to Arial.
   e. Add a blue arrow from the text box to the appropriate data point.
   f. Format the arrow line as 3-point.
   g. Adjust the formatting as necessary so that all labels are visible.
6. **Animate charts and sounds.**
   a. Animate the chart elements on slide 3 so they are introduced by series and appear as a checkerboard downward with a chime sound. Have the elements appear automatically every two seconds.
   b. Preview the animation then apply it to the presentation.
   c. Check the animation in Slide Show view.
   d. Save the presentation.
7. **Embed and format an organizational chart.**
   a. Go to slide 4 and apply the Organization Chart AutoLayout.
   b. Open the Organization Chart placeholder, then maximize the Organization Chart window.
   c. At the top level, type "Andrew Fleming" as "Book Division Manager".
   d. In the Subordinate chart boxes, type the following names and titles:
      Benjamin Wiley, Distribution Manager
      Robert Delgado, Purchasing Manager
      Evelyn Storey, Circulation Manager
   e. Change the border style for all the boxes to the third line style down in the first column.
   f. Click the Division Manager chart box, and change the border to the fourth line style down in the first column.
   g. Change the box border color to a bright blue and the box fill color to a tan color.
   h. Return to the presentation, updating the presentation, then save your changes.
8. **Modify an organizational chart.**
   a. Open the organizational chart.
   b. Click the Assistant button on the Organization Chart Standard toolbar, then click the Evelyn Storey chart box.
   c. Enter "Michael Raye" as her "Special Assistant".
   d. Add two Subordinate boxes to the Robert Delgado chart box, and enter the following:
      Katherine DeNiro, Purchase Orders
      Lynn Perry, Financial Assistant
   e. Drag the Michael Raye chart box so it is under the Katherine DeNiro chart box.
   f. Return to the Book Division Report and update the presentation.
   g. Enlarge and center the chart on the slide.
   h. Click the Slide Sorter View button, then run through your slide show in Slide Show view.
   i. Add your name as a footer on the notes and handouts.
   j. Save your changes, print the presentation as handouts, 6 slides per page, then close the presentation.

Visual Workshop

Create two slides that look like the examples in Figures F-22 and F-23. Save the presentation as "Central." Save and print the presentation slides.

FIGURE F-22

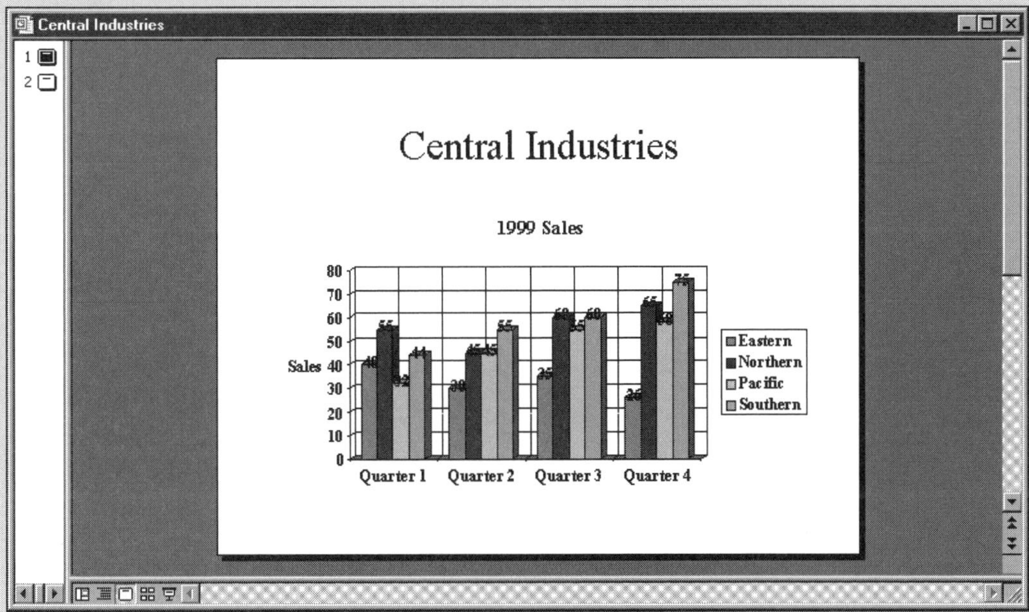

FIGURE F-23

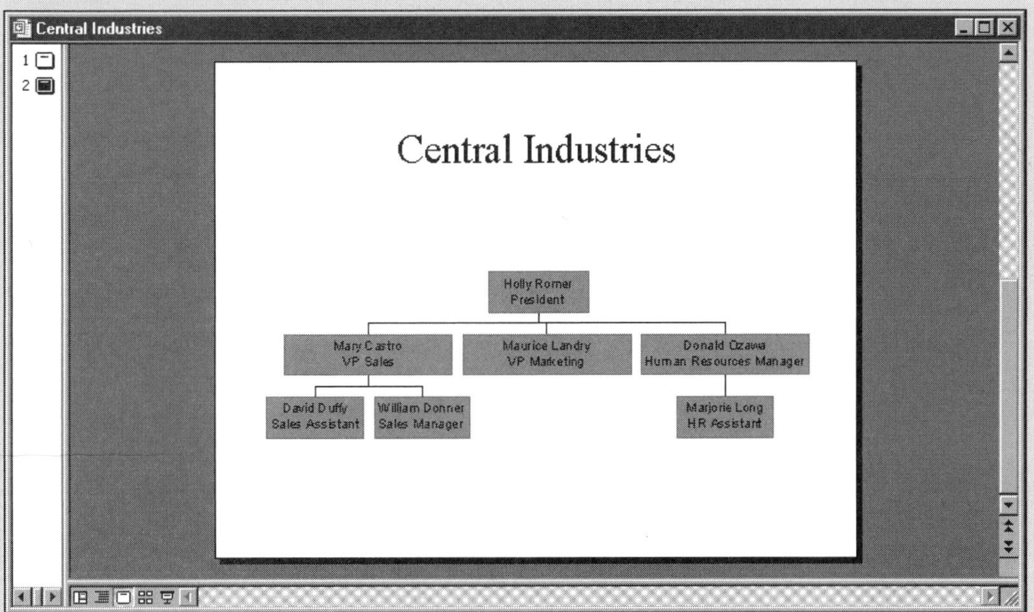

PowerPoint 2000

Working

with Embedded and Linked Objects and Hyperlinks

Objectives

- ► Embed a picture
- MOUS ► Insert a Word table
- MOUS ► Embed an Excel chart
- ► Link an Excel worksheet
- ► Update a linked Excel worksheet
- MOUS ► Insert an animated GIF file
- MOUS ► Insert a sound
- MOUS ► Insert a hyperlink

PowerPoint offers many ways to add graphic elements to a presentation. In this unit you will learn how to embed and link objects created in other programs. Embedded and linked objects are created in another program and then stored in or linked to the PowerPoint presentation. Scenario ► In this unit Maria Abbott, MediaLoft's general sales manager, uses embedded and linked objects to create a brief presentation that outlines MediaLoft's video department. She will use the presentation in a proposal she will make to a potential new video supplier.

Embedding a Picture

You can embed over 20 types of pictures using the Insert Picture command. Frequently, a presentation's color scheme will not match the colors in pictures, especially photographs. In order to make the picture look good in the presentation, you may need to adjust the slide's color scheme, recolor the picture, or change the presentation's template. **Scenario** Maria wants to embed a photograph in a slide. She will adjust the slide color scheme to make the photograph look good.

Steps

QuickTip

Click Tools, click Customize, click Reset my usage data, click Yes, then click Close to return the toolbars to a default state.

Trouble?

If the Picture toolbar does not open, right-click the inserted picture, then click Show Picture Toolbar on the pop-up menu.

1. Start PowerPoint, open the presentation **PPT G-1**, save it as **Video Division**, click the **Window** on the menu bar, then click **Arrange All**
2. Click the **slide 2 slide icon** in the Outline pane, click **Insert** on the menu bar, point to **Picture**, click **From File**, select the file **PPT G-2** from your Project Disk, then click **Insert**
   A picture of a tropical scene appears in the middle of the slide and the Picture toolbar opens.
3. Move the picture to the right side of the slide, then click on a blank area of the Presentation window
   Compare your screen to Figure G-1. A different slide color could provide a better contrast to the picture.
4. Right-click a blank area of the Presentation window, click **Slide Color Scheme** on the pop-up menu, then click the **Standard tab** in the Color Scheme dialog box
   There are seven standard color schemes from which to choose.
5. Drag the **Color Scheme dialog box title bar** to the lower-left corner of the PowerPoint window so that you can see part of the picture and the slide title
6. In the Color schemes section, click each standard color scheme option and click **Preview** after each one
   As you click a color scheme option and then click Preview, the color scheme is applied to the slide. The color scheme in the third row fits best with the picture colors.
7. In the Color Schemes section, click the **color scheme** in the third row, then click **Apply**
   Make sure you do not click Apply to All. The color scheme for slide 2 changes. A different color bullet would fit this color scheme better.
8. Press **[Shift]** and click the **main text**, click **Format** on the menu bar, click **Bullets and Numbering**, click the **Color list arrow**, click the **light green color** (third box in the second row), then click **OK**
9. Click a blank area of the slide, compare your screen to Figure G-2, then click the **Save button** on the Standard toolbar

FIGURE G-1: Slide showing embedded picture

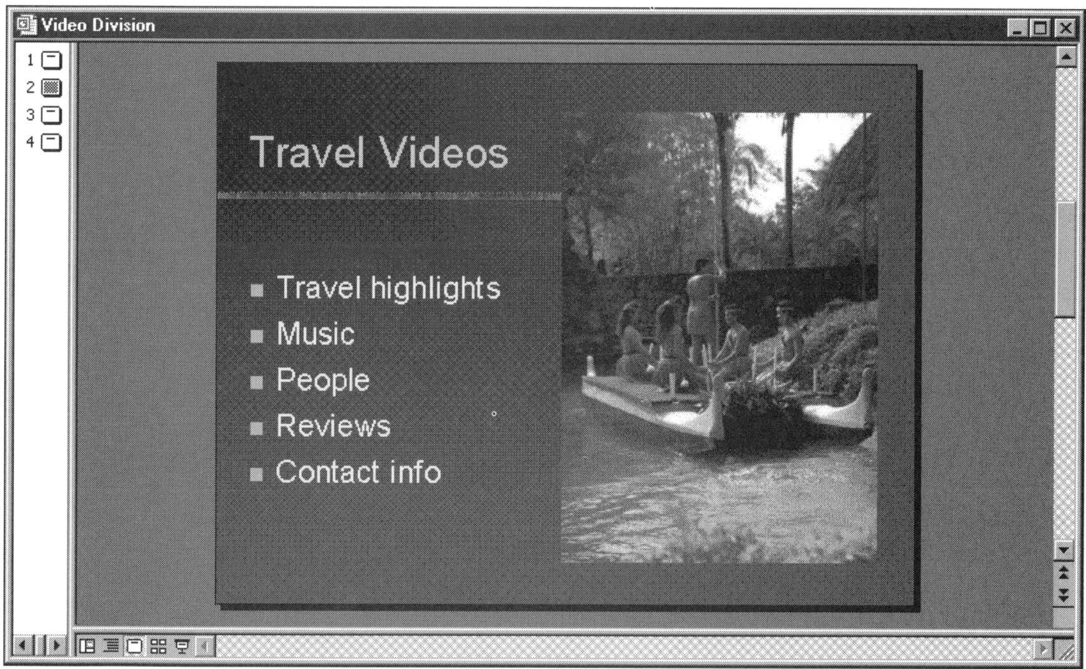

FIGURE G-2: Slide showing new color scheme

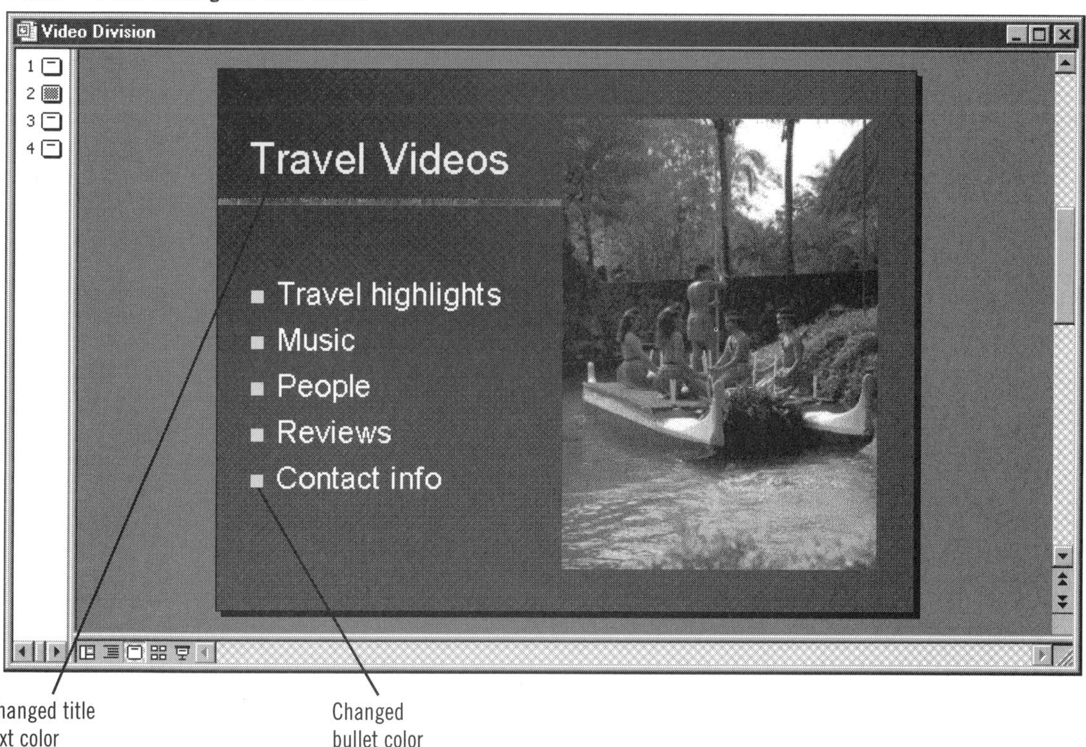

PowerPoint 2000

PowerPoint 2000

Inserting a Word Table

You can easily insert a PowerPoint table in your presentation using the Table command on the Insert menu. If you want to format a table using the Table AutoFormat command available in Microsoft Word, you can embed a Microsoft Word table in your PowerPoint slide. With an embedded Word table, you can use formatting features of both Word and PowerPoint to call attention to important information and to make the table visually appealing. Scenario Maria decides to add a new slide with a table showing the types of videos MediaLoft offers.

Steps

QuickTip

If you don't see the New Slide button, click the More Buttons button on the Standard toolbar.

1. Click the **New Slide button** on the Standard toolbar, click the **Title Only AutoLayout**, then click **OK**
   A new slide 3 appears.
2. Type **Largest Video Categories**, then click in a blank area of the Presentation window
3. Click **Insert** on the menu bar, point to **Picture**, then click **Microsoft Word Table**
   The Insert Table dialog box opens, as shown in Figure G-3.
4. Click the **Number of rows up spin arrow** once to change the number to **3**, then click **OK**
   Microsoft Word opens, and a blank table with three rows and two columns appears on the screen. The Microsoft Word menu bar and toolbars replace the PowerPoint menu bar and toolbars.
5. Enter the data shown in Figure G-4 into your blank table, pressing **[Tab]** to move from cell to cell, then click on a blank area of the slide outside the table
   After you click the slide, the PowerPoint menus and toolbars return. The table text would be easier to read with formatting to make the text stand out from the background. Because the table is embedded, you can use Word's AutoFormat feature for this.

QuickTip

To edit or open an embedded object in your presentation, the object's source program must be available on your computer or network.

6. Double-click the **table** to return to Word, click **Table** on the menu bar, click **Table AutoFormat**, in the Formats list click **Colorful 2**, under Apply special formats to, click the **Heading rows** and **First column check boxes** to remove the check marks, then click **OK**
   This table is a simple list, so it doesn't need special formatting for the first column or row. The new table format changes the contents to black text on a light yellow background. The table becomes smaller to fit the data, but the entire table object does not change size.
7. Drag to select all the table text, click the **Center button** on the Word Formatting toolbar, click **Table** on the menu bar, click **Table Properties**, click the **Cell tab**, click **Center**, then click **OK**
   The data moves to the center of the cells.
8. Drag the **right sizing handle** of the table object left so it just fits the formatted table, then click on a blank area of the slide outside the table
9. Drag the table to the lower section of the slide so that the text is centered horizontally and vertically in the blank area, click on the slide outside the table, then save your work
   Compare your screen to Figure G-5.

FIGURE G-3: Insert Table dialog box

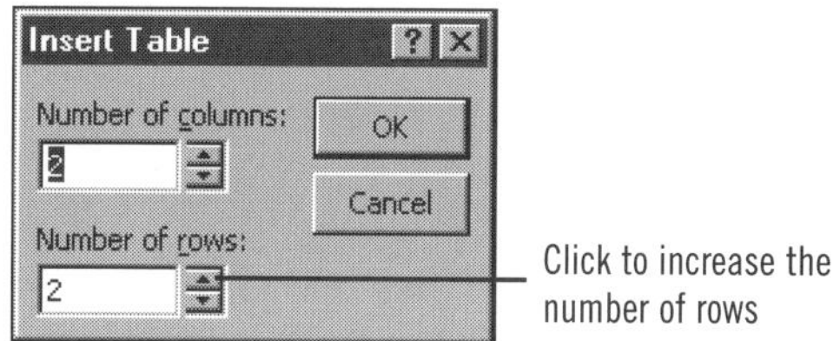

FIGURE G-4: Microsoft Word table with data

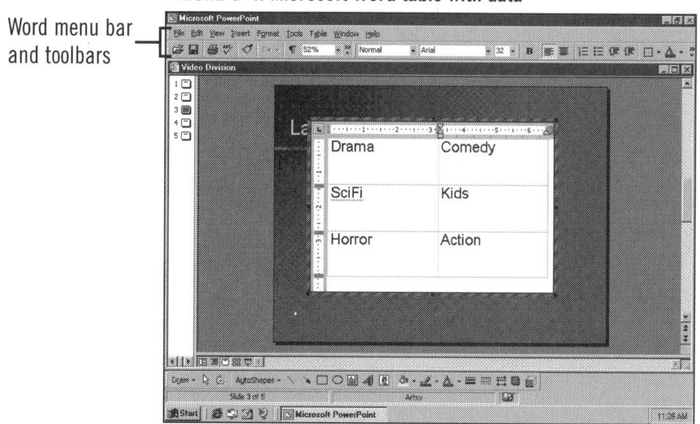

FIGURE G-5: Slide with formatted Word table

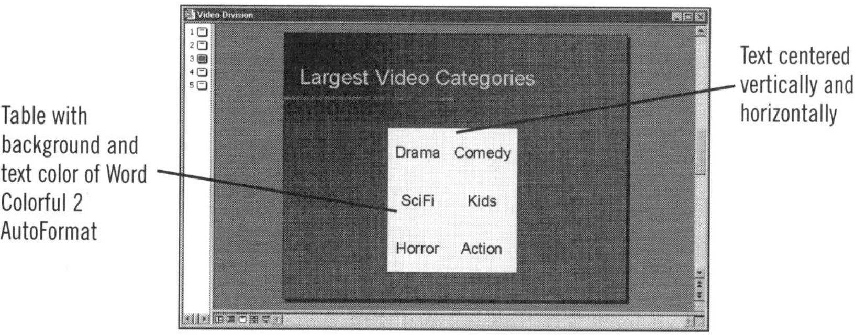

CLUES TO USE

Exporting a presentation to Microsoft Word

Sometimes you need the features of a word-processing program like Word to create detailed speaker's notes or handouts. You might also want to create a Word document based on the outline of your PowerPoint presentation. To do this, click File on the menu bar, point to Send to, and then click Microsoft Word. In the Write Up dialog box shown in Figure G-6, select one of the layout options, then click OK. A new Word document opens with your embedded presentation or outline, using the layout you selected. If you plan to modify the PowerPoint presentation and want the exported Word document to reflect your changes, click the Paste link option button.

FIGURE G-6: Write Up dialog box

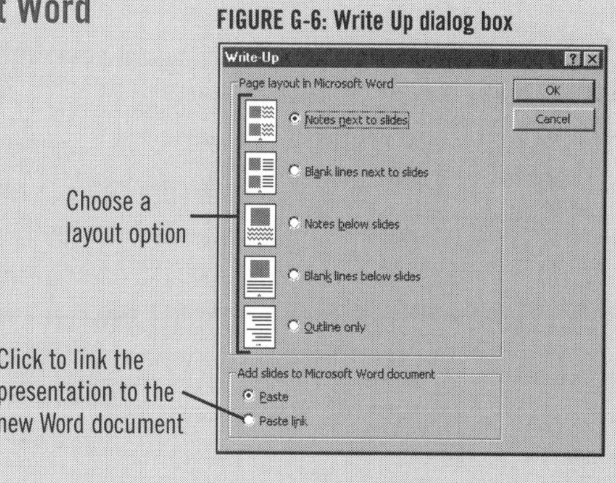

PowerPoint 2000

PowerPoint 2000

Embedding an Excel Chart

Sometimes a chart is the best way to present information that PowerPoint is not designed to create. For example, you may need to show an expense summary for each quarter of the year. For large amounts of data, it's easier to create a chart using a spreadsheet program. Then you can embed the chart file in your PowerPoint presentation and edit it using Excel tools. Excel is the chart file's **source program**, the program in which the file was created. PowerPoint is the **target program.** Scenario Maria created an Excel chart showing MediaLoft's quarterly video sales. She wants to include this chart in her presentation, so she embeds it in a slide.

Steps 1 2 3 4

1. Click the **New Slide button** on the Standard toolbar, click the **Object AutoLayout**, then click **OK**
   A new slide 4 appears.
2. Type **Quarterly Sales** in the title placeholder
3. Double-click the **object placeholder**, click the **Create from file option button** in the Insert Object dialog box, click **Browse**, locate the file **PPT G-3** on your Project Disk, click **OK**, then click **OK** in the Insert Object dialog box
   The chart containing the video data appears on the slide. Because the chart is embedded, you can edit the worksheet using Excel tools. The text labels on the chart are too small to read.
4. Double-click the **chart** to open Microsoft Excel, double-click the **chart title**, then click the **Font tab** in the Format Chart Title dialog box
5. Click **36** in the Size list, then click **OK**
   The chart title becomes larger.
6. Use the same technique to increase the text and labels on the **vertical** and **horizontal axes** and in the **legend** to **26 points**
   Compare your screen to Figure G-7.
7. Double-click the **chart background** to the right of the title, click the **Patterns** tab, click **Fill Effects**, click the **Preset option button**, click the **Preset colors list arrow**, then scroll down and click **Gold**
8. Click the **Diagonal down option button** in the Shading styles section, click **OK**, then click **OK** in the Format Chart Area dialog box
   The chart background becomes a shaded gold color.
9. Click outside the chart to exit Excel, click the **chart** once to select it, resize the **chart object** so it fills the area between the bar under the title and the bottom of the slide, center the **chart object**, click a blank area of the Presentation window to deselect the object, then save the presentation
   Compare your screen to Figure G-8.

Trouble?

You may also see the Chart Toolbar on your screen.

QuickTip

After you change the first axis, you can select the next object then press [F4] to repeat the font size increase.

FIGURE G-7: Embedded chart with resized text

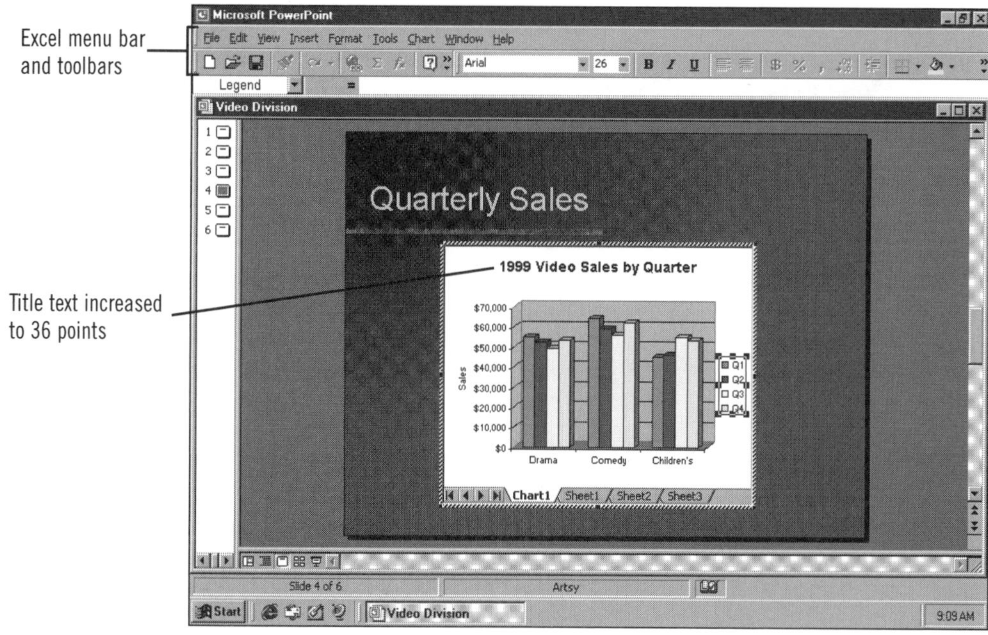

FIGURE G-8: Embedded chart with preset gold background

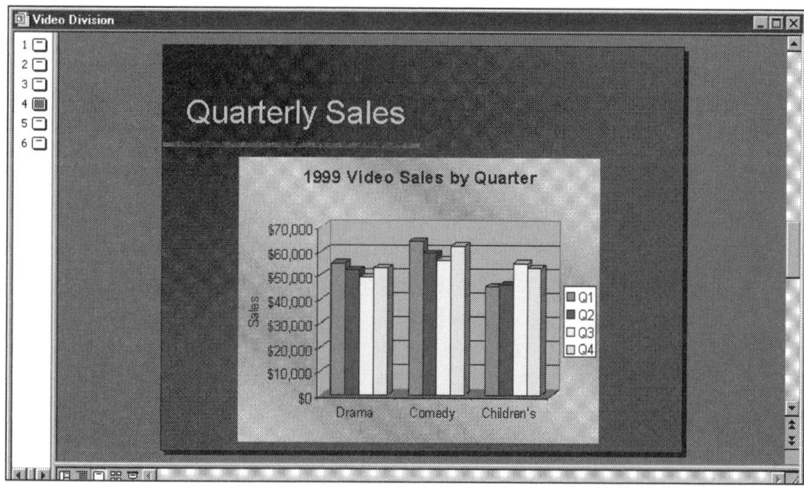

PowerPoint 2000

Embedding a worksheet

You can embed all or part of an Excel worksheet into a PowerPoint slide. To embed an entire worksheet, create a slide using the Object AutoLayout. Double-click the object placeholder, click the Create from file option button, click Browse, locate and double-click the spreadsheet file name, then click OK. The worksheet is inserted into the slide. Double-click it to edit it using Excel commands as you did in this lesson. To insert only a portion of a worksheet, open the Excel workbook and copy the cells you want to include in your presentation. Leaving Excel and the source worksheet open, open the PowerPoint presentation, click Edit on the menu bar, then click Paste Special. To paste the cells as a worksheet object that you can edit in Excel, click Microsoft Excel Worksheet Object in the Paste Special dialog box.

PowerPoint 2000

Linking an Excel Worksheet

Another way to connect objects like Excel worksheets to your presentation is to establish a **link** between the source file that created the object and the PowerPoint presentation that displays the object. When you link an object to a PowerPoint slide, a representation (picture) of the object, not the actual object itself, appears on the slide. Unlike an embedded object, a linked object is stored in its source file, not on the slide. When you link an object to a PowerPoint slide, any changes made to the source file are automatically reflected in the linked representation in your PowerPoint presentation. Some of the objects that you can link to PowerPoint include movies, Microsoft Excel worksheets, and PowerPoint slides from other presentations. Use linking when you want to include an object, such as an accounting spreadsheet, that may change over time and when you want to be sure your presentation contains the latest information. See Table G-1 for suggestions on when to use embedding and linking. Scenario Maria needs to link an Excel worksheet to her presentation. The worksheet was created by the Accounting Department manager earlier in the year.

Steps

QuickTip

If you plan to do the steps in this unit again, be sure to make and use a copy of the Excel file Video Division Budget.

1. Click the **New Slide button** on the Standard toolbar, make sure the **Object AutoLayout** is selected, click **OK**, then type **Video Division Budget** in the title placeholder
2. Double-click the **object placeholder**
   The Insert Object dialog box opens.
3. Click the **Create from file option button**, click **Browse**, locate the file **Video Division Budget** on your Project Disk, click **OK**, then click the **Link check box** to select it
   Compare your screen to Figure G-9.
4. Click **OK** in the Insert Object dialog box
   The image of the linked worksheet appears on the slide. The worksheet would be easier to see if it had a background fill color.
5. With the worksheet still selected, click the **Fill Color list arrow** on the Drawing toolbar, click the **light yellow box** (second row, fourth from the left), then click a blank area of the slide
   A yellow background fill color appears behind the worksheet, as shown in Figure G-10.
6. Click the **Save button** on the Standard toolbar, then click the Presentation window **Close button**
   PowerPoint remains open but the Presentation window closes.

TABLE G-1: Embedding vs. Linking

situation	action
When you are the only user of an object and you want the object to be a part of your presentation	Embed
When you want to access the object in its source application, even if the original file is not available	Embed
When you want to update the object manually while working in PowerPoint	Embed
When you always want the latest information in your object	Link
When the object's source file is shared on a network or when other users have access to the file and can change it	Link
When you want to keep your presentation file size small	Link

FIGURE G-9: Insert Object dialog box ready to link an object

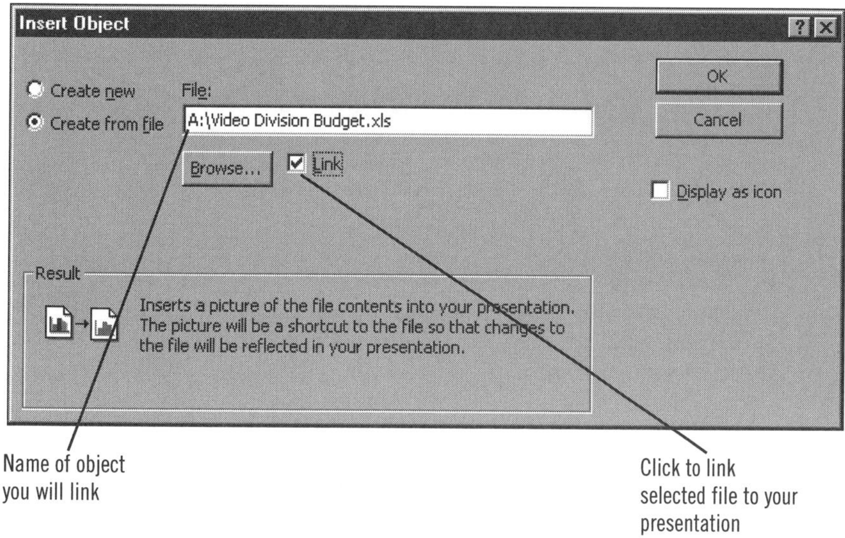

FIGURE G-10: Linked worksheet with background fill color

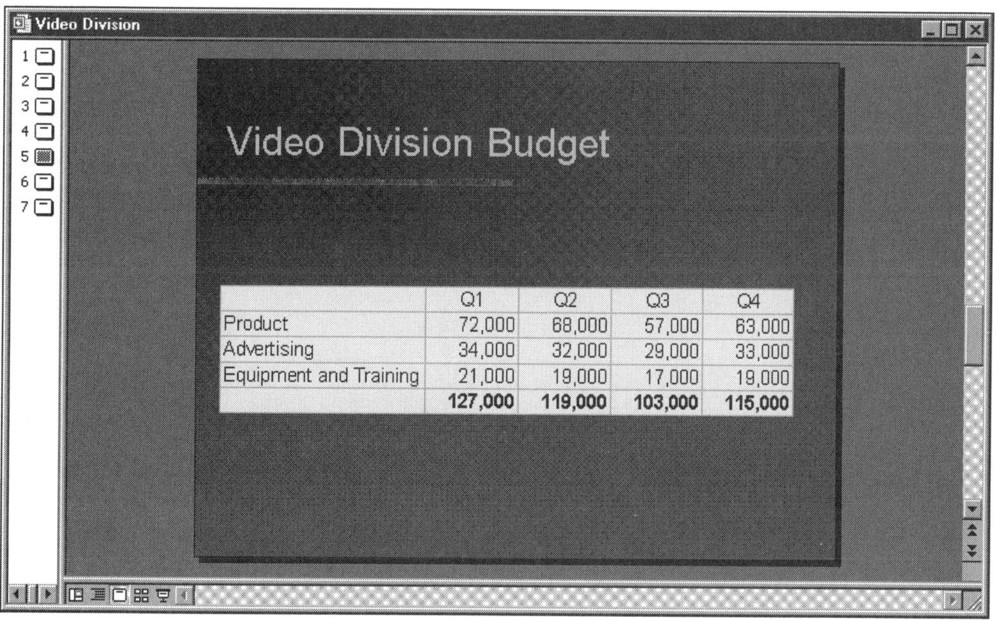

	Q1	Q2	Q3	Q4
Product	72,000	68,000	57,000	63,000
Advertising	34,000	32,000	29,000	33,000
Equipment and Training	21,000	19,000	17,000	19,000
	127,000	**119,000**	**103,000**	**115,000**

PowerPoint 2000

CLUES TO USE

Linking objects using Paste Special

You can also link an object or selected information from another program to PowerPoint by copying and pasting. This technique is useful when you want to link part of a worksheet rather than the entire file. For example, you may want to link a worksheet from a Microsoft Excel workbook that contains both a worksheet and a chart. To link just the worksheet, open the Microsoft Excel workbook file that contains the worksheet, select the worksheet, then copy it to the Clipboard. Leaving Excel and the source worksheet open, open the PowerPoint presentation, click Edit on the menu bar, click Paste Special, click the Paste link option button, then click OK.

PowerPoint 2000

Updating a Linked Excel Worksheet

To edit or change the information in a linked object, you must open the object's source program. For example, you must open Microsoft Word to edit a linked Word table, or you must open Microsoft Excel to edit a linked Excel worksheet. You can open the source program by double-clicking the linked object in the PowerPoint slide, as you did with embedded objects, or by starting the source program directly using any method you prefer. When you work in the source program, you can close your PowerPoint presentation or leave it open. Scenario Maria needs to update some of the data in the Excel worksheet and then update the linked object in PowerPoint. She decides to start Excel and the source file to do this.

1. Click the **Start** button on the taskbar, point to **Programs**, then click **Microsoft Excel**
   The Microsoft Excel program opens.
2. On the Excel Standard toolbar, click the **Open button**, locate the file **Video Division Budget** on your Project Disk, then click **Open**
   The Video Division Budget worksheet opens.
3. Click cell **C2**, type **64000**, click cell **C4**, type **18000**, then press **[Enter]**
   The Q2 total is automatically recalculated and now reads $114,000 instead of $119,000.
4. Click the **Close button** in the Microsoft Excel program window, then click **Yes** to save the changes
   Microsoft Excel closes and the PowerPoint window opens.
5. Click on the Standard toolbar, locate the file **Video Division**, then click **Open**
   A Microsoft PowerPoint alert box opens, telling you that the Video Division presentation contains links and asking if you want to update them. See Figure G-11. This message appears whether or not you have changed the source file.
6. Click **OK**.
   The worksheet in the presentation slide is updated.
7. Click **Window** on the menu bar, click **Arrange All**, then click the **slide 5 slide icon**
   Compare your screen to Figure G-12. The linked Excel worksheet shows the new Q2 total, $114,000. The changes you made in Excel were automatically made in this linked copy when you updated the links.
8. Click the **Save button** on the Standard toolbar

QuickTip

To open or edit a linked object in your presentation, the object's source program and source file must be available on your computer or network.

FIGURE G-11: Alert box to update links

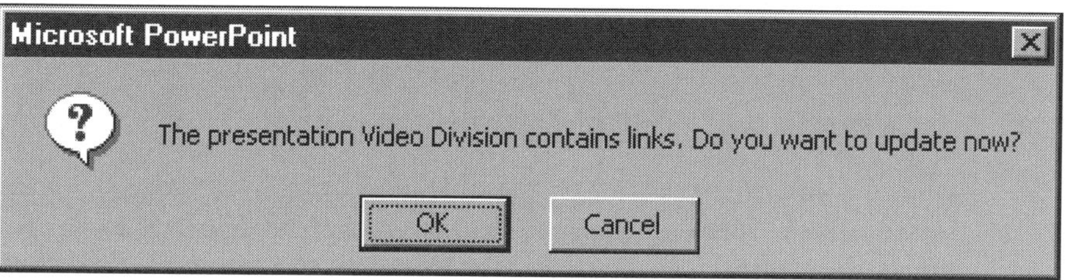

FIGURE G-12: Slide with updated, linked worksheet

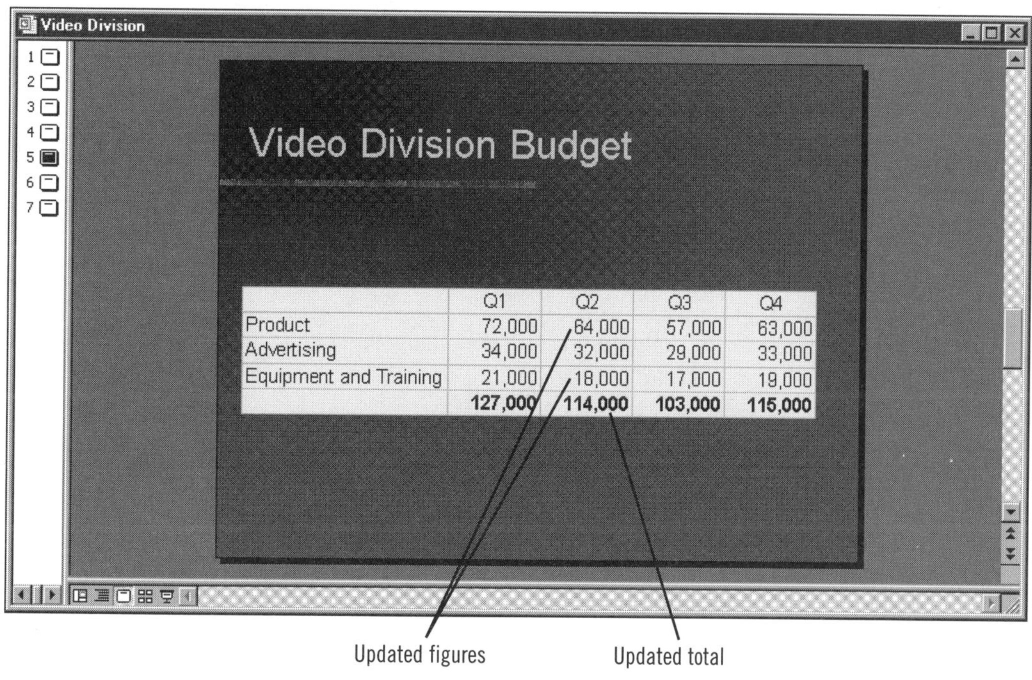

CLUES TO USE

Updating links when both files are open

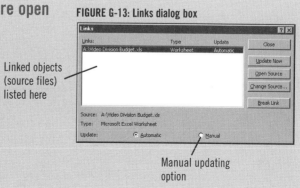

You do not have to close the target file to update the links. If you change the source file, when you switch back to the presentation file, the link will be updated. If you want to update the links manually, click Edit on the menu bar, then click Links to open the Links dialog box, as shown in Figure G-13. If the Manual check box is selected, the links in the target file will not be updated unless you select the link in this dialog box and click Update Now.

FIGURE G-13: Links dialog box

Linked objects (source files) listed here

Manual updating option

PowerPoint 2000

PowerPoint 2000

Inserting an Animated GIF File

In your presentations, you may want to use special effects to illustrate a point or capture the attention of your audience. You can do this by inserting an animation or a movie. An **animation** is a graphic such as a GIF file that moves when you run the slide show. (GIF stands for Graphics Interchange Format.) A **movie** is live action captured in digital format. Scenario Maria continues developing her presentation by embedding an animated GIF file in a slide about international videos.

Steps

1. Click the **slide 6 slide icon**
2. Click **Insert** on the menu bar, point to **Picture**, then click **Clip Art**
   The Insert ClipArt dialog box opens.
3. Click the **Motion Clips tab** in the Insert ClipArt dialog box
   The categories for motion clips appear.
4. Click the **Travel category**, then click the GIF file shown in Figure G-14
5. Click the **Insert Clip icon** on the pop-up menu, then click the **Close button** on the Insert ClipArt dialog box
   The animated GIF appears on the slide.
6. Resize the image so it is approximately the height of the bulleted list, then click a blank area of the slide
   Compare your screen to Figure G-15. The animation won't begin unless you view it in Slide Show view.
7. Click the **Slide Show button**, watch the animation, then press **[Esc]**
8. Click the **Save button** on the Standard toolbar

Trouble?

If you do not see any files in the Travel category, you may have only a basic installation. See your instructor or technical support person.

QuickTip

An animated GIF file will also play if you publish the presentation as a Web page and view it in a browser such as Internet Explorer or Netscape.

Inserting movies

You can insert movies from the Clip Gallery, Microsoft Clip Gallery Live Web site, or from disk files. Click Insert on the menu bar, point to Movies and Sounds, then click Movies from Gallery or Movies from File. If you're using the Clip Gallery, click the category then the file you want. If you're inserting from a file, navigate to the location of the movie you want. After you insert a movie, you can edit it: Click Slide Show on the menu bar, click Custom Animation, then click the Multimedia Settings tab. There you can indicate whether to continue the slide show and when to stop playing the clip. Click the More Options button to specify whether you want to loop or rewind the clip.

FIGURE G-14: Clip Gallery showing animated GIF file

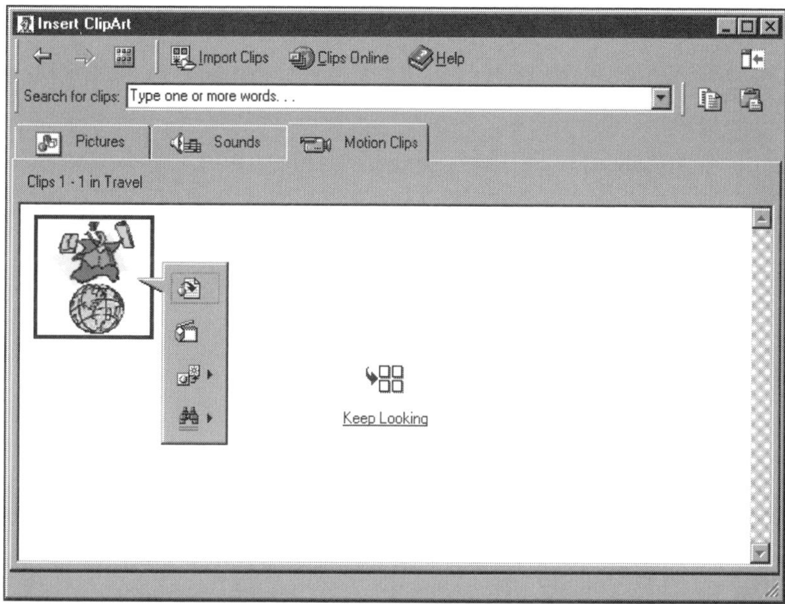

FIGURE G-15: Animated GIF in Slide Show view

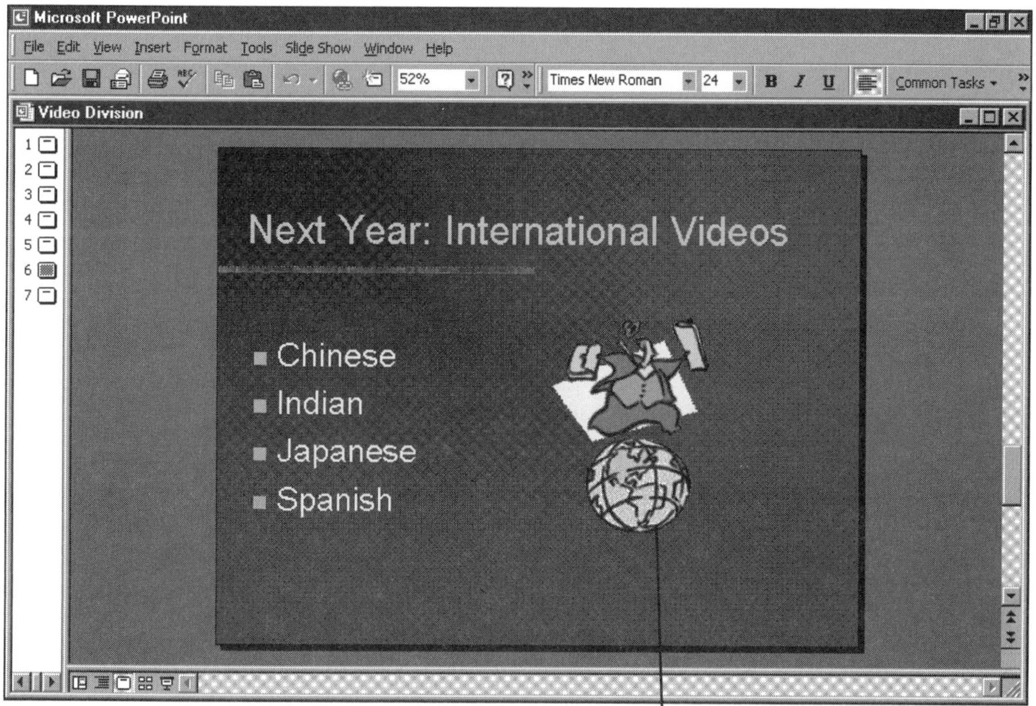

GIF image appears in Slide view but animation plays only in Slide Show view

PowerPoint 2000

Inserting a Sound

PowerPoint allows you to embed sounds in your presentation just as you embed animated GIF files or movies. Use sound to enhance the message of a slide. For example, if you are creating a presentation about a raft tour of the Colorado River, you might embed a rushing water sound on a slide showing a photograph of people rafting. To hear any sounds you embed in your presentation, you'll need a sound card and speakers installed on your computer. Scenario Maria embeds the sound of a camera click on slide 2 of her presentation to enhance the picture on the slide.

Steps

1. Click the **slide 2 slide icon**
2. Click **Insert** on the menu bar, point to **Movies and Sounds**, then click **Sound from File**
   The Insert Sound dialog box opens.
3. Select the file **PPT G-4**, then click **OK**
   A dialog box opens asking if you want the sound to play automatically or if you want it to play only when you click the icon during the slide show.
4. Click **Yes** to play the sound automatically
   A small sound icon appears on the slide, as shown in Figure G-16. The icon would be easier to see if it were larger.
5. Click **Format** on the menu bar, click **Picture**, then click the **Size tab**
   The Size tab opens in the Format Picture dialog box.
6. In the Height text box in the Scale section, double-click **100**, type **150**, then click **OK**
   The sound icon enlarges to 150% of its original size.
7. Drag the **sound icon** to the lower-left corner of the Presentation window, then click the slide background to deselect the icon
   Compare your screen to Figure G-17.
8. Double-click the **sound icon**
   The sound of a camera clicking plays.
9. Click the **Save button** on the Standard toolbar

Trouble?

The sound icon you see may be different from the one illustrated in Figure G-16, depending on your sound card software.

Trouble?

If you do not hear a sound, your computer may not have a sound card installed. See your instructor or technical support person for help.

FIGURE G-16: Slide showing small sound icon

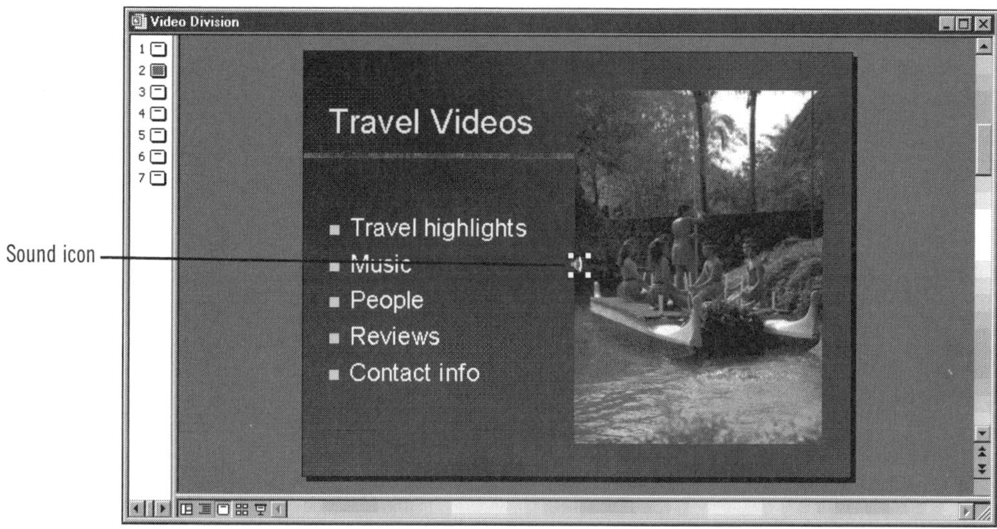

FIGURE G-17: Slide showing scaled and repositioned sound icon

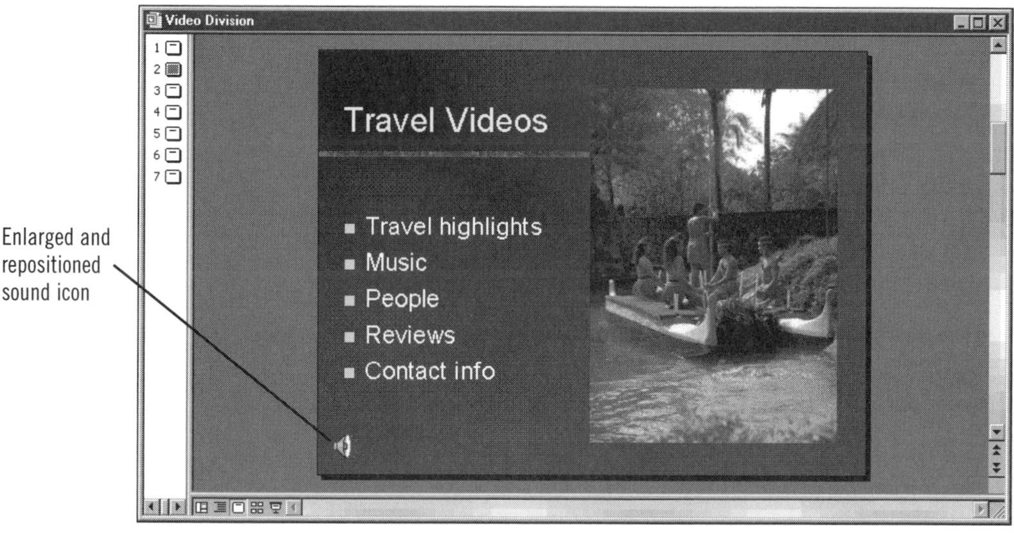

Inserting sounds and music

You can also insert sounds and music clips from the Microsoft Clip Gallery. Click Insert on the menu bar, point to Movies and Sounds, click Sound from Gallery, click the category that you want, select the clip you want to include in the presentation, then click Insert to insert it on your slide. (If you do not see any sounds in the Gallery, you may have only a basic installation. See your instructor or technical support person.) You can also add a CD audio track to play during your slide show. Click Insert on the menu bar, point to Movies and Sounds, then click Play CD Audio Track. Select the track and timing options you want, then click OK. A CD icon appears on the slide, as shown in Figure G-18. You can indicate if you want the CD to play automatically when you move to the slide or only when you click the CD icon during a slide show. You don't need to have the CD in the CD-ROM drive to insert a sound.

FIGURE G-18: CD icon on a slide

PowerPoint 2000

Inserting a Hyperlink

Often you will want to view a document that either won't fit on the slide, or that is too detailed for your presentation. In these cases, you can insert a **hyperlink**, a specially formatted word, phrase, or graphic that you click during your slide show to "jump to," or display, another slide in your current presentation; another PowerPoint presentation; a Word, Excel, or Access file; or an address on the World Wide Web. Inserting a hyperlink is similar to linking because you can change the object in the source program after you click the hyperlink. Scenario Maria decides to add a hyperlink to her presentation to show a recent product review, which is in a Word document.

Steps

1. Click the **slide 7 slide icon**
2. Press **[Shift]** and click the **main text box**, click the **Font Size list arrow**, click **48**, drag the **lower-right corner** of the text box up and to the left to resize it to fit the text, and then center the **text box** in the blank area on the slide
   The review that Maria wants to display is from *Video News* magazine.
3. Drag I across **Video News** to select it, then click the **Insert Hyperlink button** on the Standard toolbar
   The Insert Hyperlink dialog box opens. You want to hyperlink to another file.
4. Under Browse For on the right side of the dialog box, click **File**, locate the file **PPT G-5**, then click **OK**
   Compare your dialog box with Figure G-19.
5. Click **OK**, then click in a blank area of the Presentation window
   Now that you have made the magazine title "Video News" a hyperlink to file PPT G-5, the text automatically changes to hyperlink formatting, which is underlined orange text, the hyperlink color for this presentation's color scheme. It's important to test any hyperlink you create.
6. Click the **Slide Show button** , then click the **Video News hyperlink**
   The Word document containing the review appears on the screen, as shown in Figure G-20. The Web toolbar appears at the top of the screen.
7. Click the **Back button** on the Web toolbar
   The Reviews slide reappears in Slide Show view. The hyperlink is now gray, the color for followed hyperlinks in this color scheme, indicating that the hyperlink has been used.
8. Click the presentation window to make it active, then press **[Esc]** to end the slide show, press **[Ctrl][Home]**, then click the **Slide Sorter View button**
   Compare your screen to Figure G-21.
9. Run through the entire slide show, making sure you click the hyperlink on slide 7
10. Add your name to the notes and handouts footer, print the presentation slides as handouts, 6 slides per page, save your changes and exit PowerPoint, right-click the **Word program button** on the taskbar, then click **Close** on the pop-up menu

FIGURE G-19: Insert HyperLink dialog box

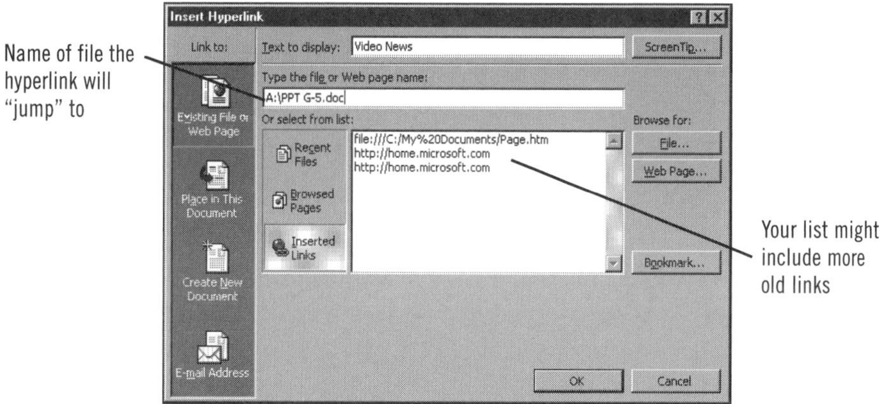

FIGURE G-20: Linked review in Word document

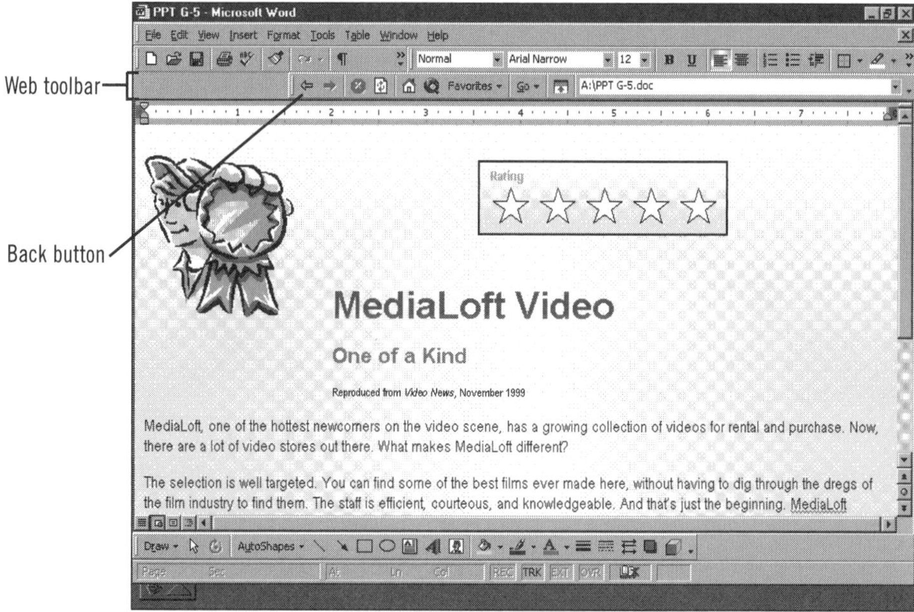

FIGURE G-21: Final presentation in Slide Sorter view

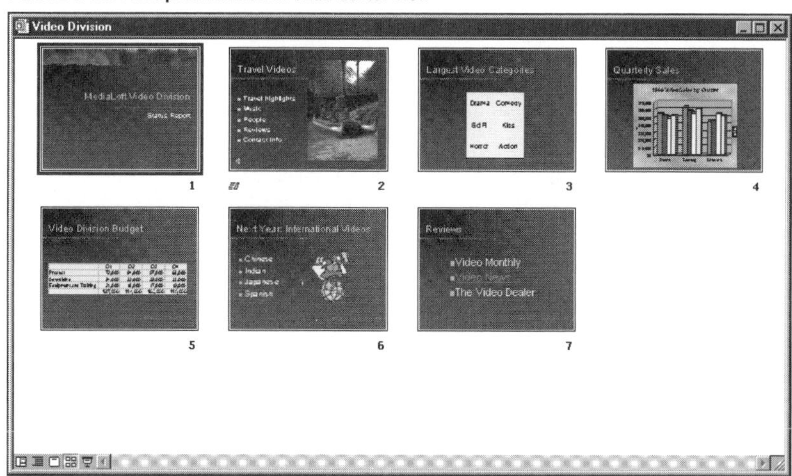

PowerPoint 2000

Practice

► Concepts Review

Label each of the elements of the PowerPoint window shown in Figure G-22.

FIGURE G-22

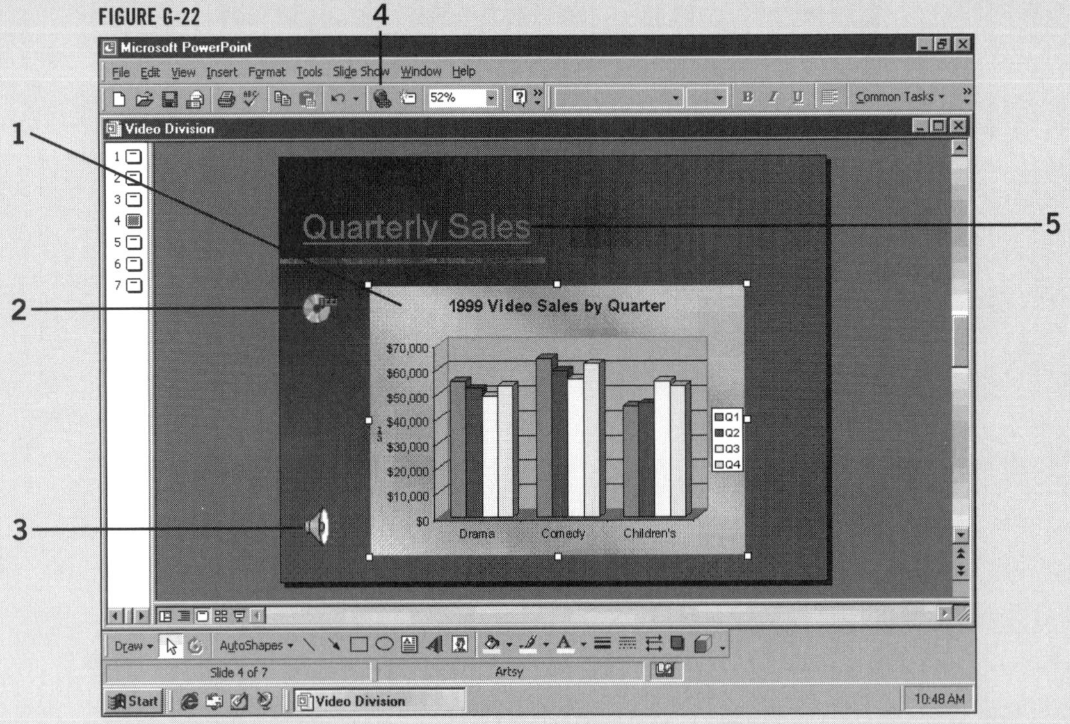

Match each of the terms with the statement that describes its function.

6. **Picture**
7. **Embedded object**
8. **Link**
9. **Source program**
10. **Hyperlink**

a. An object created in another program and then stored in PowerPoint
b. The program in which an embedded object is created
c. A scanned photograph or piece of line art
d. A word or object you click to view another file
e. The connection between a source file and a PowerPoint presentation

Select the best answer from the list of choices.

11. Which of the following objects are you able to embed into PowerPoint?
- **a.** Movies
- **b.** Photographs
- **c.** Microsoft Excel charts
- **d.** All of the above

12. Which statement about embedded objects is false?
- **a.** You can format embedded objects in their source program.
- **b.** Embedded objects are not dependent on a source file.
- **c.** Embedded objects are not a part of the presentation.
- **d.** Embedded objects increase your presentation file size more than linked objects do.

13. Which statement about linked objects is true?
- **a.** To edit a linked object, you must open its source file..
- **b.** A linked object is an independent object embedded directly in a slide.
- **c.** You can access a linked object even when the source file is not available.
- **d.** A linked object substantially increases the size of your presentation file

Skills Review

If you complete all of the exercises in this unit, you may run out of space on your Project Disk. To make sure you have enough disk space, copy files PPT G-6, PPT G-7, Projected Profit, and PPT G-8 onto a new disk and use the new disk to complete the rest of the exercises in this unit. If you do not have access to the Office 2000 CD-ROM or if the complete set of clip art images and sounds have not been imported into the Clip Art Gallery, then you should also copy the files PPT G-2 and PPT G-4.

1. Embed a picture.
- **a.** Start PowerPoint, open the presentation PPT G-6, then save it as "New Directions 2000."
- **b.** Go to slide 3 and embed the figure from PPT G-2.
- **c.** Use the cropping tool to crop about ½" from the bottom of the picture.
- **d.** Drag the picture to the right side of the slide, resize it so it is slightly taller than the bulleted list, then use the arrow keys on the keyboard to adjust its position.
- **e.** Change the slide color scheme so that it matches the picture well, customizing the scheme colors as necessary.
- **f.** Save your changes.

2. Insert a Word table.
- **a.** Insert a new slide after slide 3 with the Title Only AutoLayout.
- **b.** Title the slide "Expand Display Space."
- **c.** Insert a Microsoft Word table that is 2 columns wide and 3 rows tall.
- **d.** Enter the information shown in Table G-2.
- **e.** Click in the Presentation window, then double-click the table to return to Word.
- **f.** Select all the cells, then center the information horizontally using the Word Formatting toolbar.
- **g.** Apply the Colorful 1 AutoFormat, with no special formatting for the heading row or first column.
- **h.** Drag the right side of the table object so the border just fits the formatted table.
- **i.** Center the table entries vertically in the cells.
- **j.** Exit Word, resize the table so it almost fills the lower portion of the slide, then center it below the slide title.
- **k.** Save the presentation.

TABLE G-2

Drama	2 sections
Comedy	1 section
SciFi	1 section

3. **Embed an Excel chart.**
   a. Insert a new slide after slide 4 using the Object AutoLayout.
   b. Title the slide "Projected Video Income."
   c. Embed the chart from the file PPT G-7.
   d. Using Excel tools, enlarge the title to 28 points and the x-axis, z-axis, and legend text to 22 points.
   e. Resize and reposition the chart so it fills the lower portion of the slide and so it is centered horizontally and vertically.
   f. Give the chart a white background.
   g. Save your changes.
4. **Link an Excel worksheet.**
   a. Create a new slide after slide 5 with the Object AutoLayout.
   b. Title the slide "Projected Division Profit."
   c. Use the object placeholder to link the spreadsheet file "Projected Profit" on your Project Disk.
   d. Resize the object so that it fills the slide width.
   e. Reposition the object so it is centered horizontally. (*Hint:* To center it more precisely, hold down [Alt] while you drag, or hold down [Ctrl] while you press the arrow keys.)
   f. Fill the spreadsheet object with light blue (the Follow Accent and Followed Hyperlink Scheme Color).
   g. Save and close the New Directions 2000 presentation.
5. **Update a linked Excel worksheet.**
   a. Start Excel and open the Projected Profit worksheet.
   b. Replace the value in cell B2 with "255000."
   c. In cell D4, enter "20000."
   d. Close the Excel program, saving your changes.
   e. Open the New Directions 2000 file in PowerPoint, updating the link as you do so.
   f. Go to slide 6 and view your changes.
   g. Save the presentation.
6. **Insert an animated GIF file.**
   a. Go to slide 2.
   b. Insert an appropriate animated GIF file on the slide and resize and reposition it as necessary.
   c. Preview it in Slide Show view.
   d. Save the presentation.
7. **Insert a sound.**
   a. Go to slide 4.
   b. Insert an appropriate sound from the Clip Gallery. (If you don't have access to Clip Gallery sounds, insert the sound file PPT G-4.)
   c. In the Format Picture dialog box, scale the sound icon to 200% of its original size.
   d. Drag the sound icon to the lower-right of the slide.
   e. Test the sound in Slide Show view.
   f. Save the presentation.

8. **Insert a hyperlink.**
   - **a.** Go to the last slide in the presentation, then add a new slide with the Bulleted List AutoLayout.
   - **b.** Title the slide "Testimonials."
   - **c.** In the first line of the main text placeholder, enter "George Sanders, Medford, Oregon" and on the second line enter "Jorge Fonseca, Orem, Utah."
   - **d.** Select the entire main text placeholder, and change its font size to 48 points.
   - **e.** Resize the text placeholder to fit the text, and then center it on the slide.
   - **f.** Convert the George Sanders bullet into a hyperlink to the file PPT G-8.
   - **g.** If necessary, change the bullets on slide 7 to the triangle in the Wingdings 3 font that matches the earlier slides in the presentation.
   - **h.** Run the slide show and test the hyperlink.
   - **i.** Use the Back button to return to the presentation.
   - **j.** End the slide show.
   - **k.** Run the spellchecker, view the entire presentation in Slide Show view, and evaluate your presentation. Make any necessary changes.
   - **l.** Add your name as a footer to notes and handouts, print the slides as Handouts, 6 slides per page, save and close the presentation, then exit PowerPoint and Microsoft Word.

Visual Workshop

Create two slides that look like the examples in Figures G-23 and G-24. Save the presentation as "Year End Report." Save and print Slide view of the presentation. Submit the final presentation output.

FIGURE G-23

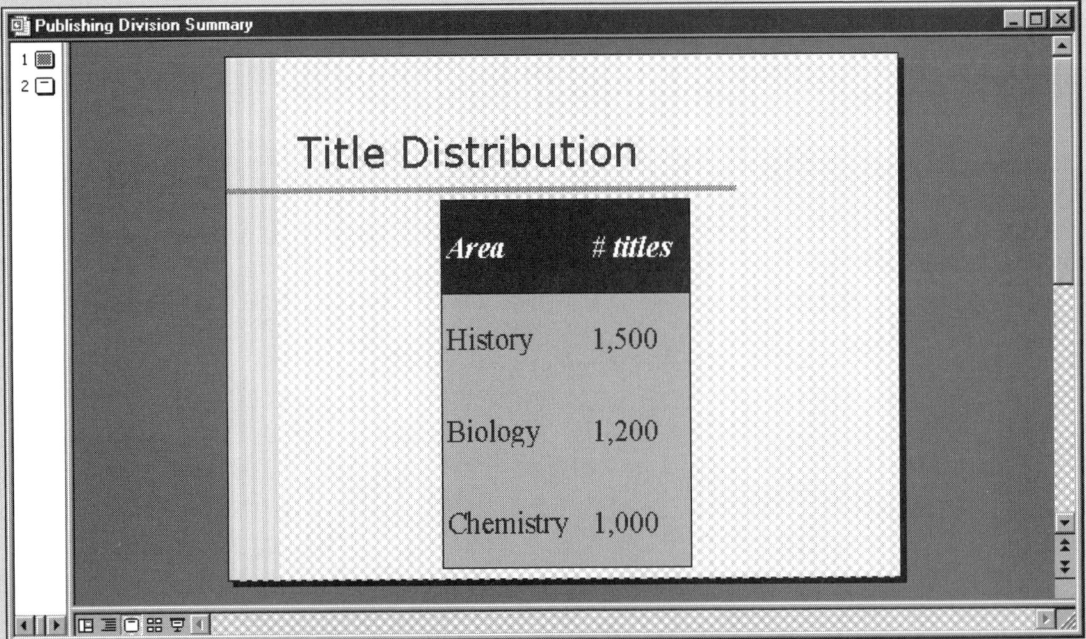

FIGURE G-24

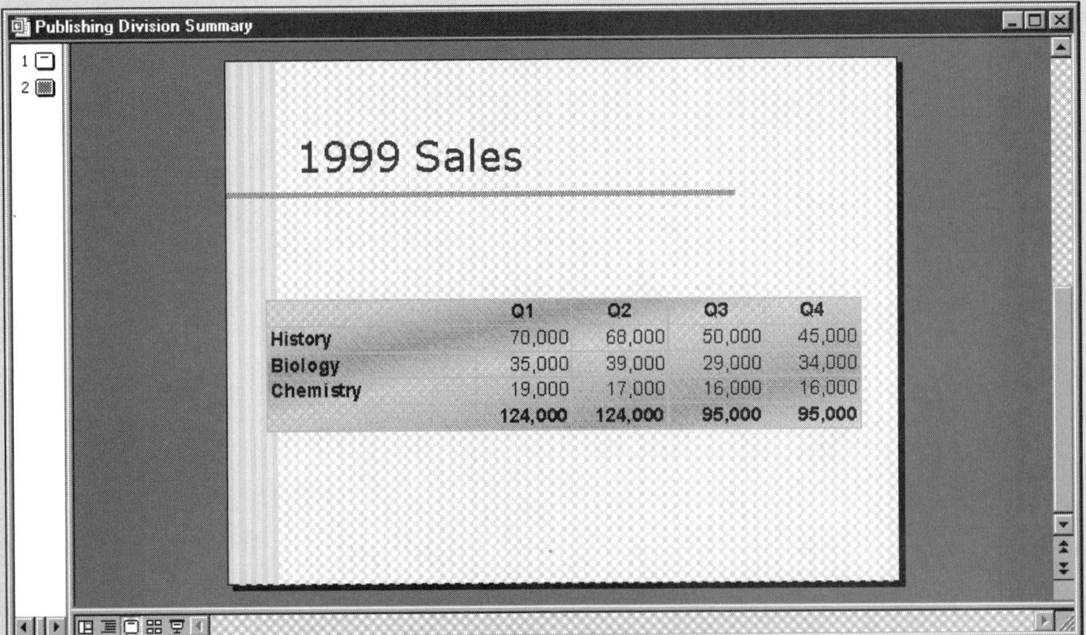

PowerPoint 2000

Using
Slide Show Features

Objectives

- MOUS ▶ Set up a slide show
- MOUS ▶ Create a custom show
- MOUS ▶ Hide a slide during a slide show
- MOUS ▶ Use the Meeting Minder
- MOUS ▶ Rehearse slide timings
- MOUS ▶ Use the Pack and Go Wizard
- MOUS ▶ Use the Microsoft PowerPoint Viewer
- MOUS ▶ Publish a presentation for the World Wide Web

After all the work on your presentation is complete, you need to produce the final output that you will use when you give your presentation. In PowerPoint, you can create 35mm slides, overhead transparencies, audience handouts, or you can show your presentation on a computer using Slide Show view. Before you use Slide Show view, you can set up custom options for your presentation so you can run it yourself or make it into a self-running slide show. You can also publish your presentation for the World Wide Web so that anyone can view it using a Web browser. Scenario ▶ Maria Abbott has finished creating the content of her presentation. She produces an on-screen slide show and publishes it for viewing on the World Wide Web.

PowerPoint 2000

Setting Up a Slide Show

With PowerPoint, you can create a slide show that runs automatically. Viewers can then watch the slide show on a public computer at a convention or trade show on a freestanding computer called a **kiosk**. You can create a self-running slide show that loops, or runs through the entire show, without users touching the computer. You can also let viewers advance the slides at their own pace by pressing the spacebar, clicking the mouse, or clicking an on-screen control button called an **action button**. Scenario Maria prepares the Video Division 1 presentation so employees can view it at a table at an upcoming company meeting.

Steps 1 2 3 4

QuickTip

To return personalized toolbars and menus to the default state, click Tools on the menu bar, click Customize, click Reset my usage data on the Options tab, click Yes, then click Close.

1. Start PowerPoint, open the presentation **PPT H-1**, save it as **Video Division 1**, click **Window**, then click **Arrange All**
2. Click **Slide Show** on the menu bar, click **Set Up Show**, and under Show type, click the **Browsed at a kiosk (full screen) option button** to select it
   The Set Up Show dialog box opens, similar to Figure H-1.
3. In the Slides section, make sure the **All option button** is selected, and in the Advance slides section, click the **Using timings, if present option button**
   This will include all the slides in the presentation, and have PowerPoint advance the slides at time intervals you set. Compare your screen to Figure H-1.
4. Click **OK**, click the **Slide Sorter View button**, press **[Ctrl][A]** to select all the slides, click **Slide Show** on the menu bar, click **Slide Transition**, in the Advance section, click the **Automatically after check box** to select it, type **5**, then click **Apply to All**
   The slide show will now advance the slides automatically at 5-second intervals or faster if someone clicks the mouse or presses [Spacebar].
5. Click the **Slide Show button**, view the show, let it start again, then press **[Esc]**
   There may be times when you want users to advance slides by themselves. You can do this by inserting a button that is actually a hyperlink that will jump to the next slide.
6. Click **Slide Show** on the menu bar, click **Set Up Show**, in the Advance slides section, click the **Manually option button**, then click **OK**
7. Double-click **slide 1** to view it in Slide view, click **Slide Show** on the menu bar, point to **Action Buttons**, click the **Action Button: Forward or Next button**, then drag the pointer to draw a button in the lower-right corner of slide 1
   The Action Settings dialog box opens. See Figure H-2.
8. Select the **Hyperlink to option button**, select **Next Slide**, then click **OK**
   The new action button appears in the lower-right corner of the title slide. Compare your screen to Figure H-3.
9. With the button selected, press **[Ctrl][C]** to copy it, click the **Next Slide button**, press **[Ctrl][V]** to paste the button on slide 2, repeat for each slide that follows, then return to **slide 1**
10. View the slide show, clicking the **action buttons** to move from slide to slide, press **[Esc]** to end the slide show once you've viewed it all the way through one time, then save your changes
   Make sure you wait for the animated objects to appear on the slides before you click the action buttons.

QuickTip

You must be in Slide Show view to use the hyperlink buttons.

Trouble?

If the Office Clipboard appears, click its Close box after you have pasted the action button on all the slides.

FIGURE H-1: Set Up Show dialog box

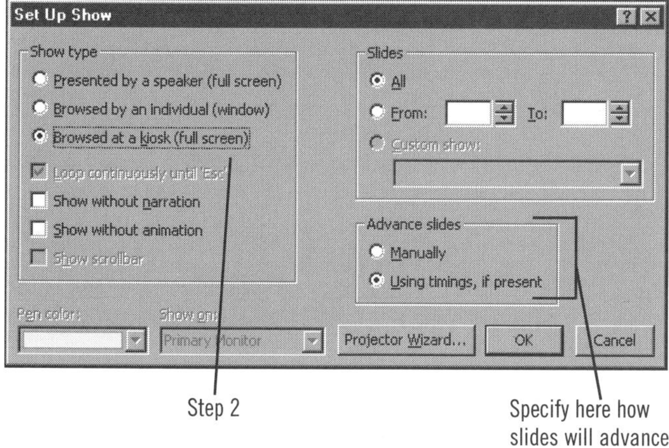

FIGURE H-2: Action Settings dialog box

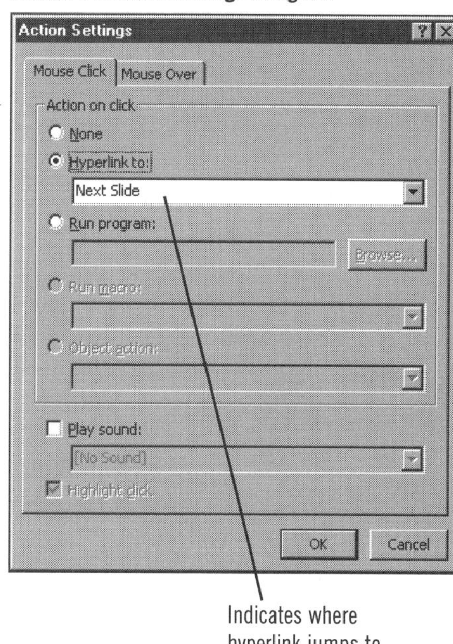

FIGURE H-3: Slide 1 with hyperlink button to the next slide

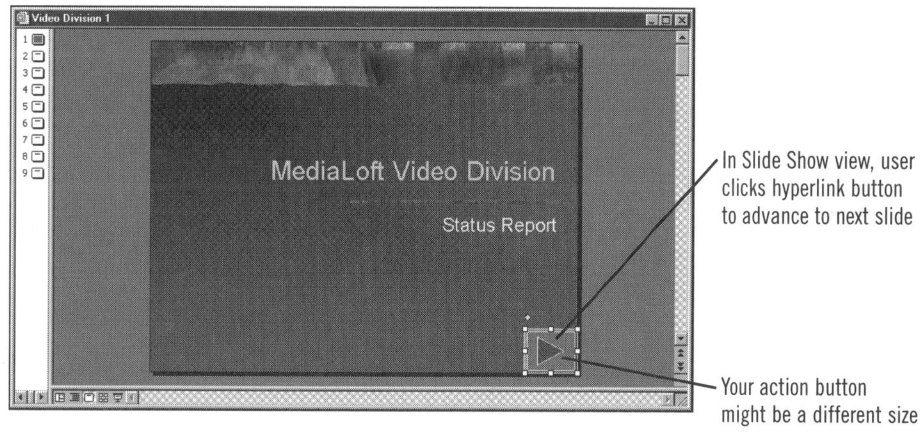

Exporting to 35mm slides

You may want to create a version of your presentation on 35mm slides to show to a large audience using a slide projector. You can create 35mm slides by sending your PowerPoint presentation electronically to a **service bureau**, a graphics business that produces and mounts slides, and then mails them to you. PowerPoint provides the Genigraphics Wizard, which prepares your presentation and sends your order to Genigraphics, a firm that performs various graphics services. First, size your slides by clicking File on the menu bar, click Page Setup, and in the Slides sized for list, select 35mm Slides, then click OK. Click File, point to Send to, then click Genigraphics. The Genigraphics Wizard takes you through several screens that ask you to choose the output format, the slides you want to send, the transmission method, as well as delivery and payment options. PowerPoint will automatically send your order and bill the credit card you specified. If you enter a credit card number and send the presentation, you will be charged, so do not complete the wizard unless you are sure you want to place the order.

PowerPoint 2000

Creating a Custom Show

Often when you create a slide show, you need to create a custom version of it for a different audience or purpose. For example, you might create a 20-minute presentation about a new product to show to potential customers who will be interested in the product features and benefits. Then you could create a five-minute version of that same show for an open house for potential investors, selecting only appropriate slides from the longer show. Scenario Maria wants to use a reduced version of the slide show in a marketing presentation, so she creates a custom slide show containing only the slides relating to the video product line. First she needs to turn off the kiosk setting.

Steps 1 2 3 4

1. Click **Slide Show** on the menu bar, click **Set Up Show**, click the **Presented by a speaker (full screen) option button**, then click **OK**
2. Click **Slide Show** on the menu bar, click **Custom Shows**, then click **New** in the Custom Shows dialog box
   The Define Custom Show dialog box opens, with the slides in your current presentation in the Slides in presentation list box on the left.
3. Press and hold **[Ctrl]**, in the Slides in presentation list, click **3. Classics**, **4. Travel Videos**, **7. Next Year: International Videos**, and **8. Reviews**, then click **Add**
   The four selected slides move to the Slides in custom show list box, indicating that they will be included in the new presentation. See Figure H-4.
4. Drag to select the existing text in the Slide show name text box, then type **Marketing Presentation**
5. In the Slides in custom show list, click **4. Reviews**, click the **Slide Order up arrow button** three times to move it to the top of the list, then click **OK**
   You can arrange the slides in any order in your custom show. The Custom Shows dialog box lists your custom presentation. To show a custom slide show, you must first open the show you used to create it. The custom show is not saved as a separate slide show on your disk even though you assigned it a new name. You then open the custom show from the Custom Shows dialog box.
6. Click **Show**, view the slide show, clicking the **action buttons** to move from slide to slide; after you view the International Videos slide, press **[Esc]** to end the custom show
   The slides appear in the new order: slides 8, 3, 4, then 7. Because the slide show is not set up to loop continuously, clicking the action button on the International Videos slide doesn't do anything. You return to the presentation in Slide view.
7. Press **[Ctrl][Home]**, click the **Slide Show button**, right-click anywhere on the screen, point to **Go**, point to **Custom Show**, then click **Marketing Presentation**, as shown in Figure H-5
8. Use the **action buttons** to move from slide to slide in the custom show then press **[Esc]** after viewing the International Video slide
9. Add your name as a footer to the notes and handouts, save your changes, click **File** on the menu bar, click **Print**, click the **Custom Show option button**, make sure **Marketing Presentation** is listed in the list box, click the **Print what list arrow**, select **Handouts**, **6 slides per page**, then click **OK**

QuickTip

If your computer has a sound card and a microphone, you can record voice narrations to play during your slide show. This can be a good choice for self-running slide shows and presentations on the Internet. On the Slide Show menu, click Voice Narrations. You can link or embed the narration.

QuickTip

You can also access the custom show in Slide Show view.

Trouble?

If you right-click the title slide and no shortcut menu appears, you probably forgot to return the Set Up Show option to Presented by a speaker (full screen). Press [Esc], click Slide Show on the menu bar, click Set Up Show, and select that option now.

FIGURE H-4: Define Custom Show dialog box

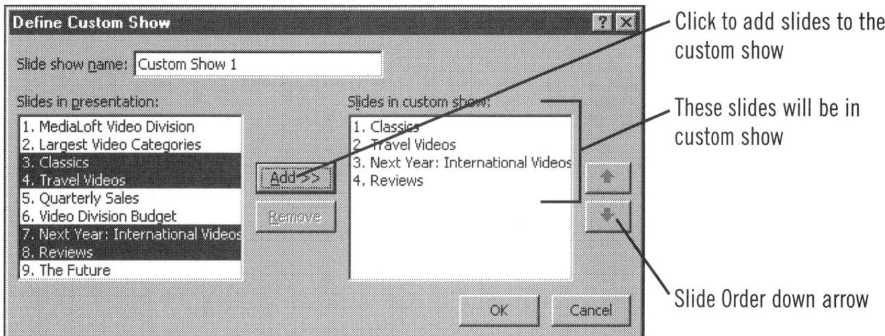

FIGURE H-5: Switching to the custom slide show

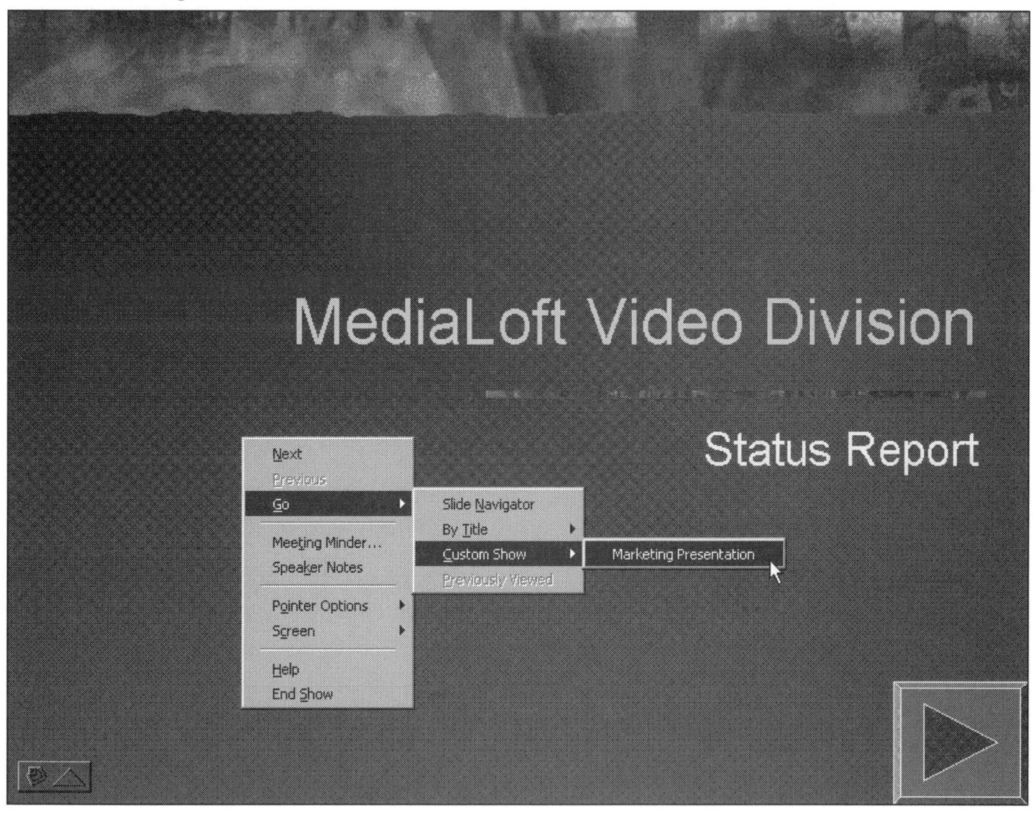

Using action buttons to hyperlink to a custom slide show

You can use action buttons to switch from the "parent" show to the custom show. Click Slide Show on the menu bar, point to Action Buttons, and choose any action button. Drag the pointer to draw a button on the slide, then, in the Action Settings dialog box, select Custom Show in the Hyperlink to list box. Select the name of the custom show to which you want to hyperlink and click OK. When you run the show, click the hyperlink button you created to run the custom show.

PowerPoint 2000

PowerPoint 2000

Hiding a Slide During a Slide Show

Another method of customizing a slide show for an audience is to hide slides you don't want the audience to see. Hidden slides are not deleted from the presentation; they just don't appear during a slide show. You know a slide is hidden when there is a line through the slide number in Slide Sorter view. Scenario Maria decides to hide the slides with financial information so she can show the presentation to a potential video supplier.

Steps 1 2 3 4

1. Click the **Slide Sorter View button**, click **slide 5**, press and hold **[Shift]**, then click **slide 6**
2. Click the **Hide Slide button** on the Slide Sorter toolbar
   The slide number under slides 5 and 6 now has the hide symbol on it, as shown in Figure H-6.
3. Click **Slide Show** on the menu bar, then click **Set Up Show**
   The Set Up Show dialog box opens, similar to Figure H-7.
4. In the Slides section, type **4** in the From box, press **[Tab]**, type **7** in the To box, compare your screen to Figure H-7, then click **OK**
5. Click **slide 4**
6. Click the **Slide Show button**, view the animation effects on slide 4, then press **[Spacebar]** once to move to slide 7
   Slide 4 (Travel Videos) appears, then PowerPoint skips slides 5 and 6, and slide 7 (International Videos) appears.
7. Press **[PgUp]** twice to see slide 4 again, press **[H]** twice to view slides 5 and 6, the Sales and Budget slides, then press **[Spacebar]** to view slide 7
   Pressing [H] causes slides 5 and 6 to appear.
8. Press **[Esc]**, click **slide 5**, press and hold **[Shift]**, click **slide 6**, then click on the Slide Sorter toolbar
   The Hide symbol no longer appears under the slide. Maria decides to reset the slide show so it shows the entire presentation.
9. Click **Slide Show** on the menu bar, click **Set Up Show**, in the Slides section click the **All option button**, click **OK**, then click the **Save button** on the Standard toolbar
   The next time you run the slide show, all the slides will appear.

QuickTip

To hide a slide in Slide view, click Hide Slide on the Slide Show menu.

QuickTip

You can start a slide show on any slide by displaying that slide in Slide or Normal view or selecting it in Slide Sorter view, then starting the slide show.

QuickTip

To view a hidden slide during a slide show, you can also right-click the slide before the hidden one, point to Go on the pop-up menu, point to By Title, then click the title of the hidden slide that you want to show.

FIGURE H-6: Slide showing Hide symbol

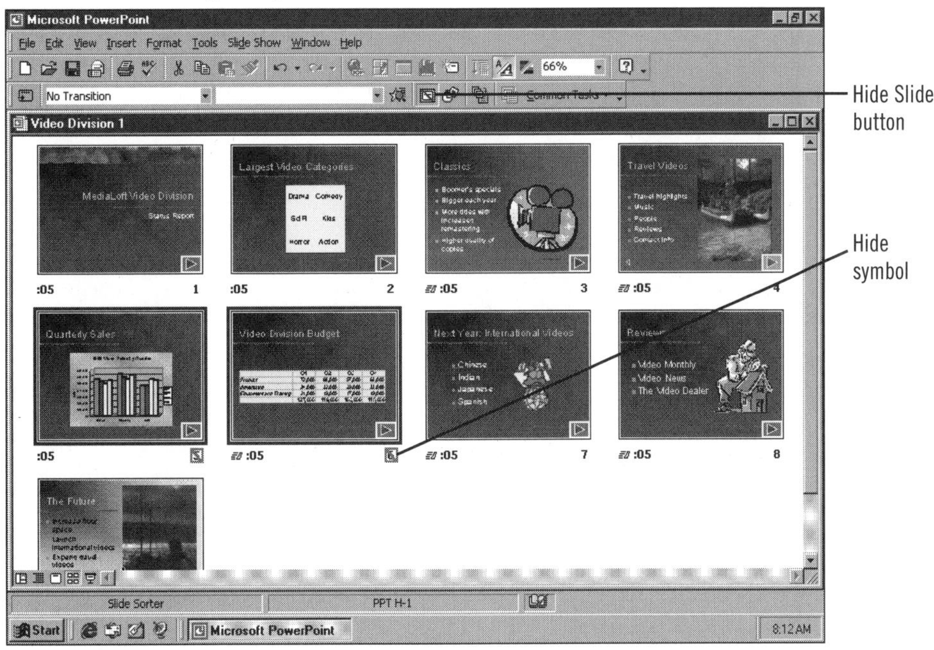

FIGURE H-7: Set Up Show dialog box

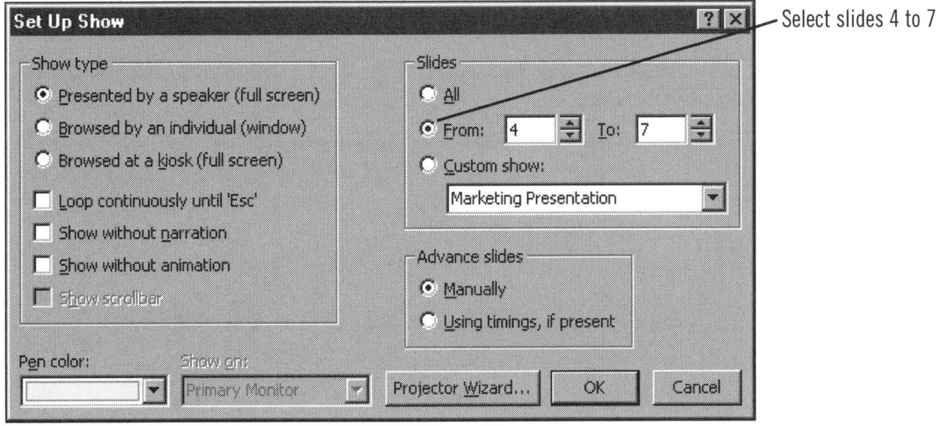

Creating summary and agenda slides

If your presentation is long, you may want to create a **summary slide**, a slide that lists the titles of each slide in the presentation. To do this, switch to Slide Sorter view or open the Outlining toolbar, select the slides you want listed on the summary slide, then click the Summary Slide button. You can also create an agenda slide using the summary slide feature. An **agenda slide** is a list of the first slide in each custom show within a presentation. First, create a custom show for each section of the presentation. In Slide Sorter view, select the first slide in each custom show. In the Slide Sorter toolbar, click Summary Slide. A summary slide is created. Switch to Slide or Normal view, select each slide title listed on the summary slide, click the Insert Hyperlink button on the Standard toolbar. In the Link to section of the Insert Hyperlink dialog box, click Place in this Document. In the list, click the plus sign next to Custom Shows to see a list of custom shows in the presentation, then click the name of the custom show you want to link to.

PowerPoint 2000

PowerPoint 2000

Using the Meeting Minder

Occasionally, it's helpful to assign tasks or take notes as you present a slide show to make sure people follow up on meeting items. PowerPoint makes this task easy with the Meeting Minder. The Meeting Minder is a dialog box you use in Slide Show view to enter information related to the slides in your presentation. The action items you enter are automatically added to a new slide at the end of your presentation. You can export the action items to a Microsoft Word document to edit them or to make them part of another document. Scenario Maria practices adding action items with the Meeting Minder so she'll know how to use it when she actually runs the presentation.

1. Double-click **slide 5** to show it in Slide view
   Slide 5 appears.
2. Click the **Slide Show button**, right-click the slide, click **Meeting Minder** on the pop-up menu, then click the **Action Items tab**
   The Meeting Minder dialog box opens, similar to Figure H-8.
3. Type **Compile detailed figures for Q1 Kids**, press **[Tab]**, type **Howard** in the Assigned To text box, press **[Tab]**, type **9/21/00** to replace today's date in the Due Date text box, compare your screen to Figure H-8, then click **Add**
   The action item you entered appears in the list box on the Action Items tab. If you were to enter any more action items, they would be added to this list.
4. Click **OK**
   Action items are added to a new slide at the end of the presentation.
5. Right-click the slide, point to **Go** on the pop-up menu, point to **By Title**, then click **10 Action Items** on the list of slides
   The new Action Items slide appears, with the action item you entered in the Meeting Minder. See Figure H-9.
6. Right-click the slide, select **Meeting Minder** on the pop-up menu, click the **Action Items tab**, click the item in the list, then click **Export**
   The Meeting Minder Export dialog box opens.
7. Make sure that the **Send meeting minutes and action items to Microsoft Word check box** is selected, click the **Post action items to Microsoft Outlook check box** to deselect it, then click **Export Now**
   Microsoft Word starts and opens a new Word document containing your Meeting Minder action items. See Figure H-10. Word assigns a temporary file name that begins with PPT to the document. You can edit and print this document just as you would any Word document.
8. Add your name as the first line in the document, click the **Print button** on the Word Standard toolbar, click **File** on the menu bar, click **Save As**, save the document as **Video Action Items** to your Project Disk, then click the **Close button** in the Word program window
   Word saves the action item to your Project Disk in Rich Text Format, which is readable by other word processors. Your PowerPoint presentation reappears in Slide Show view.
9. Click **OK** in the Meeting Minder dialog box, then click the left mouse button twice to end the slide show

FIGURE H-8: Meeting Minder dialog box

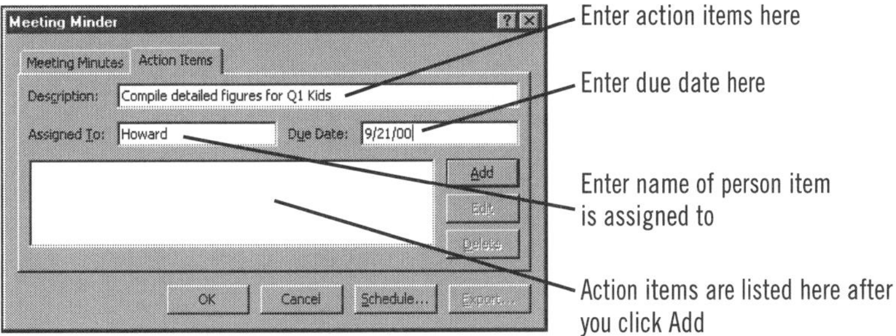

FIGURE H-9: New Action Items slide at end of presentation

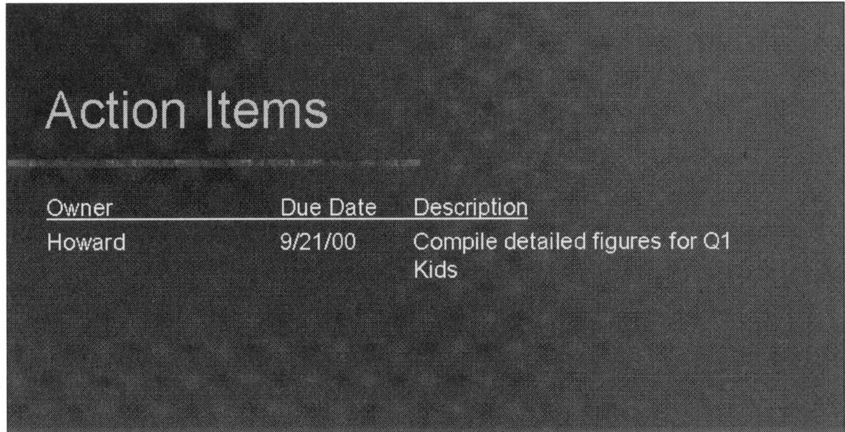

FIGURE H-10: Action items after exporting to Microsoft Word

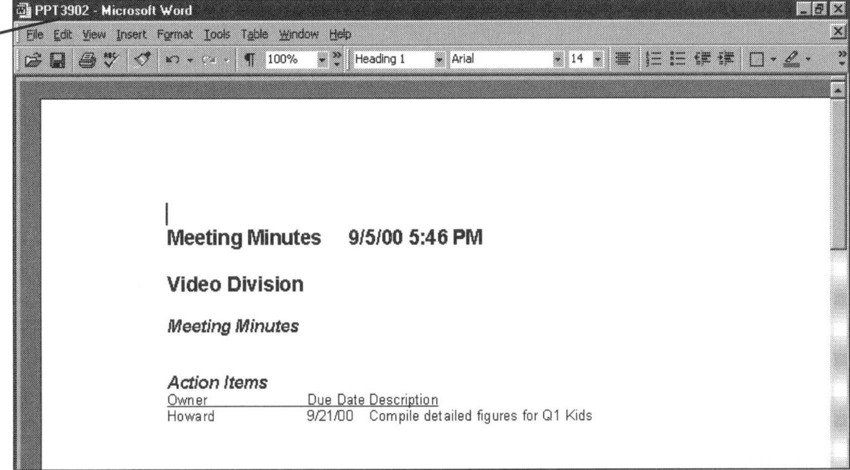

Keeping track of meeting minutes and speaker notes

You can also use the Meeting Minder to keep a record of meeting minutes you type during the slide show. Right-click any slide in Slide Show view, click Meeting Minder, click the Meeting Minutes tab, then type notes in the text box. You can export meeting minutes to Microsoft Word the same way you export action items. You can also create speaker notes by clicking the Speaker Notes command on the Slide Show view pop-up menu. Type any items you want to remember, and they will automatically be transferred to the Speaker Notes section of that slide.

PowerPoint 2000

PowerPoint 2000

Rehearsing Slide Timings

Whether you are creating a self-running slide show or you're planning to talk about the slides as they appear, you should rehearse the **slide timings**, the amount of time each slide stays on the screen. If you assign slide timings to your slides without actually running through the presentation, you will probably discover that the timings do not allow enough time for each slide or point in your presentation. To set accurate slide timings, use the PowerPoint Rehearse Timings feature. As you run through your slide show, the Rehearsal toolbar shows you how long the slide stays on the screen. When enough time has passed, click the mouse to move to the next slide.

Scenario Maria rehearses the slide timings.

1. **Click the Slide Sorter View button, then click slide 1**
   Before you continue through the steps of the lesson, you may want to read the steps and comments that follow first, so you are aware of what happens during a slide show rehearsal.
2. **Click the Rehearse Timings button on the Slide Sorter toolbar**
   Slide Show view opens, and slide 1 appears. The Rehearsal toolbar appears in the upper-left corner of the screen, as shown in Figure H-11.
3. **When you feel an appropriate amount of time has passed for the presenter to speak and for the audience to view the slide, click the Next button on the Rehearsal toolbar or click your mouse anywhere on the screen**
   Slide 2 appears.
4. **Click at an appropriate interval after slide 2 appears, then click again to view slide 3**
5. **Continue setting timings for the rest of the slides in the presentation**
   Be sure to leave enough time to present the contents of each slide thoroughly. At the end of the slide rehearsal, a Microsoft PowerPoint message box opens asking if you want to save the slide timings. If you save the timings, the next time you run the slide show, the slides will appear automatically at the intervals you specified during the rehearsal.
6. **Click Yes to save the timings**
   Slide Sorter view appears showing the new slide timings, as shown in Figure H-12. Your timings will be different. When you run the slide show, it will run by itself, using the timings you rehearsed. The rehearsed timings override any previous timings you set.
7. **Click the Slide Show button, view the presentation with your timings**
8. **Save your changes, click File on the menu bar, click Print, click the All option button, click the Print what list arrow, click Handouts, 6 slides per page, click OK, then close the presentation**

QuickTip

If too much time has elapsed, click the Repeat button to restart the timer for that slide. You can also set the time for each slide by typing it in the Elapsed Time box.

QuickTip

You can also view the next slide by clicking the slide itself.

QuickTip

To move to the next slide before your rehearsed slide timing has elapsed, click the slide to advance to the next slide or open the slide show pop-up menu.

FIGURE H-11: Rehearsal toolbar

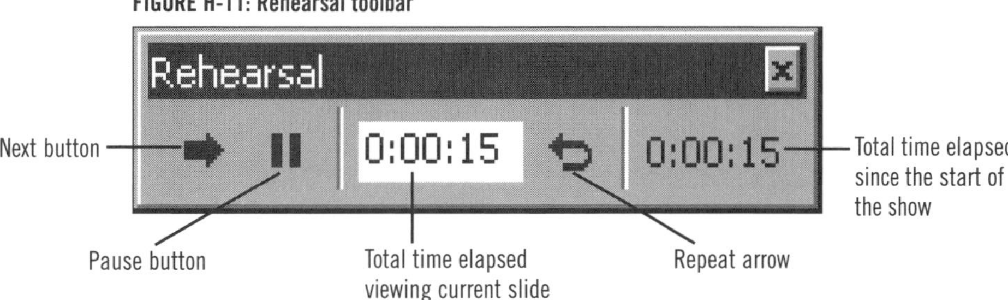

FIGURE H-12: Final presentation in Slide Sorter view showing new slide timings

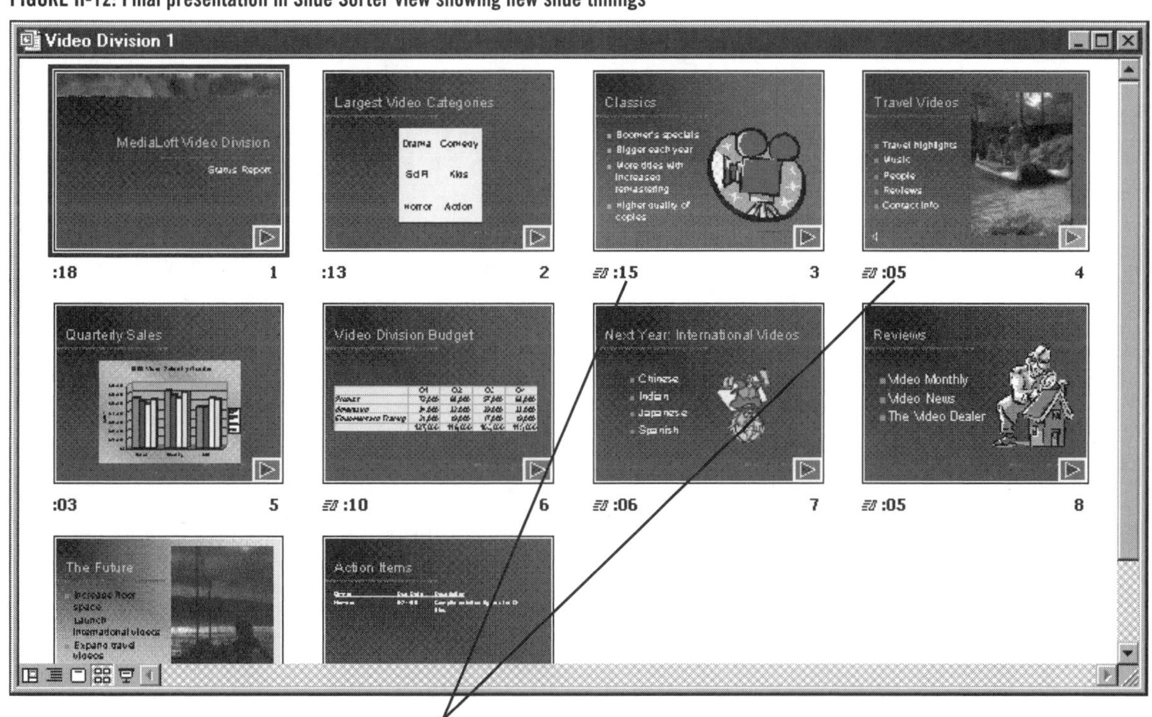

PowerPoint 2000

PowerPoint 2000

Using the Pack and Go Wizard

Occasionally you need to present your slide show using another computer. To transport everything (including your presentation, embedded objects, linked objects, and fonts) to the new computer, you use the Pack and Go Wizard. The Pack and Go Wizard compresses and packages all the necessary files that you'll need to take a presentation on the road. You can also package the PowerPoint Viewer with the presentation. **PowerPoint Viewer** is a program that allows you to view a slide show even if PowerPoint is not installed on the computer. Scenario Maria packages the Video Division 1 presentation using the Pack and Go Wizard so she can present it at an off-site meeting at a conference center.

Steps 1 2 3 4

1. **Create a new folder on your hard drive called PackNGo**
   When you run the Pack and Go Wizard, you will save your packaged presentation in this new folder. You will delete this folder from your hard drive at the end of the next lesson. PowerPoint Viewer is available in several versions. Older versions of the Viewer will not run PowerPoint 2000 presentations.

2. Open the file **Video Division Offsite** from your Project Disk, click **File** on the menu bar, click **Save As**, change the Save in list box in the Save As dialog box to the **PackNGo folder** on your hard drive, click the **Save as type list arrow**, click **PowerPoint 97-2000 & 95 Presentation**, edit the File name so it is **Video Division Offsite Viewer Version**, click **Save**, then click **Yes** in the warning box
   If your original presentation is on your hard disk, you can place the packaged version directly on a floppy disk. If the presentation is too big for one disk, PowerPoint lets you save across multiple floppy disks.

3. Click **File** on the menu bar, click **Pack and Go**, read the screen, then click **Next**
   The Pick files to pack screen opens, as shown in Figure H-13. You indicate here which presentation you would like to package.

4. Make sure the **Active presentation check box** is selected, then click **Next**
   The Choose destination screen opens. See Figure H-14.

5. Click the **Choose destination option button**, click **Browse**, locate and click the **PackNGo folder** you created, click **Select**, then click **Next**
   The Links screen opens. There aren't any links in this version of the presentation.

6. Click the **Embed TrueType fonts check box** to select it, then click **Next**
   The Viewer screen opens. You want to package the PowerPoint Viewer with your presentation so you can run it from any compatible computer. The PowerPoint Viewer program is available on the Office 2000 CD-ROM.

7. Insert the Office 2000 CD-ROM into the disk drive, click the **Viewer for Windows 95 or NT option button**, click **Next**, read the Finish screen, then click **Finish**
   The Pack and Go Wizard packages the Video Division Offsite presentation. After the presentation is packaged, a message box opens telling you that the Pack and Go Wizard has finished.

8. Click **OK**

9. Close the presentation, then exit PowerPoint

Trouble?

If you decide to place the PackNGo folder in a different location, make sure the folders in the path name have a maximum of eight characters and contain no spaces.

Trouble?

If you see a dialog box telling you that the Pack and Go feature isn't installed, insert the Office 2000 CD-ROM to install it or consult your instructor or technical support person.

QuickTip

If you are working on a network, ask your instructor or technical support person where you can locate the PowerPoint Viewer file. You can also download the latest version of Viewer from the Product News link on the Microsoft Web site (http://www.microsoft.com).

FIGURE H-13: Pick files to pack screen in the Pack and Go Wizard

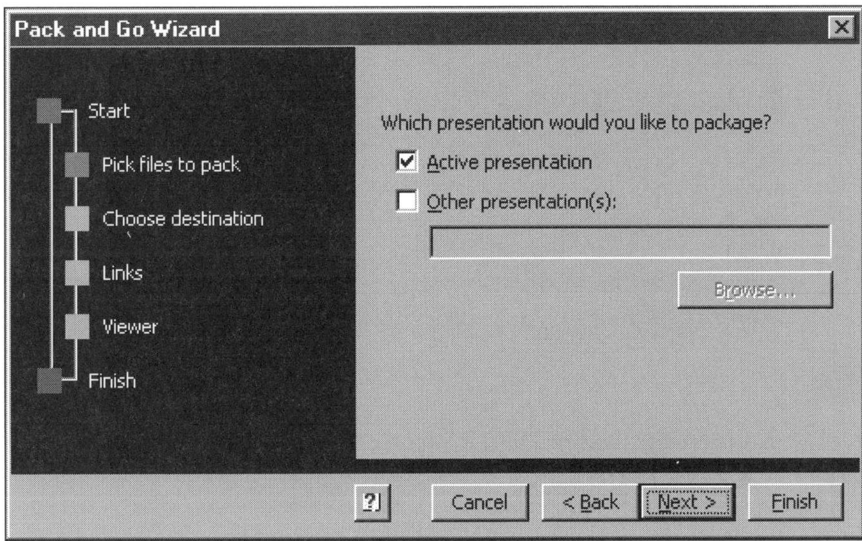

FIGURE H-14: Choose destination screen in the Pack and Go Wizard

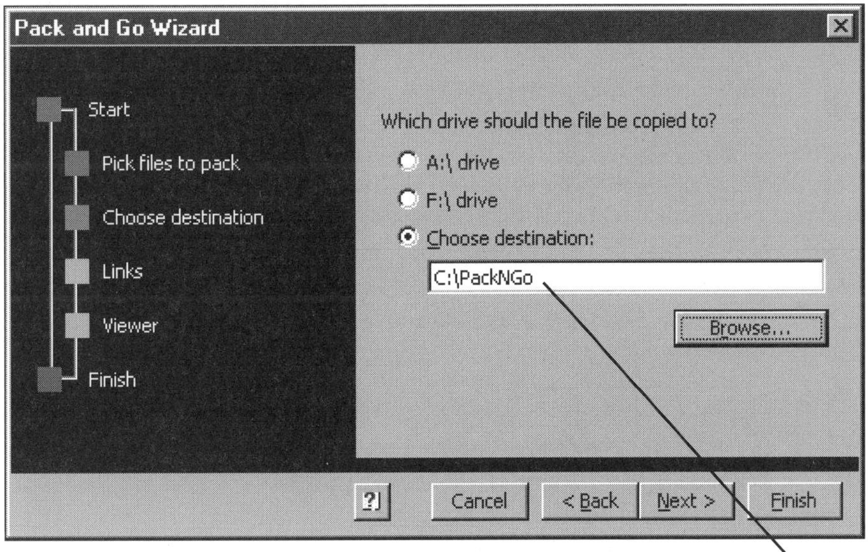

Your destination path may be different

Send a presentation via e-mail

You can send a single PowerPoint slide as the body of an e-mail message or you can send an entire presentation as an e-mail attachment. You can also route a presentation to a list of recipients. To send an individual slide, view it in Slide view, and click the E-mail button on the Standard toolbar. A message header appears below the Slide Sorter toolbar. Fill out the To and Subject lines, then click Send this Slide. To send an entire presentation, click File, point to Send to, then click Mail Recipient (as Attachment). A new e-mail message opens with the open PowerPoint file attached to it. Fill out the To and Subject lines, then click the Send button. To view a slide sent as the body of an e-mail message, the recipient must have an e-mail program that can read messages in HTML format. To view an attachment, the recipient must have PowerPoint 2000. (You cannot send an entire presentation as an e-mail attachment in HTML format.)

PowerPoint 2000

Using the Microsoft PowerPoint Viewer

The Microsoft PowerPoint Viewer is a program that shows a slide show on compatible computers that do not have PowerPoint installed. It is a free program distributed by Microsoft that can be copied onto any compatible computer. All you need to show a presentation using the Viewer is a computer running Windows 95, Windows 98, or Windows NT, a copy of PowerPoint Viewer, and the PowerPoint presentation itself. The content of a presentation cannot be altered using the Viewer. Scenario Maria practices locating and using the PowerPoint Viewer to show her presentation.

Steps 1 2 3 4

1. Open the **PackNGo folder** you created in the previous lesson
   The Pack and Go Wizard supplies a special setup program that automatically decompresses the packaged file.
2. Double-click the **pngsetup** icon in the PackNGo folder window
   The Pack and Go Setup dialog box opens.
3. In the Destination folder text box, click after the backslash, type the path to your PackNGo folder ending with the folder name **PackNGo** (the same way it appears in the Source Folder line), compare your screen to Figure H-15, click **OK**, then click **Yes** in the warning box that opens
   The presentation you previously saved as a PowerPoint 97-2000 & 95 presentation has been overwritten with the newly unpacked files. Next a message box opens telling you that the installation was successful and asking if you want to view the slide show.
4. Click **Yes**
   When you use Viewer, you should always preview your slide show before the actual presentation to make sure everything works the way you expect. The Viewer shows the Video Division presentation without opening PowerPoint. The presentation runs with the slide timings set during a rehearsal. When the presentation is complete, the presentation and the Viewer close. You can adjust the settings so you can advance the slides manually.
5. In the PackNGo folder window, double-click the **Ppview32 icon**
   The Microsoft PowerPoint Viewer dialog box opens, similar to Figure H-16, with the name of the viewer file listed.
6. Select the file **Video Division Offsite Viewer Version**
   A preview of the Video Division Offsite presentation appears in the Preview window shown in Figure H-16. You want to have access to the pop-up menu and end with a black slide. Because this will not be a kiosk presentation, you won't need to protect it with a password.
7. Click **Options**, select the check boxes **Popup menu on right mouse click**, **Show popup menu button**, and **End with black slide**
   Presentations viewed with PowerPoint Viewer do not automatically end with a black slide, so you have to check this option.
8. Click **OK**
9. Under Advance slides, click **Manually**, click **Show**, then click the left mouse button to progress through the slide show
   PowerPoint Viewer runs your show. The timing of the appearance of the animated objects was overridden by selecting the Manually option. After you view the black slide, you are returned to the Microsoft PowerPoint Viewer dialog box.
10. Click **Exit**, then delete the **PackNGo folder** and its contents from the hard drive

QuickTip

You may see messages that the Viewer cannot play the sound you embedded. Click OK and continue.

QuickTip

If you see a truncated file name, for example Videod~1, in the PowerPoint Viewer dialog box, select it and continue with the steps.

QuickTip

PowerPoint Viewer does not support picture bullets; it substitutes character bullets.

FIGURE H-15: Pack and Go Setup dialog box

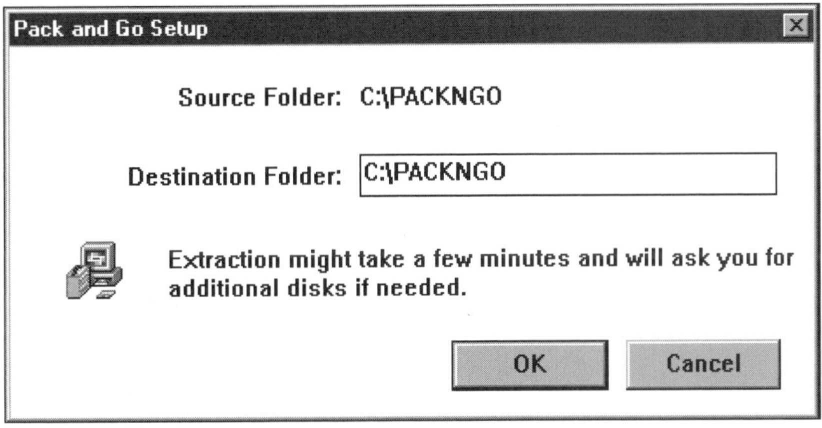

FIGURE H-16: PowerPoint Viewer dialog box

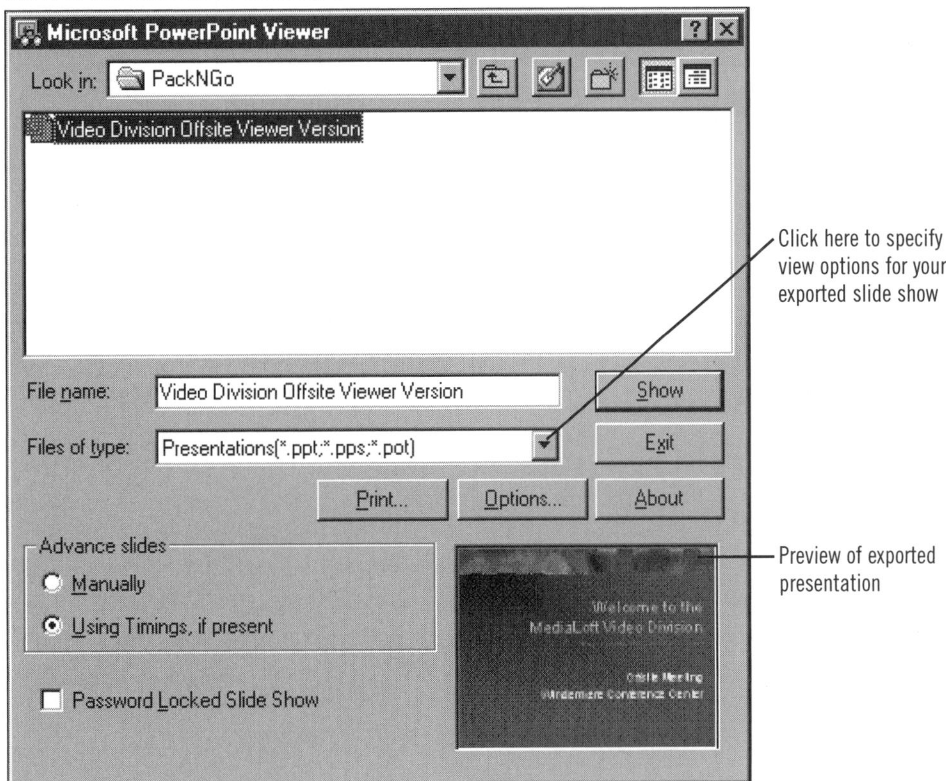

PowerPoint 2000

PowerPoint 2000

Publishing a Presentation for the World Wide Web

You can use PowerPoint to create presentations for viewing on the World Wide Web by using the Publish feature. When you **publish** a presentation, PowerPoint automatically saves a version of it in Hypertext Markup Language (HTML) format, which you can then copy to a Web server. Others can view (but not change) the presentation over the Web. Scenario Maria wants to create a version of her Video Division 1 presentation that can be viewed on the MediaLoft intranet page. She does not want to include the financial information on slides 5 and 6, so she uses the Publish feature to publish the custom show she created earlier.

1. Start **PowerPoint**, then open the presentation **Video Division 1**
2. Click **File** on the menu bar, then click **Save as Web Page**, click the **Save in list arrow**, then select the drive containing your Project Disk

   A dialog box titled "Save As" opens, similar to the Save As dialog box.
3. Click **Publish**

   The Publish as Web page dialog box opens, similar to Figure H-17.
4. In the Publish what? section, click the **Custom Show option button**, then click the **Display speaker notes check box** to deselect it
5. In the Browser support section, click the **Microsoft Internet Explorer or Netscape Navigator 3.0 or later option button**

   Now you want to make sure the HTML file can be viewed by most browsers. At the bottom of the dialog box, notice that the default file name for the HTML file you are creating is the same as the presentation file name, and that it will be saved to the same folder that the presentation is stored in. See Figure H-17.
6. Deselect the **Open Published Web page in browse check box**, Click **Publish**

   PowerPoint creates a copy of your presentation in HTML format and your original presentation remains open on the screen. This may take several minutes.
7. Open your Internet browser and choose the **Work Offline option**
8. Click **File** on the menu bar, click **Open**, click **Browse**, click the **Look in list arrow** and switch to your Project Disk, double-click the **Video Division 1.htm** file, then click **OK**

   There are two files called Video Division in your Project Disk folder. One is a PowerPoint file and has the PowerPoint icon associated with it; the other is the HTML file you just created and has the icon for your browser, probably Internet Explorer or Netscape Communicator, associated with it. There is also a folder called Video_Division_files that contains the supporting files the HTML file needs. The presentation opens in your default browser, similar to Figure H-18, which shows the presentation in Internet Explorer 5. You can navigate through the presentation using the navigation arrows at the bottom of the screen, by clicking the hyperlink representing each slide on the left side of the screen, or by clicking the action buttons on the slides.
9. Use the arrows at the bottom of the screen or the hyperlinks on the left side of the screen to view the presentation slides
10. Close your browser window, save the PowerPoint presentation, then close the presentation and exit PowerPoint

Trouble?

Be sure you click Save as Web Page, not Save As. You can use the Save As command to save a presentation in HTML format, but you can only save the whole presentation, you don't get to choose a browser, and users will be able to edit it.

QuickTip

To change the format of elements on the Web page, click Web Options in the Publish as Web Page dialog box, and make your changes.

QuickTip

Once you publish a presentation and create the HTML files, you'll need to copy it to a Web server so others can open it from the Web. See your system administrator for instructions on how to do this. This presentation has already been copied to the MediaLoft intranet site, and you view it online at *www.course.com/illustrated/MediaLoft*. Click the Marketing link, then click the Video Division presentation link.

FIGURE H-17: Publish as Web Page dialog box

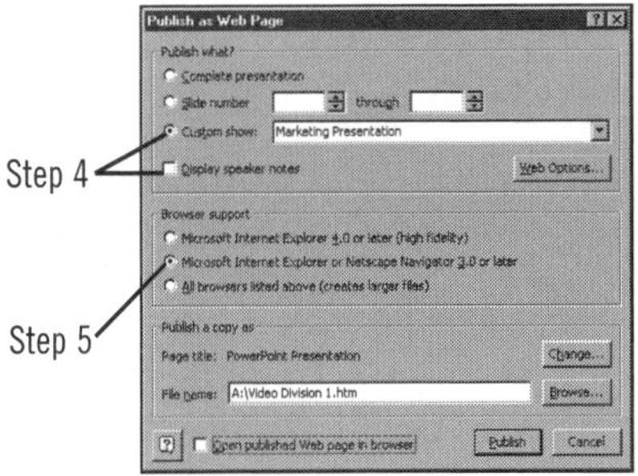

FIGURE H-18: Custom show from Video Division presentation in Internet Explorer

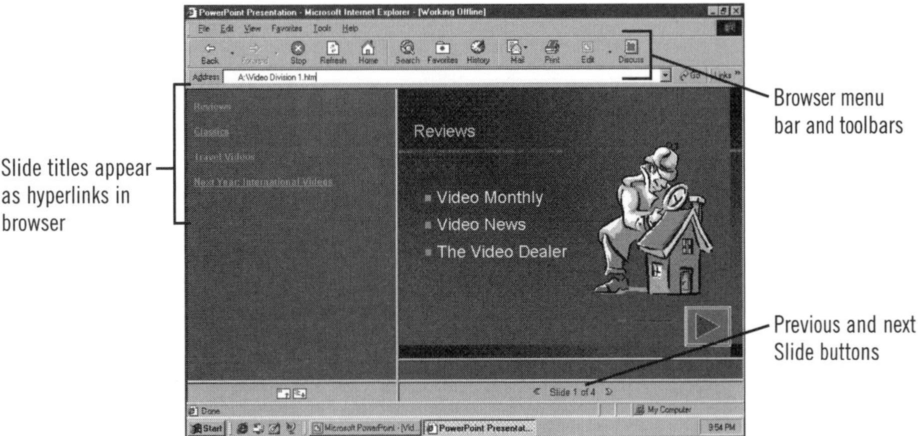

Using PowerPoint to collaborate with workgroups

You can use PowerPoint as a communication tool within a workgroup by broadcasting presentations or by setting up online meetings to collaborate on presentations.

Use NetMeeting to schedule a broadcast or a meeting: If you are on a network, you can use NetMeeting to broadcast presentations or host meetings over the World Wide Web or an intranet. To schedule a broadcast, click Slide Show on the menu bar, point to Online Broadcast, then point to Set Up and Schedule. In the Schedule a New Broadcast dialog box, click the Broadcast Settings tab and indicate your audio, video, e-mail, and recording preferences. Use the Server Options tab to enter your server information. On the Description tab, enter the text that you want other users to see in your online "lobby" page before the broadcast starts. Then click Schedule Broadcast. To schedule a meeting, point to Online Collaboration on the Tools menu, then click Schedule Meeting. A dialog box similar to an e-mail message box opens. Add participants' e-mail addresses to the To box, type a subject, then click Send button on the toolbar.

Begin a presentation broadcast: Once you have scheduled a presentation broadcast, you initiate the broadcast by clicking Slide Show on the menu bar, pointing to Online Broadcast, then clicking Begin Broadcast. When you want to start the broadcast, click Start. If you have an audience of 16 or more people, you need a NetShow server. For more information on NetShow, see your system administrator. To use online collaboration, Outlook will send you a reminder 15 minutes before the meeting is scheduled to start. To start the meeting, click the Start The NetMeeting button in the Reminder dialog box.

View a presentation broadcast: When you participate in an online broadcast, you receive an e-mail reminder 15 minutes before the presentation start time. On the reminder, you'll see a View this NetShow button, which you click to view the lobby page in your browser. At the start time, you see the presentation on your screen. If you are invited to participate in a meeting, the Reminder dialog box will have a Join This NetMeeting button. During the meeting, you will be able to chat with other people who are participating in this meeting and send e-mail messages to the presenter.

Practice

► Concepts Review

Label each of the elements of the PowerPoint window shown in Figure H-19.

FIGURE H-19

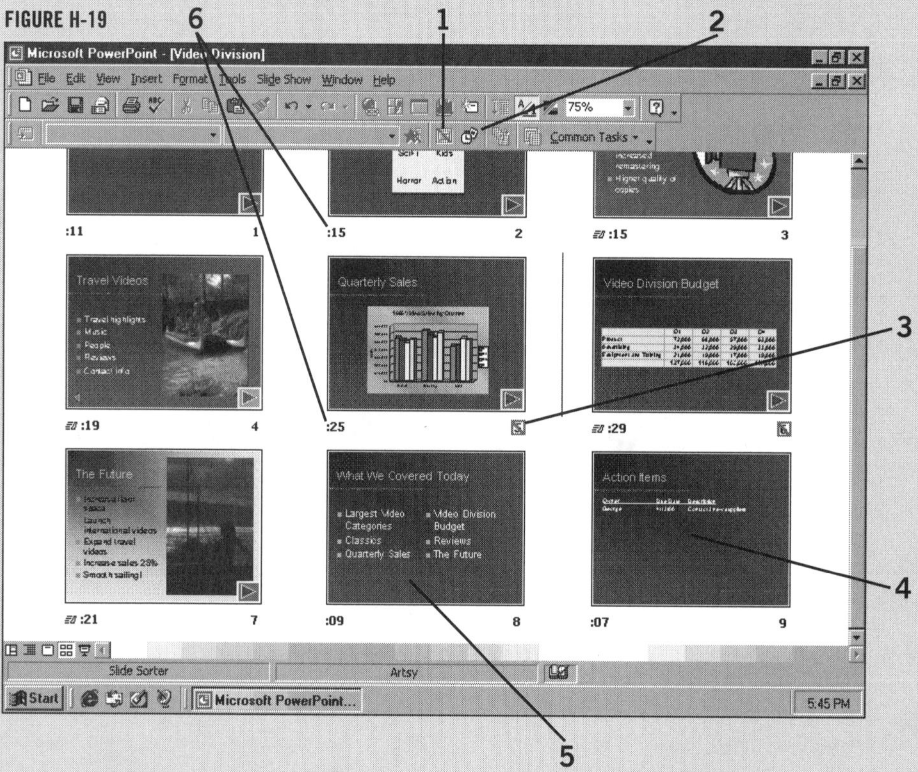

Match each of the terms with the statement that describes its function.

7. **Microsoft PowerPoint Viewer**
8. **Kiosk**
9. **Custom show**
10. **Pack and Go Wizard**
11. **Meeting Minder**

a. A dialog box that lets you keep track of meeting minutes and action items during a slide show
b. A program that runs a slide show on other computers
c. A freestanding public computer that runs a slide show
d. A presentation created from selected slides in a presentation
e. A feature that packages a presentation to take it to another computer

Select the best answer from the list of choices.

12. **In Slide Sorter view, what does a box with a line through it indicate when it is over a slide number?**
    a. The slide won't appear in a slide show.
    b. The slide is deleted.
    c. The slide appears last in a slide show.
    d. The slide is first in the presentation.

13. **Which of the following is *not* a Meeting Minder feature?**
    a. You can print the text you enter in the Meeting Minder.
    b. You can export text to Microsoft Word.
    c. You can enter text that is placed on a new slide in your presentation.
    d. You can enter text directly to the notes pages of your presentation.

14. **Which of the following statements is true about rehearsing your slide timings?**
    a. If you rehearse your presentation, someone on another computer can set the slide timings.
    b. During a rehearsal, you have no way of knowing how long the slide stays on the screen.
    c. If you give your slides random slide timings, you may not have enough time to adequately view each slide.
    d. Rehearsing the slides in your presentation gives each slide the same slide timing.

15. **When you want to have a slide show run continuously and automatically at a kiosk, you should**
    a. Add a voice narration and save the presentation using the Pack and Go Wizard.
    b. Click Custom Animation on the Slide Show menu, and choose the Automatically option button.
    c. Insert hyperlink buttons on all the slides.
    d. Use the Set Up Show dialog box to choose the appropriate settings.

Skills Review

If you complete all of the exercises in this unit, you may run out of space on your Project Disk. To make sure you have enough disk space, copy files PPT H-2, PPT H-3, and PPT H-4 onto a new disk and use the new disk to complete the rest of the exercises in this unit.

1. **Set up a slide show**
   a. Open the presentation PPT H-2 and save it as "KC Series Proposal."
   b. Set up a slide show that will be browsed at a kiosk, using slide timings.
   c. Set the slides to appear every three seconds.
   d. Run the slide show all the way through once and then stop it.
   e. Set the slide show to run manually, presented by a speaker.
   f. Put a Forward or Next action button, linked to the next slide, in the lower-right corner of slide 1, to the left of the page number.
   g. Copy the action button, then paste it onto all of the slides except the last one.
   h. Move to slide 2 and place an Action Button: Back or Previous in the lower-left corner. Have it link to the previous slide. Resize the button so it is the same size as the button you created in step f, and place it at the bottom of the slide, about an inch from the left side.
   i. Copy the Back button, then paste it on all of the slides except the first one.
   j. Run through the slide show from slide 1 using the action buttons you inserted. Move forward and backward through the presentation, watching the animation effects as they appear.
   k. When you have finished viewing the slide show, save your changes.

2. **Create a custom show**
   a. Create a custom show called "New Series Format" that includes slides 3, 4, 5, 6, and 7.
   b. Move the two performance slides above the lecture slides.
   c. View the show from within the Custom Shows dialog box, using the action buttons to move among the slides and waiting for the graphics animations. Press [Esc] to end the slide show after viewing the Financing Lectures slide.
   d. Move to slide 1, begin the slide show, then when slide 1 appears, go to the Custom Show.
   e. View the custom slide show, then return to slide view and save your changes.

3. Hide a slide during a slide show

- **a.** In Slide Sorter view, hide slide 8.
- **b.** Set up a custom slide show that includes only slides 7, 8, and 9, and name it "Sample".
- **c.** View the slide show Sample and verify that Slide 8 does not appear.
- **d.** Run the Sample slide show again and press [H] to view slide 8.
- **e.** In Slide Sorter view, set slide 8 to be visible during a slide show.
- **f.** Add a summary slide after the title slide, containing the titles of all the ensuing slides. Two slides will be created. Edit the slides so that there are four bullets on each one.
- **g.** Add forward and back action buttons like the ones on the other slides.

4. Use the Meeting Minder

- **a.** Run the slide show beginning at slide 2, then open the Meeting Minder.
- **b.** Display the Meeting Minutes tab and enter the following items, pressing [Enter] after each one:
  "Work with community liaison committee."
  "Do research on literary/cultural profile."
- **c.** Display the Action Items tab.
- **d.** Enter an action item with the description "1. Speak to Marketing for their ideas." Assign the task to yourself, then change the Due Date to one week from today's date. (Note: The Assigned To text box will accept a maximum of 15 characters including spaces.)
- **e.** Add the note to the Action Items list then click OK.
- **f.** Open the Meeting Minder again.
- **g.** Enter another action item with the description "2. See recent survey for format ideas", then enter your name and make the due date a week from today's date. Add the item to the Action Items list.
- **h.** Add a Forward or Next action button to slide 11, and a Back or Previous action button to slide 12.
- **i.** In Slide Show view, go through the presentation starting with slide 9 until the Action Items slide appears.
- **j.** Open the Meeting Minder, then export the meeting minutes and action items to Word. (Do not post the action items to Outlook.)
- **k.** Add your name as the first line of the Word document. Save the Microsoft Word document as "ML Action", print the document, then exit Word.
- **l.** Close the Meeting Minder dialog box and end the slide show.

5. Rehearse slide timings

- **a.** Open the Rehearsal toolbar, go through the presentation setting new slide timings, then save your new timings and review them.
- **b.** Add your name as a footer on notes and handouts, then save your changes.
- **c.** Print your New Series Format custom show without animations, as handouts, 6 slides per page.
- **d.** Print all the slides in the presentation as handouts, 6 slides per page.

6. Use the Pack and Go Wizard

- **a.** Create a new folder on your hard drive and name it "PackNGo2".
- **b.** Save the presentation in the PackNGo2 folder you created, naming it "KC Series Proposal – Viewer".
- **c.** Open the Pack and Go Wizard and specify that you want to pack the active presentation.
- **d.** For the destination, navigate to the PackNGo2 folder on your hard drive.
- **e.** Indicate that you want to Embed TrueType Fonts.
- **f.** Include the Viewer for Windows 95 or NT option (insert the Office 2000 CD-ROM if necessary), then end the Wizard.
- **g.** Close the KC Series Proposal – Viewer presentation.

7. View a packaged presentation

- **a.** Open the PackNGo2 folder, start the Pngsetup program, then in the Destination Folder text box, type the path to your PackNGo2 folder.
- **b.** Show your packaged presentation.
- **c.** Open the Pptview32 program in the PackNGo2 folder.
- **d.** Select the file name representing the KC Series Proposal presentation. Indicate that you want to view the pop-up menu when you right-click, and that you want to end with a black slide.
- **e.** Specify that you want to advance the slides manually, then view the show.
- **f.** Exit the show, then delete the PackNGo2 folder from your hard drive.

8. Publish a presentation for the World Wide Web

- **a.** Publish the entire KC Series Proposal presentation for the World Wide Web. Make the page title "Kansas City Series Proposal". Do not include speaker notes, and make it viewable using Microsoft Internet Explorer or Netscape Navigator 3.0 or later. On the General tab in the Web Options dialog box, include the slide navigation controls, and make sure the color is Presentation Colors (accent color). Show the slide animations and resize the graphics to fit the browser window.
- **b.** Working offline, open the HTML file in your browser, navigating with the hyperlink buttons you created and with the slide title hyperlinks.
- **c.** Close your browser and close the presentation and PowerPoint.

Visual Workshop

Create the slides shown in Figures H-20 and H-21. The clip art is in the Clip Gallery. The design template has been modified from its original colors. (*Hint:* You will need to view the slide master.) Adjust the background to match the figures. Set transitions, animations, and slide timings. Adjust the hyperlink color by modifying the slide color scheme. Insert a hyperlink and create a target slide for the hyperlink to jump to. Create a title slide. Print the presentation as handouts, 6 slides per page.

FIGURE H-20

FIGURE H-21

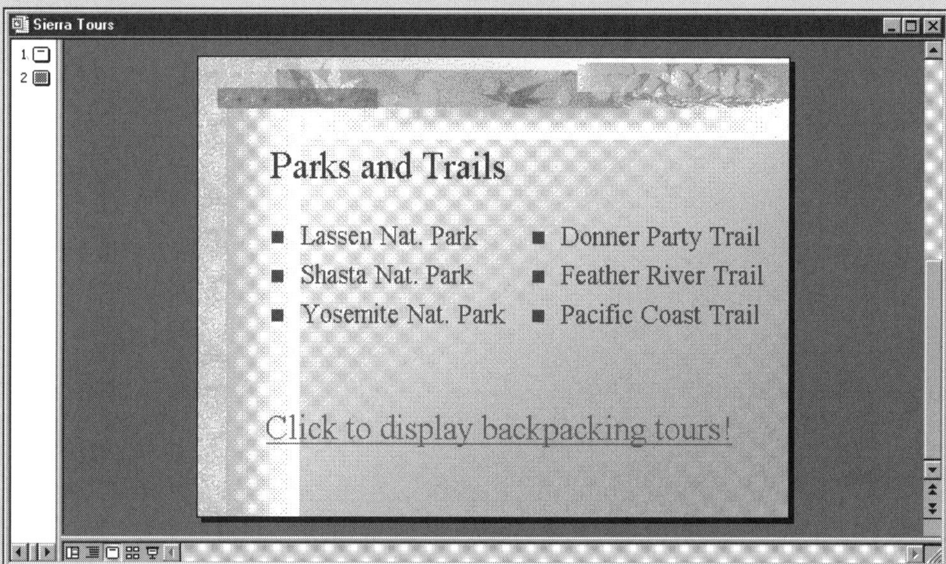

Glossary

Action button An object on a screen that you click to perform an activity, such as advancing to the next slide.

Active cell A selected cell in a Graph datasheet or an Excel worksheet.

Adjustment handle A small diamond positioned next to a sizing handle that changes the dimensions of an object.

Agenda slide A list of the first slide in each custom show within a presentation.

Align To place objects' edges or centers on the same plane.

Animation A graphic such as a GIF (Graphics Interchange Format) file that moves (like a cartoon) when you run the slide show.

Annotation A freehand drawing on the screen made by using the Annotation tool. You can annotate only in Slide Show view.

AutoContent Wizard A wizard that helps you get your presentation started by supplying a sample outline and a design template.

AutoLayout A predesigned slide layout that contains placeholders for titles, main text, clip art, graphs, and charts.

Background The area behind the text and graphics on a slide.

.bmp The abbreviation for the bitmap graphics file format.

Bullet A small graphic symbol, usually a round or square dot, often used to identify items in a list.

Cell The intersection of a column and row in a worksheet, datasheet, or table.

Chart A graphical representation of information from a datasheet or worksheet. Types include 2-D and 3-D column, bar, pie, area, and line charts.

Chart boxes In Microsoft Organization Chart, the placeholders for text. The placeholders will contain names and positions in an organization's structure.

Clip art Professionally designed pictures that come with PowerPoint.

Clip Gallery A library of art, pictures, sounds, video clips, and animations that all Office applications share.

Clipboard toolbar A toolbar that shows the contents of the Office Clipboard; contains buttons for copying and pasting items to and from the Office Clipboard.

Color scheme The basic eight colors that make up a PowerPoint presentation; a color scheme assigns colors for text, lines, objects, and background color. You can change the color scheme on any presentation at any time.

Common Tasks menu A menu located on the Formatting toolbar that contains commands for common tasks performed in PowerPoint.

Control boxes The gray boxes along the left and top of a Graph datasheet that contain the row and column identifiers.

Crop To hide part of a picture or object using the Cropping tool.

Data label Information that identifies the data in a column or row in a datasheet.

Data series A column or row in a datasheet.

Data series marker A graphical representation of a data series, such as a bar or column.

Datasheet The component of a graph that contains the information you want to depict on your Graph chart.

Design templates Prepared slide designs with formatting and color schemes that you can apply to an open presentation.

Dialog box A window that opens when more information is needed to carry out a command.

Drawing toolbar A toolbar that contains buttons that let you create lines and shapes.

Embedded object An object that is created in another application and is copied to a PowerPoint presentation. Embedded objects maintain their identity as files in their original application for easy editing.

File format A file type, such as .wmf or .gif.

Folder A subdivision of a disk that works like a filing system to help you organize files.

Formatting toolbar The toolbar that contains buttons for the most frequently used formatting commands, such as font type and size.

.gif The abbreviation for the graphics interchange format

Graph The program that creates a datasheet and chart to graphically depict information.

Grid Invisible, evenly-spaced horizontal and vertical lines that help you align objects.

Group To combine multiple objects into one object.

Hyperlink A specially formatted word, phrase, or graphic that you can click during a slide show to "jump to," or display, another slide in your current presentation, another PowerPoint presentation, a Word, Excel, or Access file, or an address on the World Wide Web.

Indent levels Text levels in the master text placeholder. Each level is indented a certain amount from the left margin. You control their placement by dragging indent markers on the ruler.

Indent markers Small triangles on the ruler that indicate the location of indent levels, which determine how far text is indented from the left.

Keyword A word you use to quickly find an object.

Kiosk A freestanding computer used to display information, usually in a public area.

Leading The spacing between lines of text in a text object.

Link A "live" connection between a source file and its representation in a target file; when one is updated, the other is updated automatically. Can also refer to a hyperlink (see also *hyperlink*).

Main text Sub-points or bullet points on a slide under the slide title.

Main text placeholder A reserved box on a slide for the main text points.

Master text placeholder The placeholder on the Slide Master that controls the formatting and placement of the Main text placeholder on each slide. If you modify the Master text placeholder, each Main text placeholder is affected in the entire presentation.

Master title placeholder The placeholder on the Slide Master that controls the formatting and placement of the Title placeholder on each slide. If you modify the Master title placeholder, each Title placeholder is affected in the entire presentation.

Menu bar The bar beneath the title bar that contains menus that list the program's commands.

More Buttons button A button you click to view toolbar buttons that are not currently visible.

Movie Live action captured in digital format.

Normal view A presentation view that divides the presentation window into Outline, Slide, and Notes panes.

Notes pane In Normal view, the pane that shows speaker notes for the current slide; also in Notes Page view, the area below the slide image that contains speaker notes.

Object The component you place or draw on a slide. Objects are drawn lines and shapes, text, clip art, imported pictures, and embedded objects.

Office Assistant An animated character that appears to offer tips, answer questions, and provide access to the program's Help system.

Office Clipboard A temporary storage area shared by all Office programs that can be used to cut, copy and paste multiple items within and between Office programs. The Office Clipboard can hold up to 12 items collected from any Office program. See also *Clipboard toolbar*.

Organization chart A diagram of connected boxes that shows reporting structure in a company or organization.

Outline pane The presentation window section that shows presentation text in the form of an outline with a small slide icon representing each slide.

Outline view A presentation view that lists the titles and main text of all the slides in your presentation. Also shows a small version of the current slide.

Outlining toolbar The toolbar that contains buttons for the most-used outlining commands, such as moving and indenting text lines.

Pane A section of the presentation window, such as the Outline or Slide pane.

Placeholder A dashed line box where you place text or objects.

PowerPoint Viewer A special program designed to run a PowerPoint slide show on any compatible computer that does not have PowerPoint installed.

PowerPoint window A window that contains the running PowerPoint application. The PowerPoint window includes the PowerPoint menus, toolbars, and Presentation window.

Presentation software A software program used to organize and present information.

Presentation window The area or "canvas" where you work and view your presentation. You type text and work with objects in the Presentation window.

Publish To save a version of a presentation in HTML format. You can save the HTML files to a disk or save them directly to an intranet or Web server.

Scale To change the size of a graphic a specific percentage of its original size.

Scroll To move within a window to see parts of a document that are not currently visible.

Selection box A slanted line border that appears around a text object or placeholder indicating it is ready to accept text.

Service bureau A graphics business that produces and mounts slides, and then mails them to you.

Sizing handles The small squares at each corner of a selected object. Dragging a handle resizes the object.

Slide icon A symbol that appears next to a slide in Outline view.

Slide indicator box A small box that appears when you drag the vertical scroll box in Slide and Notes Page view identifying which slide you are on.

Slide Master A template for all slides in a presentation. Text and design elements you place on the slide master appear on every slide of the presentation. The title slide has its own master, called the Title Master (see also *Title Master*). There is also the Notes Master for Notes Page view and Handout Master for Slide Sorter view.

Slide miniature A reduced version of the current slide that appears in a small window.

Slide pane The presentation window section that contains a single slide, including text and graphics.

Slide Show view A view that shows a presentation as an electronic slide show.

Slide Sorter view A presentation view that provides a miniature picture of all slides in the order in which they appear in your presentation; used to rearrange slides and add special effects.

Slide timings The amount of time slides stay on the screen during a slide show. You can assign specific slide timings to each slide, or use the PowerPoint Rehearse Timings feature to simulate the amount of time you will need to display each slide in a slide show.

Slide view A presentation view with a large Slide pane and a reduced Outline pane.

Source program The program in which a file was created.

Stacking order The order in which objects are placed on the slide. The first object placed on the slide is on the bottom, the last object placed on the slide is on the top.

Standard toolbar The toolbar containing the buttons that perform some of the most frequently used commands.

Status bar The bar at the bottom of the PowerPoint window that contains messages about what you are doing and seeing in PowerPoint, such as the current slide number or a description of a command or button.

Summary slide A slide that lists the titles of each slide in the presentation, acting as a summary of the presentation content.

Target program The program in which a file is placed using linking, embedding, or pasting.

Text anchor The location in a text object that determines the location of the text within the placeholder.

Text label A text object you create using the Text Box button.

Text object Any text you create using the Text Box button or enter into a placeholder. Once you enter text into a placeholder, the placeholder becomes a text object.

Text placeholder A box with a dashed border and text that you replace with your own text.

Timing The time a slide stays on the screen during a slide show.

Title The first line or heading on a slide.

Title Master A template for all title slides in a presentation. Text and design elements you place on the Title Master appear on all slides in the presentation that use the title slide layout.

Title placeholder A box on a slide reserved for the title of a presentation or slide.

Title slide The first slide in your presentation.

Toggle button A button that turns a feature on and off.

Transition The effect that moves one slide off the screen and the next slide on the screen during a slide show. Each slide can have its own transition effect.

View A way of looking at your presentation, such as Slide view, Normal view, Notes Page view, Slide Sorter view, and Slide Show view.

View buttons The buttons next to the horizontal scroll bar that you click to switch among views.

Window A rectangular area of the screen where you view and work on presentations.

Wizard An interactive set of dialog boxes that guides you through the process of creating a presentation; it asks you questions about presentation preferences and creates the presentation according to your specifications.

.wmf The abbreviation for the Windows metafile file format, which is the format of much clip art.

Word-processing box A text object you draw using the Text Box button that automatically wraps text inside a box.

Index

Index